THE R FACTOR

THE R FACTOR

**Michael Schluter
and
David Lee**

Hodder & Stoughton
LONDON SYDNEY AUCKLAND

British Library Cataloguing in Publication Data
A record for this book is available from the British Library

ISBN 0 340 58892 6

Printed and bound in Great Britain by
Mackays of Chatham PLC, Chatham, Kent

Hodder and Stoughton Ltd
A Division of Hodder Headline PLC
338 Euston Road
London NW1 3BH

To
Roy Clements
who launched this voyage of discovery

Contents

Preface

The decade of the 1980s has proved to be an ideological watershed. It has been marked by a huge resurgence of the power and efficacy of the capitalist market system ... the capitalist world is racing ahead ... never again will any considerable body of opinion seriously doubt its wealth-producing capacity or seek to replace it with something fundamentally different.[1]

Such is the judgement British historian Paul Johnson issues on his own times. Few have quibbled with it. Soviet state Communism posed the only serious challenge to Western political economy, and Soviet state Communism is dead. Indeed, claimed Francis Fukuyama, if history indeed has a direction it will culminate "not as Marx thought, in a Communist society, but in modern liberal democracy, which has seen such a broad acceptance in the past generation ..."[2]

It was for making this point in a short article called "The End of History?" in 1989 that Fukuyama, then a US State Department official, fell under the spotlight of the international media. Looking back in 1992, he notes that "One of the most striking facts about the original debate on 'The End of History?' was that not one single critic put forward the vision of a society fundamentally different from contemporary liberal democracy and at the same time better ..."[3]

The sad thing about these arguments from Johnson and Fukuyama is the virtue they ascribe to necessity. True enough, the collapse of the Soviet economy was a posthumous poke in the eye for all those Bolshevik technocrats who thought happiness was a Five Year Plan. But there is a touch of hubris in the idea that, through the natural selection of political economies, market capitalism and liberal democracy have been singled out as fittest to survive. You could picture the message scratched on a schoolboy's desk: ours worked, yours didn't.

Does ours "work"?

The Western system has notched up extraordinary accomplishments all the way from microwave ovens to open-heart surgery. Democracy is clearly a vast improvement on dictatorship. And there is no doubt that, as a mechanism for setting prices and furthering the efficient use of resources, the market is vastly superior to state planning. Yet praising the Western system in this way should not require us to ignore its patent instability and extensive social costs.

It will seem strange to someone born outside the West that Westerners are so meekly accepting of the price they pay for economic development. The incurable economic booms and busts, the precipitous swings of the money markets, the structural poverty, long-term unemployment, environmental damage, crime, stress and loneliness: all these are dysfunctions in the system to which the system itself has no answer. The fact is only too plain to the Eastern European and Third World leaders now ideologically stranded by the demise of Marxism. Yet in one sense, at least, Johnson and Fukuyama are right. Having won by default, the Western system holds a world monopoly. We lack even the language to critique it.

We speak of, and in a deep way comprehend, the significance of the individual's right to basic amenities, dignity, freedom of speech and conscience. But our willingness to recognise such rights – itself a towering accomplishment – goes hand in hand with a more general willingness to promote individual interests over group interests. And this shift in social ethos, which is carried forward by the momentum of Western economic growth, becomes visible in developments as different as serial marriage/cohabitation and the financial scandals over the Maxwell pension funds and BCCI.

One way of dealing with such things is to resort straight to words like "responsibility" and "values". But not only can such language be used in the West only at the risk of moralising; even if you agree, as most people probably would, that responsibility and values are social necessities, you will not find it easy to sustain them given the confinement and channelling of relationships imposed by our shared institutions.

It is the influence of a society on its relationships that provides the starting point for this book. For we do not, first and foremost, exist either as individuals, with rights against society, or as members, with responsibilities to society. We are persons in mutual relationship. Not only respect for rights and responsibilities, but also the entire edifice of our political economy, rest on the way we relate. And yet conditions in a post-industrial society make relating highly problematic. Mobility often causes us to lose touch even with close friends and family; key political and economic transactions have to be conducted between individuals who barely know one another; and the market, the heart of the capitalist economy, is now almost completely impersonal. We can no longer take for granted, as we have until now, the stability of the West's Relational infrastructure.

The significance of relationships has been stressed by writers as diverse as Tolstoy, Buber, Durkheim, and Solzhenitsyn. Indeed the idea that relationships matter is implicit in any commonsense view of human life. But expanding it, as this book begins to do, into a full conceptual and interdisciplinary framework is clearly a massive undertaking. Such a framework – let us call it Relationism – will have to encompass a critique of Western society not just at the level of its underlying political philosophy but also in terms of its social institutions and patterns of economic life. It will also (in some ways a more demanding task) have to give a coherent picture of what government and the markets look like when they are reformed along proRelational lines.

As authors, therefore, we do not regard this book as a definitive statement. No two individuals could hope between them to command the immense literatures on politics, philosophy, society and economics, even if, like Marx, they spent their lives in the British Museum. We present it in the hope that others will be stimulated to expand and develop its ideas further.

Two further comments should be made. The reader will notice almost immediately that the two authors of the book refer to themselves throughout as "I". This is a stylistic device adopted for the reader's greater comfort and convenience. The personal stories "I" tell are drawn from two different lives, and except in this preface the pronoun "we" is only ever used in a general, all-inclusive sense.

Second, we should perhaps confess to an embarrassment about publishing a book on relationships when in writing it we have been made so aware of our own Relational shortcomings – of how poorly we have mastered the intricacies of human interaction and communication, and how disadvantaged we are simply to be writing as men. We are the last people, our wives assure us, who should produce a book on this subject. They are right.

Nevertheless, that *The R Factor* has been published indicates that Relationism has become something of a personal quest. The quest began in Africa during the 1970s, in discussions with students who were seeking a framework for economic and social life that went beyond the prevailing ideologies of capitalism and Marxism, and many of the ideas born at that time have since become the foundation for the Jubilee Centre in Cambridge, a Christian research and campaigning group whose concerns include Relational perspectives on the criminal justice system, the ethics of consumer credit and debt, the contribution of the older person to social development, and the issue of Sunday trading.

Many friends have discussed the ideas in *The R Factor*

with us over the years, and, more recently, commented on the numerous drafts of the manuscript. We would especially like to thank Auriel and Loralee, Roy Clements, Paul Mills, Nicholas Miller, David Porteous, Michael Ovey, John Barton, Mark Scholefield, Jeremy Ive, Will Candler, Shirley Dex, Jonathan Chaplin, John Ashcroft, Stuart Buisch, Fiona Lillee, Peter Coxon, Marlene Finlayson and Gordon Graham. Whatever faults remain cannot be blamed on our competent and patient advisors. Thanks are due also to our research assistant Helen Hayward, and to Marilyn Collins, who co-ordinated communication between Cambridge and St Andrews.

We hope only that this book will be as life-changing for others as it has been for us.

Michael Schluter,   David Lee,
Cambridge   St Andrews

Notes

1 Paul Johnson, "The Capitalism & Morality Debate", *First Things*, March 1990, p.18.
2 Francis Fukuyama, "The end of history is still nigh", *Independent*, Feb. 3, 1992.
3 *ibid.*

1

The Mega-Community

Don't We Know Each Other?
Encounter and Contingency

At a reception I attended recently – one of those faintly arty affairs run on Ritz crackers and white wine decanted from a cardboard box – I found myself talking to a professor of English literature. He was an accomplished socialite, which is to say he put about 10% of his mind into the conversation and used the rest to look around the room. Three full minutes elapsed before his eyes finally settled on me and he said, "Hey, don't we know each other?"

Don't we *know* each other? It's a question you could only ask in a society like ours. We know so many people that we no longer know who we know. Nor are we clear about what it means to know them: the word has multiple connotations, stretching from the archaic sense of carnal knowledge to the merest acquaintance with a name.[1] You know Bill Clinton? Of course. We all know Bill Clinton.

Knowledge of this sort is a slippery commodity. Reading this sentence you hear my voice, or a voice that doubles as mine. But which of the two authors of this book am I? How do you know I'm trustworthy, that the story I have just told you is true and not something I have made up? Well, you don't. The medium of the printed word allows you only limited knowledge of me, and me almost no knowledge of you. A book is simultaneously a bridge and a wall. Consequently, such a relationship as we form through it is remote, mediated, impersonal, sterile. It gives us scant grounds for liking or trust. We really don't know each other. How could we? We've never met.

This distinction between meeting and non-meeting, between relationships growing in *encounter* and relationships of *contingency*, is, I would argue, among the most crucial of our time.[2]

I am not concerned here with drawing boundaries through the foggy region between them. There is plenty of room for disagreement about whether a taxi driver and the passenger he chats to between Holborn and Bank can truly be said to have encountered one another. Yet a five-minute chat, and even a nod or exchange of glances, opens up a path of direct communication that makes a relationship qualitatively different from one in which the partners never interact. We cannot say that someone who has seen Bill Clinton on television, and someone who has worked with him, know him in quite the same way. There is knowing of, and there is knowing. Or at least there is beginning to know, since encounter always carries the potential for extension and growth.

This might seem to imply that contingent relationships are of little consequence. But that is not so. A contingent relationship is one mediated through social, economic and political institutions. It demands no knowledge of the other partner, indeed no knowledge by either party that contact exists. Nevertheless my contingent relationships affect me because social, economic and political institutions often create asymmetries of power, making me, whether I like it or not, a lord to some people and a vassal to others.

The patterns of contingent relationships in a high-income society are extremely complex. Like phone lines they mass and merge through particular institutions, too numerous to count, too tangled to sort out, and yet active because they represent real power relations and carry real power transactions. These contingent relationships link us to almost every other person on the planet. I may never have met George Bush, but his decision to commit American forces to the Gulf in 1990/91 had quantifiable effects on my conversation, my television viewing, my thinking about Middle Eastern affairs, and the price I paid for petrol.

A more subtle example can be drawn from Britain's main generator of wealth: the public limited company. As part owner of a plc – a shareholder – your relationship with the directors is almost exclusively economic. You are unlikely to encounter them in any meaningful way even if you attend the annual general meeting. Not that you will; if you hold shares through a unit trust the chances are you don't even know which companies you've invested in. Nevertheless, since the company's performance affects your savings you clearly have an interest in its profitability, and this interest is communicated to the directors, without any effort on your part, as pressure to maximise returns on capital.

Of course the company carries out many non-economic functions as well, in relation to its workers, the workers' families, the surrounding community and the environment, but as a shareholder you have scant reason to think of them. You may sign a petition to protect the ozone layer, but when it comes to a showdown between your pension fund and, say, the welfare of the workers at a mercury treatment plant in southern Africa, the pension wins every time – and the directors know it.

For this reason it is misleading to cite the neglect of safety precautions that led to Piper Alpha and the Exxon *Valdez* simply as proof of callous management. Most corporate bosses are not monsters. But in the plc they are hemmed into two sets of contingent relationships. In one, with the corporate shareholders, they are generally the weaker party and know they may be penalised heavily for favouring conscience over market forces. In the other – with the company's ground personnel and those affected by its operation – they are generally the stronger party and able to get their way with relative ease. Unless he has very strong principles indeed almost anyone in such a position will tend to take the line of least resistance. If directors appear stingy, then, remember that their stinginess serves your interests as an investor. The real culprit isn't the person behind the MD's desk; it is a corporate structure that relies too heavily on contingent relationships.

We can see already the nature of the problem with contingency. Power without personal contact invites abuse and division. In factories where a senior executive turns up on the shop floor only to show a visiting delegation what a tight ship he runs, it is hardly surprising to find industrial relations drifting towards the instrumental and dialogue drying up in wrangles over wages and productivity. In an economy where the welfare system represents the only link between the community and the long-term unemployed, it is hardly surprising that a young person who has never held a job will experience a loss of dignity and self worth.

In contrast we can make the rather general observation that proRelational qualities like trust, sympathy, respect, understanding, self-restraint, loyalty and co-operation really do seem to come more easily where encounter occurs. You work more efficiently with colleagues once you have got to know them. You feel greater loyalty to your firm or regiment or school if you have belonged to it for a number of years. More poignantly, to trek through an encampment of starving people is a more deeply life-changing experience, and more likely to break your heart, than watching someone else do it on the six o'clock news.

Exploding the Village
The Mega-Community

Why encounter works like this is a question we will return to later. The point is that conditions in Western, post-industrial society have put encounter at a premium.

Here we could tap a formidable literature on the various Jekyll-and-Hyde transmutations "traditional" agrarian society is supposed to have gone through to produce what we have today: military to industrial (Comte), gentle to teleological (Ward), folkways to institutions and laws (Sumner), status to contract (Maine), natural will to rational will (Tönnies), mechanical to organic (Durkheim), kinship to citizenship via despotism (Hobhouse), traditional to rational-legal (Weber), community to mass society (Mannheim). The feeling such intellectual constructs attempt to explain – of being in some fundamental way out of touch with oneself and one's surroundings – is seldom disputed, and it is true to say that around the turn of the century social scientists in general went through a rather weepy phase about that comfortable world industrialisation blew away.

Of course there are dangers in trying to score points with history. The myth of the village as an Eden the city-dweller in her skyless, clock-driven exile longs to return to pivots against the counter-myth of a pre-industrial countryside seething with poverty and unspeakable Boschian horrors. Talk of "recovering community" is therefore ambiguous. What sort of community do we want to recover? Did it ever exist?

Of all the changes accompanying industrial development, probably the most significant from the standpoint of encounter is that the scale of community we relate to has expanded beyond recognition. As a villager almost anywhere in twelfth-century Europe you would have known a limited number of people very well simply because you were stuck with them. It is difficult to imagine in the age of the car just how much isolation results from having to go places on foot – the nearest town becomes the equivalent of a hundred-mile drive. Not surprisingly, therefore, pre-industrial communities tended to be self-sufficient, the village blacksmith and the village baker providing the nearest and most convenient source of their respective services as perhaps only the village pub does today. Everybody knew everybody else; everybody relied on everybody else.

Of course there were larger settlements where these conditions didn't hold. Yet even in London (and twelfth-century

London had an estimated population of between 20,000 and 35,000 – surely big enough to get lost in) men and women were thrown into daily contact with their neighbours to a far greater degree than we are today. Without taps, municipal rubbish vans or flush toilets, basic functions had to be serviced in public space. There were no televisions or paper boys – you got your news through gossip and official proclamation, or, when printing arrived and if you were literate (which you probably weren't), by reading notices. The mere fact that you had to walk everywhere put you constantly on the verge of encounter, particularly as relatively low rates of residential mobility left more or less the same people next door to one another for years on end.

In the city almost as much as the village, therefore, localism ruled. For most of the people most of the time the larger scales of social organisation (other settlements, nations, distant lands) arrived on the doorstep only in the shape of passing merchants and beggars. The real world – the world in which everyday life was lived – consisted in the main of a small geographical area containing, in the main, people you *knew*.

It is to a large extent the remnants of this "knownness" that attract us to small communities today. Socially, our terms of reference have blown wide open. We talk of the "global village" as though the globe had somehow shrunk to village proportions; yet the reverse is true – the network of dependencies traditionally confined within grasping distance of the villager has exploded towards the global scale. Advances in transport technology bring us into contact with huge numbers of people. When a Westerner thinks of the others who resemble her in owning a laptop PC, liking jazz or suffering from breast cancer, she thinks of those not in the same street or town, but in the same country or the same world.

At the close of the second millennium Westerners are citizens first, neighbours second. Most of us read the national press before the local, watch more national than regional news on television. And by the same token the populations we sense ourselves as somehow belonging to contain far more people than we can ever hope to meet, let alone befriend. The village has inflated around us, billowing with a mass of contingent relationships that give our senses of identity and belonging a wholly different slant. Insofar as we identify with a geographical community at all we identify with England, Scotland, Wales, Britain, Europe or the world — what we might call the *mega-community* — rather than the 10,000 or so individuals who happen to occupy our own suburban district.

It might be argued, of course, that contingency and encounter have existed in every age, and that the recent resurgence of nationalism represents a move away from rather than towards higher levels of political organisation. But while both these observations are true, one should also note that nationalism (in the case of the Scots or the Israelis) and regionalism (in the case of the Basques or Quebecois) are strong precisely because these ethnic units fear absorption into and engulfment by the wider culture. The common purpose on which each of them relies (supported in Quebec, for instance, by complex legal requirements in the use of the French language), itself stands under constant threat of corrosion not just by the values of the mega-community — notably, that one should be able to opt out of local loyalty if one wishes to — but also by the sheer pressure of the mega-community's political and economic structures.

It is within these common structures, developed on ever broader scales as communications improve, that contingency has snowballed. Contingent relationships are by far the most widespread, and in many ways by far the most influential. How deeply they penetrate in any one region will decide how visible the mega-community is. In Britain, where there is a high degree of centralisation and communications are pervasive, the individual will have a strong sense of participation in the mega-community and a weak sense of participation in the locality; in a more self-contained settlement in rural India, links with the mega-community will be more attenuated and sense of participation in local affairs proportionally stronger.

Of course the kind of contingent relationships operating, and therefore the individual's experience of the mega-community, will vary considerably from place to place. Nevertheless, as liberal democracy and capitalism fasten their grip across the globe, absorbing the old Soviet wing of the mega-community into the Western wing and unifying the world in a single political and business ethos, that experience is becoming increasingly uniform. To live anywhere in the mega-community is to have your relating shifted slowly and persistently into contingency. At the centre of it, in the West, we find ourselves scattered too far and moving too fast to maintain a strong base of encounter relationships. Relationship is less and less a matter of sharing the same patch of earth and the same block of air. We meet many more people, but less frequently; we still have friends and families, but on the whole these relationships are fewer, more intermittent, less stable. Instead we feel millions of tiny threads tying us into general and indirect relationship with people we will never touch or talk to, people who as individuals we know nothing about, nor ever will. And this has a profound effect on the way we live. For it means that in the mega-community we live among strangers.

White Monkeys, Safe Sex
Life Without Encounter

The status of stranger is a precarious one at the best of times. You have little immediate knowledge of a stranger's intent, indeed little knowledge of who, or even what, he or she is. For example:

The late Doctor Stutterheim, Government Archaeologist in Java, used to tell the following story: somewhat before the advent of the white man, there was a storm on the Javanese coast in the neighbourhood of one of the capitals. After the storm the people went down to the beach and found, washed up by the waves and almost dead, a large white monkey of unknown species. The religious experts explained that this monkey had been a member of the court of Beroena, the god of the sea, and that for some offence the monkey had been cast out by the god whose anger was expressed in the storm. The Rajah gave orders that the white monkey from the sea should be kept alive, chained to a certain stone. This was done.[3]

Stutterheim claimed actually to have seen this stone. Roughly scratched on it in Latin, Dutch and English were the name of a man and details of a shipwreck. Apparently the large white monkey had been a European sailor. Being trilingual, however, had not helped him communicate with his captors. It probably never occurred to him that they doubted his humanity – though, as Stutterheim concluded, he probably doubted theirs.

Apocryphal or not, the story marks the outer limits of the stranger's predicament. Stutterheim's Javanese treated the sailor inhumanely because they did not recognise him as human. If this seems to be an unusual and rather extreme case it is worth reflecting that more familiar instances of inhumanity carry much the same implication. Inhumane treatment of another is that which denies him or her a place within the network of our own duties, loyalties and affiliations. It keeps the stranger at arm's length, reserves our right to apply double standards, subverts the sense of equality which is one of encounter's basic preconditions. The old contention of white racists that blacks are somehow less evolved, closer to the apes than Caucasians, should serve as a reminder that Westerners are as able as Stutterheim's Javanese to legitimate such behaviour on the grounds of literal distinctions of species. "They're not like us" has provided the rationale to almost every race riot, civil war, pogrom and "final solution" ever devised. Stutterheim's story is a footnote to a long tale of ignorance and cruelty.

But although this sort of thing is still common – and in some ways has become more common as larger numbers of people move and individual states accommodate larger ethnic minorities – the problem of the stranger persists in the mega-community even where populations remain relatively homogenous. Whereas in the typical pre-industrial setting the arrival of strangers constituted an extraordinary event, a break in routine demanding special protocols, in the mega-community with its massive urban concentrations and rapid mobility the stranger has become the norm. Seldom in the West is the stranger another person coming in; rather he is every one of us going out. Step into public space – the street, the park, the shopping mall, the beach – and suddenly you are just a face in the crowd.

Anyone who has travelled on the London Underground at rush hour will have noticed the extraordinary ability of Westerners to ignore each other even in situations of extreme physical intimacy. This deliberate refraining from encounter is one of the most striking features of the modern city. Most of us have internalised a complex set of rules governing our avoidance of encounter, and implement it mercilessly.

It goes without saying that body-contact of the kind you may be suffering now on the Central Line to Epping is a definite no-no when you're queuing for a ticket. We go to considerable trouble, in fact, to avoid touching strangers – pausing at doorways, calculating yards in advance which side we're going to pass on a narrow pavement – and are programmed to apologise if we slip up and invade another's personal space. We wear privacy like a pressure suit. Given half the chance we'll stuff the seat next to ours in a café with raincoats and umbrellas, stare unremittingly at posters about measles in a doctor's waiting room, sidestep tin-rattlers and buskers, flee from friendly drunkards and Jehovah's Witnesses and people who seem to be having an epileptic fit. Anything but invite encounter; anything but get involved.

Of course individuals vary, as do cultures. Go to an

American supermarket and the cashier will likely turn on a thousand-watt smile and tell you to "Have a nice day". You may, as I once did, think this slightly fraudulent and suspect that in her heart of hearts the cashier couldn't care less whether you had a nice day or fell under a bus the moment you left the store. But both the action and the reaction illustrate the same principle. We learn what we need to know about others in the mega-community not by meeting them – they're too numerous for that – but by signals picked up at a distance from their appearance and behaviour. Not just smiles, but long hair, stubble on the chin, slash-back lapels, pinstripe trousers, slouching, nervous ticks and Oxbridge accents (to mention but a few) all furnish us with instant clues as to the "kind of person" we are looking at. Hence the importance traditionally attached to first impressions, dressing for success and walking tall, and our surprise on being told that, for example, the woman we'd tagged as an account executive or corporate lawyer in fact earns her living as a hospital cleaner.

That mistakes of this sort are possible highlights a dilemma. However efficiently you avert encounter in the mega-community, you cannot avoid strangers. Everywhere you go you share space with them, interact with them; even those you now count as friends were strangers at the first meeting. In such a world a lot has to be taken on trust. Or perhaps a better way of saying it is that trust – surely the preferred basis of relationship – becomes a lot riskier; the incentive grows to bolster or replace trust with security.

It is because you don't know who else your lover has slept with (or who previously slept with him) that you practise "safe" sex. It is because you cannot be sure a financier's word is his bond that you hedge your deal around with threats of litigation. It is because you don't meet your neighbours or the people who pass down your street that you put locks on your windows and think twice before letting your children go unaccompanied to the playground. Probably the people you see today will not be child rapists, pickpockets or psychotic serial killers. But you can't be sure. You worry enough to take precautions. Not walking alone at night if you are a woman. Staying out of Harlem if you are white. In the mega-community the old adage that "what you don't know won't harm you" is summarily upended. Ignorance isn't bliss. It is Relational dysfunction.

The Western Voyeur
The Bounds of Caring

A certain set of problems, then, arises in the mega-community because we have to share space with people we do not encounter. Another set arises for a different reason: that contingent relationships link us with people we never meet.

Take, for example, Maria Costa Ferreira, who plants cocoa saplings on a plantation in north-east Brazil. She is paid piece rates: one tenth of a Brazilian cruzado for each sapling, enough to buy 2% of a single 40g chocolate bar. There are only so many saplings a person can plant in one day, and not surprisingly her children go hungry.

Now I don't know this woman personally – I just happened to read about her in a magazine.[4] Nevertheless I have to take seriously the relationship a worldwide market gives me with people like Maria Ferreira. How many private tragedies do I have a bit-part in as the price-conscious consumer of Third World agricultural commodities? What lights flash and wheels turn at the other end of the engine of international trade when I exercise my right to buy cheaper brands of food? The economic strings leading back from my consumption attach me to injustices I know nothing about. Not just foodstuffs but almost any produce traded within the mega-community could turn out to be morally allergenic.

That most of us in fact do not worry ourselves over such matters demonstrates that the mega-community, and in particular the economy and communications, expand our Relational horizon far beyond the range of felt responsibility.

Logic is powerless here. Granted the peculiar Relational structure of the plc, for instance, managers in a multinational will almost inevitably take the short-term view and tend to resist wage rises or improvements to working conditions in countries where such things are not strictly enforced by law. An increase in production costs could, after all, only jeopardise the profit margin and the ability to compete. Consequently, ownership of shares through an insurance policy or pension fund may give me, if only to the nth decimal place, a percentage stake in somebody else's suffering. But do I feel badly? No: set against my own demonstrable and concrete needs the whole argument seems unreal. What happens to someone like Maria Ferreira, what happens to the blue whale or the African elephant, what happens to earthquake victims in Mexico, are questions of marginal concern to me. There's no encounter involved. Even the argument — beloved of the Brandt Report — that I am my brother's keeper because I depend on *him* to keep *me* makes little impression if I have never seen him.

In terms of such psychology the difference between decision-makers and other interested parties — between managers and owners, ministers of state and electors — is one of degree, not kind. The issues are just more explicit. Distance still has its anaesthetic effect; self-interest still chisels away at moral inhibition. How much moral or emotional leverage does the death of African children through diarrhoea exert on an executive whose company markets expensive pharmaceutical treatments in full knowledge that better results are obtained by mixing water, sugar and salt? Very little, unless he spends time with the children himself, or their cause is taken up by someone he knows and respects. But encounter of this sort is unlikely to occur when he lives on another continent. If it did occur the moral dimensions of his relationship with them would emerge in unwelcome clarity: he would either have to respond humanely, by, for instance, taking a stand against company policy, or become a monster.

For this reason, perhaps, political leaders prefer not to prolong their visits to zones of urban deprivation. To linger, to let encounter develop, would be to acknowledge a challenge to their integrity and the moral claims of weakness on power. The conversion of those who do linger is a theme more common in literature and film than in real life. In real life it is too easy to insulate yourself. If you have money you can move away when times get hard, protect yourself to some extent even from the effects of global warming or ozone depletion. It is unusual to find someone with the means to live elsewhere voluntarily exposing himself or his family to as much as a theoretical risk to health. How many board members in British Nuclear Fuels would go swimming within a mile of Sellafield?

This may appear cynical. The success of charity organisation in the 1980s — telethons, sponsored fun-runs, satellite-borne musical extravaganzas, red nose days — surely proves the competence not just of the economy to channel together vast pools of small donations but of the media to sensitise us by proxy to the suffering of others. That is true enough; the strength of the photographic or televised image lies in its ability to make us respond emotionally to the starving mother and crying child as though we encountered them directly. But it is also in the nature of such images that their intensity is time-bound, that they give way a moment later to other images, other messages. Hence the stress laid on immediate response: don't wait, phone now.

More damaging in the long run is the tendency of this continuous particle bombardment to cause media-burn. No subsequent broadcast has had the impact of Michael Buerk's harrowing report from the refugee camp at Korem, Ethiopia, screened in October 1984. In fact the multiplication of images and the competition of charities in the race to shock tends inevitably to push the urgent, fathomless needs of strangers to the edge of our attention — especially if those strangers are elderly, disfigured or mentally sick, and thus, in the language of the media-driven aid industry, unmarketable. Where the image fails, self-interest moves in. We support the causes we ourselves are most likely to benefit from. After all, anybody can get cancer; but cerebral palsy? Out of sight is out of mind. What makes this retreat from involvement possible, and in some senses perhaps necessary, is the sheer size of the mega-community. A recent unpublished government study showed air pollution over Britain to have risen by 35% in just five years, nox (oxides of nitrogen) levels now exceeding EC guidelines in a third of 353 test sites.[5] More than half our nox emissions come from road traffic. But whose fault is that? The government's for not regulating exhaust emissions? The vehicle manufacturers' for not pioneering cleaner engines? Ours for using private cars and not going to work on the bus?

The truth is, it is everyone's fault, and nobody's. Nox production, like the instability of cocoa prices on the world markets, like inflation or nuclear proliferation, arises from a complex blend of interests interacting through the economy and the media. No single individual ordained Black Monday or the collapse of the Eastern Bloc. Which is why these mega-issues – dramas played out at the scale of the mega-community – seem to have lives of their own, to be as resistant to human control as tides and typhoons. Equipped only with a pen for writing to the press and the Herculean power to stuff paper into a ballot box perhaps three times a decade, the individual feels – understandably – helpless.

Apparently whatever he or she does or fails to do matters not one whit.

Deaf Paper
The Plight of the Individual

Here we have arrived at one of the fundamental questions in the mega-community: power, and who has it.

Such power as you possess in the mega-community derives in large measure from the value the mega-community (and in particular the Western liberal tradition) places on you as an individual. It is as an individual that you bear rights, as an individual that you vote, as an individual that you apply for jobs, pay taxes, watch commercials, buy a house, open a bank account. So much stock is set by your individuality that you are free to register disapproval of the system by an individual decision to, say, support the Scottish Nationalists and buy free-range eggs.

If exercising this freedom seems futile, that is not because your entitlements as an individual are counterfeit and worthless, but only because in the mega-community you are one among millions of voters and buyers and therefore, numerically, a blip. But the problem doesn't end there. The mega-community contains correspondingly large-scale institutions which, through their ability to claw together substantial amounts of political, economic or media power, often make one individual far more influential than another. In other words the mega-community isn't a flat field: it is a jumble of hierarchies.

Hierarchy frustrates encounter. Complain to the chairman of a large corporation and you will usually receive a polite reply from someone in customer services. Naturally, you say; the chairman gets too many letters to reply to them all in person. But that's exactly the point: hierarchies have a narrow pinnacle and a broad base. As you are at the bottom of one hierarchy (the consumer lobby) and he is at the top of another (a plc), the structure prevents you meeting.

It also makes you invisible. At least it allows you to be visible only in a limited range of aspects. The facts the people at the top of a hierarchy want to know about you – indeed in the age of advanced information technology the only facts they can handle – are those that can be quantified: age, sex, address, net earnings, post code, whether you are a B1 or a C2, single or married, a smoker or a non-smoker. It is as though in order to be seen at the higher levels you have to be broken up into bits and most of you thrown away.

The result is Relational constriction, a channelling of relationship into isolated and specific streams by means of meshes and valves so fine that often only numbers can slip through them. Insofar as it precludes any real possibility of dialogue, the form you fill out under a credit-scoring system is like the transcript of a lecture; but it differs from a transcript in the important respect that where personal finance is concerned your motives for wanting to answer back have to do not just with intellectual curiosity but with basic wellbeing. The form has no box for extenuating circumstances. In effect it permits you to say only that you're a bad credit risk, not that your marriage is in trouble or that with just a two month extension on a loan you could pull your business back from insolvency. Paper is deaf.

And of course deafness isn't only an affliction of stationery. Who hasn't at some time belaboured a railway official or a traffic warden or a DSS clerk, and been met with a patient (and, one suspects, gleeful) insistence on working by the book? *But my train leaves in two minutes.* Wait your turn in the queue. *But my wife's having a baby.* All I know is you're parked on a yellow line. *I told you I can't find my birth certificate.* Sorry, there's nothing we can do without documentation. And on and on. Infuriating as it may be, however (and it is very infuriating), petty officialdom doesn't run entirely on dyspepsia and grudge. True enough, the chips of institutional power are stacked high on the other side of the table. But the limits to your encounter with, for example, a station ticket clerk are set with equal firmness by the fact that you can relate to him only through a panel of reinforced glass, in terms of his function in the hierarchy. You don't see him at home; you don't know his interests, or his children. Your relationship with him has been pared down to the exchange of some coins for a piece of card. He could be a machine. Indeed, he often is.

This division of the whole person into a series of slot-like roles is characteristic of the mega-community. We no longer describe our doctor as a friend of the family, or seek her advice on such non-medical matters as making a will. She exists only to treat our illnesses (or some of them: the trickier cases she refers), and if she doesn't keep pumping patients through the consulting room, those of us left waiting for our appointments begin to cast grim and meaningful glances at the clock.

Borne with stoicism, such experiences of what we usually nickname bureaucracy seem to prove what a little thought would suggest is obvious: that the institutions of the mega-community deal more readily with the capacities in which people are all the same than those marking each of them out as individual and unique. Handing the pensioner the weekly allowance that is every pensioner's due takes less time than sitting down for a cup of tea and listening to his story.

It is hardly surprising that big institutions do not foster a sense of belonging. If encounter occurs within them it occurs in spite of them, through sheer force of human decency, and not thanks to the Relational conditions they set up. The house of administration, as one writer has dubbed the welfare state, is not one to party in.[6]

Watching the Golden Goose
Fear and Economics

The mega-community is held together mainly by the twin networks of economy and communications. There are, of course, some very obvious ways in which communications allow dialogue to be conducted with reasonable speed even over large distances (air transport, telecommunications), and some equally obvious ways in which economy relies on communications (container haulage, on-screen monitoring of share prices) and is in some ways a sub-category of it. Nevertheless economy and communications have distinct functions and influences in the mega-community, and these invite further exploration.

We say money talks. But we've also grown accustomed to talking through money. In fact on all scales the economy is the principal medium through which we conduct our countless contingent relationships. Thus the Canadian philosopher Michael Ignatieff, reflecting on his dealings with pensioners in North London:

> My encounters with them are a parable of moral relations between strangers in the welfare state. They have needs, and because they live within a welfare state these needs confer entitlements – rights – to the resources of people like me. Their needs and their entitlements establish a silent relation between us. As we stand together in line at the post office, while they cash their pension cheques, some tiny portion of my income is transferred into their pockets through the numberless capillaries of the state. The mediated quality of our relationship seems necessary to both of us. They are dependent on the state, not upon me, and we are both glad of it. Yet I am also aware of how this mediation walls us off from each other. We are responsible for each other, but we are not responsible to each other.[7]

Ignatieff catches well the psychological nuances involved in linkage through the economy. Through contingency the tax-payer has a relationship not just with one old lady in one post office but with every old lady in every post office. His attentions are scrupulously divided between them. And if he never posted a letter and never met a single old-age pensioner face to face the state would still doggedly dispense his responsibility to them through the ubiquitous medium of money. The system doesn't preclude encounter, certainly; but it doesn't need it either. The little encounters it provokes in the post office queue are incidental and could be prevented entirely if pensions were credited direct to the recipient's bank account. At the very least, people standing in the queue like Ignatieff are left with one less reason to start chatting. Knowing that their debts to the claimant are paid up in advance via the Inland Revenue may throw simple decencies like smiling and saying hello a long way down their already full lists of priorities.

The operation of the economy in general keeps encounter within strict bounds. We have already noted the example of the station ticket clerk. As a more or less universal medium of exchange, money creates a whole genre of such function-based relationships – postal clerk, bank teller, taxman, insurance salesperson – each controlling a small tap in the infinitely complicated plumbing of the Western economy.

In a minimalist sense they qualify as relationships of encounter. Yet you don't stop to pass the time of day with these people. On the plane to Italy the first phrase you look up in the Berlitz guide is "How much?" not "How are you?" and in shops at home, where you could say much more, you will often say less. You can perform the entire ritual of payment-by-card without so much as a glance at the person serving you. Even without a twenty-yard line-up at your back it takes a conscious effort to act as if the cashier is a human being and not merely an extension of the till. Once again the system, while not precluding encounter, fails to encourage it. And once again, with the increasing popularity of mail-order and television shopping, technology offers the prospect of encounterless purchase.

Economics impacts on us in other ways too. In a society linked together by money, the concept of monetary value soon bubbles through the language. We talk about a job paying thirty grand, damage estimated at five billion, the prize money at a golf tournament, a man with a price on his head. We express admiration of a car or a house by speculating about its cost. We reduce art to a saleable good, remarking on a Van Gogh because it fetches a record sum at Sotheby's, saving Maori war dances and goodness knows how many other culturally endangered species from extinction by paying to see them.

Somewhere in the midst of this a very old belief is revived

– the belief that when all is said and done it is monetary value that counts. Price becomes a shorthand for quality. Parents feel a subtle pressure (judiciously reinforced by the advertising industry) to measure their love for children in the amount they spend on schooling, camps, toys, books and computer games. It follows that the happy man is one who can afford to live well, and accordingly success is defined as the knack for turning skill into profit. A successful actress isn't in the first instance one who is good at acting or one who enjoys her work, but one who has secured a string of leading roles at Hollywood. That she may be desperately lonely or commit suicide at the age of thirty-five isn't deemed to make her less "successful". Nobody thinks of Marilyn Monroe as a flop. Yet, arguably, if she had been a flop commercially she wouldn't have died.

Considered in the context of individual behaviour this amounts to a fairly conventional critique of materialism. The obsession with the economic, however, also applies in the public realm.

All the major Party campaigns in the 1992 General Election were dominated by the single issue of economic management. Despite the obligatory huffing and puffing, this did not reflect a contrast in the proposals put forward for coaxing the economy back to life. Rather it betrayed a widespread consensus on the economy's importance to national and individual wellbeing. On two very fundamental points the Conservative, Labour and Liberal-Democratic Parties were in complete agreement: first, that every need politics can address is addressed through the apportioning of cash, and second, that the ability of politics to address any need at all depends on maintaining economic growth.

The second, of course, follows directly from the first. Not only among Party campaign managers but throughout Western society in general the economy is perceived as delivering both what we positively value (prosperity, education, health) and the resources to manage problems we would rather be without (unemployment, crime, personal debt). Almost every developed state, for example, has trimmed its definition of welfare needs to five things for which specific claims can be made against a national budget: food, shelter, clothing, warmth and medical care. No growth, no welfare. Keeping wealthy is the key to everything.

It is entirely consistent with such thinking that the maximisation of returns on capital should be the inherent goal-structure and exclusive aim of the plc, and that successive political administrations in Britain should have treated the economy as though it were the golden goose on life support.

Outside Marxism and Green fundamentalism, arguments over social issues almost never challenge the aims of the economy. The patient is too ill to allow that kind of hubbub to be carried on around the bed. Instead, argument is framed, by all major Parties, in terms of varying degrees of commitment to public sector spending. Labour policy-makers generally think we can squeeze out a few more eggs than Conservative policy-makers do. But both would say that the amount we can give to the inner cities or the NHS is limited by what we can afford given the dodgy condition of the goose.

It is easy to see how tempting the inverse logic can be. If the goose shows signs of lapsing, the first thing you must do is keep visitors away, cut back on unnecessary expenditures of its strength. You shed workers, increase efficiency, give pep talks about belt-tightening and foreign competition. Such anxiety is infectious. There is little doubt that most of us judge a political administration successful primarily on the basis of economic indices like the rate of inflation, the balance of payments and the strength of the currency.

Consequently, although certain more searching questions are occasionally raised by the media, doubters have no place in the darkened room of political realism. No one in earshot of the goose will take seriously the proposition that real and substantive needs – needs like dignity or fraternity, for instance, which do not thrive naturally in the mega-community – might lie beyond the reach of money, or that by neglecting such needs, leaving them to look after themselves, the state will gradually let the social costs of the economy build up to the point where even rapid growth will no longer suffice. And this effect is exacerbated by the tendency of ministers who may be out of office at the next election to concentrate on projects that will bear fruit quickly. The long-term is perpetually sacrificed to the short-term.

And yet, as we'll see, this argument for what we might call the Relational unsustainability of growth is a very powerful one. The endless rising welfare needs of the British population have already stretched government resources to near breaking point, so that present levels of support can be maintained only by raising taxes, with an attendant threat to international competitiveness, or by reducing per capita expenditure on welfare, health and education.

Nevertheless the official line is still that growth achieves all. If you only have money, the rest will pan out. Dig deep enough in the literature and you will find, occasionally, the belief taken to its illogical conclusion: that one day money will have the power to make us *good*.[8]

The Case against Milo Radulovich
Media in the Mega-Community

In 1951 the broadcaster Edward R. Murrow, whose reports to CBS's revolutionary *World News Roundup* from wartime London had made him a media hero, collaborated with producer Fred Friendly to put out the hard-hitting television current affairs show *See It Now*.

It made its name for a programme screened on October 20, 1953, title: *The Case Against Milo Radulovich*. In the gathering paranoia of the McCarthy era Radulovich had been dismissed from the Air Force on the strength of suspected Communist sympathies in his family. It was a clear case of guilt by association. But with a group of ex-FBI vigilantes recently having named 151 suspected Communists in the media, the network bosses were sitting tight, afraid that they would be next in McCarthy's sights. Murrow was the only media personality with the guts to pick up on it.

Six months later, in a follow-up for which CBS refused to finance advertising in the *New York Times*, Murrow created a sensation by taking on Senator McCarthy direct. He did not blackball McCarthy. That the show marked the beginning of the end for the anti-Communist purges followed simply from McCarthy's own effect on the viewers. The results were emphatic: intense public interest in the televised Army – McCarthy hearings that started in April 1954, and a Senate vote later the same year censuring McCarthy by a margin of 67 to 22 for breach of constitutional privilege.

Joseph McCarthy succeeded in alarming the American people, and ultimately failed to convince them, for one and the same reason: the news media. If Orson Welles' radio adaptation of *The War of the Worlds* could cause a national panic, it was no big deal during the cold war for McCarthy to persuade Americans that the country was riddled with Communist infiltrators. Is someone on your street a terrorist? In the mega-community you can never be sure. What you can be, though,. is well informed, and it was by trading on the efficiency of the news media in transmitting accuracies as well as falsehoods that Murrow helped precipitate McCarthy's downfall.

The news media, the fulcrum of Western communications, is efficient because it is omnipresent. Without it the mega-community shatters like a windscreen. The instant view it offers of world events and the way it projects back at us through the opinion polls our own political and social preferences sharpen our sense of involvement even when – as is normally the case – we have no direct interest in the affairs it portrays. For most of us the fall of Margaret Thatcher, entry into Europe and the 1992 Earth Summit have little bearing on the negotiation of daily life. Yet we are aware of them as relevant to us; we gossip about them, express opinions about them, fall in and fall out about them. And we do so because we are wired up to the same machine and occupy the same psychological space. Hardly a day goes by but we scan the headlines, catch a bulletin on the radio or slump onto the sofa for the evening news. We want to know what is going on in the mega-community. We belong to it.

The media can promote encounter. The fact that TV programmes and newspaper reports form part of our shared experience makes them potential subject matter for conversation. At the other end of the airwaves, American public-access TV, radio phone-ins, studio debates and to a lesser extent correspondence columns all bring ordinary people together in dialogue. But such encounters are characteristically partial and brief, squeezed into short bites by the premium on studio time or page space. And always between producer and consumer falls the shadow of screen, loudspeaker and printed page – insurmountable barriers to reciprocation that separate star from fans and impose passivity on the masses, redefining them as listeners, viewers, readers, subscribers.

In the end the only way to be known in the mega-community is to use the mass media – to project yourself and hence to become, in effect, a celebrity. The competition is stiffer than it was. As the media industry has expanded, so the number of occupational groups eligible to produce celebrities has increased. The traditional mainstays, film stars and "society" people – the only ones the public heart missed a beat for when the *Titanic* went down – now have to jostle on the platform with rock musicians, politicians, TV chat show hosts, footballers, lesser royals, weather forecasters and moguls – not least the Richard Bransons and Silvio Berlusconis whose assets have included significant portions of the media industry. If writers less often achieve celebrity status it is only because they spend less time in the public eye. You would probably recognise Shakespeare; but would you know Norman Mailer or David Lodge if you passed them in the street?

If cultivating yourself as a celebrity gets you heard in the mega-community, however, it can also take the privacy out of private life. Of course there are plenty of people for whom being stared at in restaurants is the ultimate trip and who like nothing better than posing for the paparazzi. But whatever the famous get out of fame, and whatever the obscure admire them for, there is certainly no encounter taking place. Such is the elevating power of media attention that if you're a celebrity and I'm not I will be hard put to meet you on level ground. The weight of your reputation in the mega-community will tend to unbalance any personal exchanges between us. If I did achieve real encounter with you – encounter of the uncompromising kind that catches you before you've put your mascara on or brushed your teeth – I would soon confront the disappointing truth that having your name up on Broadway doesn't make your laundry smell sweet.

But that's a big if. Celebrities aren't the sort of people you bump into walking the dog on a Sunday afternoon. The lifestyles of the rich and famous warrant their own TV show precisely because, like mountain gorillas, they are the sort of thing the ordinary punter doesn't see. A celebrity's work and leisure, her courtships, face-lifts and divorces, seem to happen in a fantasy world where everyone has money, and nothing, not even death, is a serious problem. In one sense the solid flesh-and-blood human being is irrelevant. Seen only through the media she functions as an icon – a symbol of social, political or economic aspiration – and in the role of icon achieves a sort of immortality. Elvis *is* alive – and living on a postage stamp. Garbo is alive; JFK is alive; Leonardo da Vinci would be alive too if Andy Warhol had only been around to paint him.

In Party campaign offices across the world the art of being a celebrity is, of course, treated very seriously indeed. When you can be known to the electors only through the mass media, your adeptness in front of the cameras will decide whether you're in or out of the White House – a lesson

Ronald Reagan learned long before Walter Mondale did
in 1984. Much care is taken in the construction of media
events and shielding the unreliable candidate (all candidates
are unreliable) from situations where he may blow a gaffe
– one result of which is that the media, suspicious of being
manipulated for propaganda purposes, tends to give gaffes
undue prominence. "The travelling press," Jimmy Carter
once complained in an interview to *Playboy*, "have zero
interest in any issue unless it's a matter of my making a
mistake."[9]

In this and other ways celebrity electioneering shifts
attention away from issues and on to personalities. But
what's new? Personalities fit the screen better. A TV clip
showing the Prime Minister and the Leader of the Opposition
shouting at one another about farm subsidies is infinitely
more interesting – though considerably less informative –
than finding out exactly how much Britain pays to prop
up European agriculture. To be seen to win the argument
matters more than to have a coherent view. The term news
story is thus a literal description of the way that television
in particular reports events. It implies that news isn't about
issues at all, but about characters, conflicts, developments,
resolutions. Political debate, shaped and filtered by the
media for consumption in the mega-community, begins to
look suspiciously like entertainment.

And of course entertainment, not news coverage or documentary, takes up most of the time we devote to the media.
Ironically, in view of his triumph over McCarthy, it was
when Edward Murrow stood at the height of his success
and had won more awards than any other broadcaster that
CBS allowed *See It Now* to be edged from its prime time
slot by game shows, westerns and entertainment spectaculars,
finally dropping it in 1958. The escapist programming that
bulks out the schedules today on practically every channel
still links the viewer with the mega-community, but, as
it were, through curved mirrors. The families contending
amiably for a food mixer or a set of garden furniture

aren't malnourished, missing limbs, or dressed in cast-offs. The cops and the lawyers fighting their sixty-minute battles always seem to win, or to learn from their mistakes. The heroes and heroines seldom have crooked teeth, seldom have less than completely satisfying sex. And perhaps that is what escapism means. We cannot take too much social realism, too much honesty about relationships, routine, and disappointment. We want, and we are offered, harmonies and variations on the real world, punctuated by short, sly appeals to spend money. The object isn't to learn, only to relax and enjoy.

As technology hightails down the road of media entertainment, and the VCR is loaded with videos and the desktop computer with games, the screen's significance as a link with the mega-community vanishes almost completely. Not too far ahead lies the ultimate denial of encounter: the live-in fantasies of virtual reality, where the individual, grotesquely masked, hacks at virtual dragons with a virtual sword, to win the favours of maidens who don't exist.

Mega-Community and Humanity
Conclusion

I have used the term mega-community to describe an arrangement of personal relationships that has resulted from the Western transition from "traditional" to "modern" society.

The community to which we feel we belong no longer centres on face-to-face encounter relationships largely contained within the immediate town or neighbourhood. Our encounter has become wider spread and more diffuse, and our sense of community, informed now by the millions of contingent relationships where people have indirect contact but never meet, has expanded to include the nation and the world.

One important consequence of the contingency created by large-scale institutions is that some people have power over other people they have never seen. The individual, then, will often feel helpless in relation to government and big business, and both helpless and in some sense guilty in relation to those victimised by a world political and economic order of which he, as a Westerner, is usually a net beneficiary.

The use of the word "individual" here is more significant than might first appear. In the philosophical sea-change that has occurred in the emergence of the mega-community we take it for granted that we are individuals first, social members second. We have a highly developed language of rights, and a native suspicion of anyone or anything that seems to place constraints on our freedom. Beneath the mega-community – in other words, fostering it, reinforced by it and embodied in it – is a deeper movement that has to do with our understanding of what kind of creatures human beings are, and what forms of social organisation do their nature justice.

It is this level – a few floors down in the philosophical elevator – that we now need to explore.

Notes

1　Shakespeare was already punning with alternative meanings of the word at the turn of the seventeenth century: ". . . that is Angelo," says Mariana in *Measure for Measure* (Act 5, scene 1), "/Who thinks he knows that he ne're knew my body,/But knows, he thinks, that he knows Isabel's."

2　For an explanation of the use of the pronoun "I" in this book please refer to the Preface.

3　Jurgen Reusch and Gregory Bateson, *Communication: The Social Matrix of Psychiatry* (W. W. Norton & Co. Inc., New York, 1951), pp. 204–5, n.1.

4　Sue Branford, "Plantations and Planes", *New Internationalist*, no. 204, February 1990, p. 21.

5　Nicholas Schoon, "Soaring pollution blamed on cars", *Independent*, May 15, 1992.

6 Ronald Fletcher, *The Shaking of the Foundations* (Routledge, London, 1988), p. 191.

7 Michael Ignatieff, *The Needs of Strangers* (Chatto & Windus, The Hogarth Press, London, 1984), p. 10.

8 John Maynard Keynes once expressed such a view. See "The end of laissez-faire" in *Essays in Persuasion* (London, 1926).

9 Ronald Berkman and Laura Kitch, *Politics in the Media Age* (McGraw-Hill, New York, 1986), p. 129.

2

Mapping the Relational Universe

Danes Are Like That
Choice and Obligation, Commitment and Constraint

When he visited the anthropology department at a Danish university, Professor Prakesh Reddy, a social anthropologist from India's University of Sri Vankarewara, made a discovery that surprised him: of all the pins on the wall-chart marking where the department sent its field workers, not one was in Denmark. Why not? Simple: "There's nothing here to study," a colleague explained. Apparently Professor Reddy didn't believe him, because he went on to write *Danes Are Like That* – probably the first study of a small Western community to be made by an anthropologist from the Third World.[1]

Actually Professor Reddy had some difficulty applying the word *community* to the 104 occupants of the Jutland village of Hvilsager. Where he hailed from – Tiruptati in Andhra Pradesh – neighbours were constantly in and out of his house and relatives two a penny. Social conditions approximated to those of the pre-industrial society in allowing high rates of encounter. But in Hvilsager some people didn't even know their neighbours. Children appeared to leave home as soon as possible, and by all accounts their parents were relieved to see them go. Even more surprising, the elderly seemed happy to be put in an old people's home, complaining only that they'd like to see their children as well as talk to them on the telephone. Denmark, the professor concluded, had become a place of independence, loneliness and spiritual aridity.

He was accused of moralising. Yet the way of life he found so strange in Hvilsager will probably strike you, a Westerner, as pretty much par for the course. Danes *are* like that. So, on average, are the British. And the Americans. With the emergence of the mega-community, neighbourhood networks of the kind noted in Young and Willmott's classic study of East London[2] have become increasingly rare. Strong encounter relationships – the sort a person is raised with – now occur mostly inside the home. Furthermore, the home itself has grown lean and mean, wider families being broken up into nuclear and single-parent units where the individual's desires and interests characteristically take precedence over those of the group. Unable to stop treading on each other's toes in the mega-community, we have stepped into our separate houses and closed the door, and then stepped into our separate rooms and closed the door. The home becomes a multi-purpose leisure centre where household members can live, as it were, separately side by side. Not just the gas industry but life in general has been privatised.

To appreciate fully how significant a development this is you have to move a few squares back and look at the way individuals and society connect.

Philosophically speaking, individualism is very much the new kid on the block. Take Plato off the shelf and you will find he takes it for granted that the individual's place and purpose are defined by society, much as the place and purpose of the branch are defined by the tree. The idea that in essence the individual is complete on his own – that the tree does not exist until the branches agree to create it – appeared for the first time in post-Reformation Europe and remains, from the historical point of view, an enigma. To have imagined a civilisation where almost every individual has a sense of his or her own unique worth, and where this sense is mirrored in real economic and political freedoms, would have blown Plato's highly capable mind.

History has left us, then, with two very different concepts of society. We can see it as an organic whole (described by analogy as a family or a body politic) which has claims on us as its constituent members; or, and perhaps at the same time, we can see it as a social construct, whose institutions exist (albeit implicitly) only by consent, and thus have no absolute claim on us. In the first, emphasis is laid on responsibilities; in the second, on rights.

A cursory examination of Western attitudes will reveal that while we do not always distinguish the two clearly as ways of seeing society, we do recognise a corresponding distinction in values. We realise that there are some benefits we can obtain only by means of co-operation and linkage with others – benefits as diverse as love, security, motorways, air-sea rescue services and tinned pears – and that co-operation and linkage imply certain claims against our freedom. This idea is so deeply rooted in our society – indeed the very existence of "society" as such presupposes it – that we often fail to notice it at work. Nevertheless it is strongly present in what we refer to as obligations: obligations to the state enforced by the law, obligations to parents and children, and so on.

You will see immediately that some obligations are imposed on us without reference to our own preferences or feelings. Nobody asks me if I want to drive under 30 mph in an urban area: I am simply expected to do it. Nobody asks me if I want to care for my elderly mother or father: social convention simply urges that I should. At the same time, you will see also that some types of obligation form part of a transaction where certain freedoms are traded for others. By taking a job, you agree in effect to suspend your freedom to do as you like during working hours in exchange for the economic freedoms conferred on you by a wage packet. Obligation, therefore, is not always a unilateral act of sacrifice performed for the good of a social group. There is exchange. Indeed, without that exchange such things as friendship and motorways could hardly exist.

Pre-industrial societies tended to be dominated by obligation. They also provided the individual with few opportunities to step out of line. In fact for a long time the very idea of leaving your place in society, of dropping the obligations that both bound you and sustained you, was inconceivable: only the eccentrics did it: the hermits, the madmen. It wasn't as though you could take a plastic card with you and draw cash in another town. Your life and wellbeing were almost entirely constituted by the obligations linking you to your own community. It is not coincidental that the roots of individualism go back to thirteenth-century England and beyond, where the path to its development was laid by economic structures which allowed relatively high levels of mobility.[3]

Alongside individualism in Europe, then, there arose, both feeding it and being fed by it, an extension of options in the economic and political spheres. The belief that options are good and should be extended has become the dominant ethos of the mega-community. It underlies our understanding of society as a social contract. It is embodied in our democratic institutions, in the operation of the economy, in the drift of the post-modern arts toward pastiche, parody, eclecticism, and deconstruction. We are accustomed to having a choice of residences, a choice of schools and universities, a choice of cosmetics, a choice of jobs, investments, restaurants, companions for a date. Not all options are resourced, to be sure; on a Saturday night the ill-starred, spotty teenager may find himself conspicuously alone at the disco. Nor is the ideal of extending options by any means consistently applied across the social structure. As the Leeds University Professor of Sociology Zygmunt Bauman succinctly points out, freedom to choose is a social relation distinguishing the more privileged from the less.[4] How many options the supermarket offers me for Sunday lunch depends on whether or not I am in work. Nevertheless, in theory at least, choice rules. A woman can choose whether and when to conceive. Any kid can end up Prime Minister.

In the social sphere, of course, the extension of choice very often involves a relaxing of obligations. Our social trajectory is no longer determined by the site of the launch pad. We do not meekly follow our fathers into the family firm or our mothers into the kitchen. We do not take a job with the intention of staying in it for life, nor would this be assumed by an employer. On average, children are now given far greater discretion than they once were in behaviour toward adults and in the development of their own social lives.

It is partly because many obligations in the past were created and maintained for the benefit of small elites that choice has such a hold on the popular imagination, and that its extension for the ordinary individual has gathered so much moral force. Unionisation. Universal suffrage. Right of assembly. Such extensions of individual choice against centralised power and political patronage are a priceless achievement. It is thanks to our insistent belief in the right of the individual to choose that we have such humane documents as the United Nations Charter for Human Rights, and are so profoundly moved by the image of a solitary protestor confronting the tanks in Tienanmen Square. Deeply, absolutely, and irrefutably, choice matters.

The problem is, however, that choice becomes self-justifying. Given the extraordinary speed with which social change and technology have multiplied certain kinds of options, it is worth reminding ourselves just how recently choice has been embraced as something close to a necessity. It is hard to imagine now what life was like with only one television channel; how we survived without shopping centres; and how people buying an old Model-T could, in the words my father is so fond of quoting from Henry Ford, have it in any colour they liked provided it was black.

And yet the question of how much choice we need has no ready answer. There seems to be no a priori reason why people should feel happier with more rather than less choice. It is quite possible to be content in a society where there is only one colour of car; it is possible, in fact, to be content in a society that offers the individual almost no choices at all, in cars, shops, television channels or anything else. Were that not the case we would have to suppose that most people in pre-industrial times, who had far fewer choices than we do, were by the same token significantly more miserable – a contention anthropologists have so far not succeeded in proving.

Nevertheless choice tends to create an impetus for self-extension regardless of arguments over whether extension is necessary or a good idea. You might say it becomes addictive, both in the sense that once you have it you cannot think what you would do if it were taken away, and also in the sense that, if anything, you will want the dose increased. Of course there may be no objection to this so far as choice is an independent variable unrelated to the social structure – to do with the number of dresses you want in your wardrobe or the quality of the CD player in your living room. But choice also impacts directly on obligation. Or, more precisely, it impacts on our willingness to fulfil obligation.

This willingness can have two sources. The first, which we can call *commitment*, is more or less equivalent to moral conscience, the inner mechanism that makes the fulfilment of an obligation a natural reflex because we believe the obligation to be morally binding. The second, *constraint*, can occur without the other and represents, in essence, the conclusion that failure to fulfil a particular obligation would not be in our interest, the action resulting in censure or possible censure by others, either through the enforcement of formal regulations (firing, fining, imprisonment) or informally through some expression of social disapproval (ridicule, criticism, ostracism). Company expense accounts are an obvious example. Anybody who has had one will know how tempting it is to throw a couple of his own personal expenditures in with those made for the company. If he refuses to make false claims, therefore, it will be either because he considers it wrong or because he reckons he can't get away with it. In the first case his willingness springs from commitment, in the other from constraint.

That so few people consider false claiming to be wrong ("The company can afford it," "It's one of the perks") or traceable ("Everyone does it," "They don't bother to check") illustrates fairly clearly the weakness of our motivation given the underlying social conditions of the mega-community. When the heat is on, there is a tendency for obligations of all kinds (moral, contractual, marital) to be seen as secondary to the securing of personal advantage. Not only that, but in time this relative devaluing of obligation as an ethos moves sideways into the social structure and begins to transform the nature of the obligations we take on. The limited responsibility of the shareholder in his contingent relationship to the factory operative reflects precisely this development, as indeed do all relationships mediated through the financial markets.

This move toward looser, more limited, often less defined obligation accords with our view of obligation as a net in which the free-choosing individual should be wary of entangling herself. Yet this is clearly a partial view. Not all obligation is oppression. On the contrary, obligation forms as indispensable a foundation for the good society as the natural environment does for life generally. There is no such thing as a society without obligation; nor, since obligation can be just or unjust, is the issue simply whether we should have less or more of it. What matters is the nature of the obligation and, crucially, the ability of individuals to fulfil obligation where it has a legitimate claim on them.

But although commitment and constraint are valuable social resources, conditions in the mega-community do not foster them. Quite the opposite.

One way of tracing their demise is to look at the changes occurring in Western attitudes to marriage. In the free-choosing mega-community, relationships themselves turn into consumer goods. Surrounded by so many potential relationships we are forced to select and cultivate those most to our liking. This is proverbially true of romance. Going into a social situation with people you don't know can resemble a visit to the supermarket. You submit those you meet to examination before committing a mental act of purchase:

"Give me a call some time . . ." or "Let's keep in touch
. . ." – downpayments destined to culminate, perhaps, in
that desperate all-or-nothing bid, "I love you." Few words in
the English language can describe such beauty as these three,
or have suffered such systematic abuse. Either way, however,
they remain our culture's most sacred vow of commitment,
and, as you would expect, it is a vow based squarely on
mutual and voluntary choice.

Yet because such obligations as marriage is now seen to
invoke are generated from choice and do not come independently credentialled in the form of a vocation, choice can
also nullify them. In several very familiar ways, the exercise
of choice has become a factor in relationship breakdown: wit-
ness the legal shift to no-fault divorce in the UK and the US,[5]
the growth of extra-familial institutions that provide alternative sources of financial security, satisfaction and leisure,[6]
and the availability of paid employment for women.[7]

Naturally, one effect of these is to rectify structural injustices which otherwise would keep people tied into bleak and
unworkable relationships, and to this extent they are to be
welcomed. But clearly choice is more than a guardian of
justice. So deeply has it penetrated our thinking, and so
firmly do we set the right of individual choice above the moral
and religious systems which supply authoritative reasons to
choose, that tolerance for the idea of dissolving a marriage or
cohabiting relationship has become almost second nature to
us. It is entirely consistent with the value of choice to make
legal preparations for divorce before you marry; it is agreed
as commendable not to vow loyalty if you cannot regard the
vow as binding.

Particularly as applied to marriage and the family, this
suck-it-and-see approach to obligation has come under heavy
attack from the conservative wing on both sides of the
Atlantic. Social commentators talk in pejorative terms of
"hedonism", "narcissistic withdrawal" and "the flight from
commitment".[8] Even granted the pain occasioned by the
dissolution of a relationship, of course, it might appear to

a divorcing couple that more is being gained than lost in the sacrifice of obligation. They can choose again, and, who knows, maybe the next choice will be luckier.

But whatever your feelings about the conservative social critique, terms like "flight from commitment" are not too wide of the mark where the obligations involved are those of the strong for the weak. That adults will profit from the termination of the marital relationship says nothing about the interests of the child. And although many parents in failing relationships take conscious steps to protect their children, it seems safe to predict that a norm of greater provisionality in relationships between parents will only leave children more vulnerable. What happens where commitment to the weak breaks down entirely can be seen in the number of elderly people dumped at hospital gates, deliberately shorn of ID, and with the name-tags cut out of their clothes. It happened no less than 70,000 times in the United States in 1991.[9]

Neither granny-dumping nor divorce can be seen as simple abdications of responsibility. They occur for numerous reasons, and against the background of the immense pressures the mega-community places on its families and carers. Yet they also mark that slowly shifting point of equilibrium beyond which, in accordance with our culture's prevailing values, freedom of choice is, however reluctantly, asserted against the interests of another individual – that is, asserted over obligation.

Things Fall Apart
The Weakness of Association

These developments have not passed unnoticed. In quietly subversive mood, Oxford's Ralf Dahrendorf recently suggested that "in the free societies of the OECD world . . . the task of the liberal has to do with that most vexing of social objectives, building ligatures, encouraging the creation of norms, reconstituting the social contract."[10]

Being rooted in the struggle to wrench the individual free from the clutches of the state, liberalism has not much concerned itself with promoting obligation, commitment and constraint. *Social contract* is perhaps the closest liberalism can come to naming ideas for which other traditions have a far more developed vocabulary: fraternity, belonging, love, communion, solidarity. Terms like these occupy a rich vein of socio-political thinking which we can trace through Emile Durkheim, British guild socialism, the co-operative movement, T. H. Green's civic humanism, and the lode-stars of European Christian Democracy, Jacques Maritain and Emmanuel Mounier.

All these thinkers could be described as communitarian; that is, they urge the necessity of bringing individuals together in relationships of community. As such, communitarians form the well-they-would-say-that-wouldn't-they constituency in the modern critique of liberalism, and Dahrendorf, as a liberal, is able to share an intellectual bed with them only through his concern for what he calls *ligature*, or social bonding. In at least one other and very important respect, though, communitarians tend to buy not just into Dahrendorf's thinking but into the liberal tradition generally, and this has left both schools with the same problem.

This can be illustrated in the light of recent political history. The sentiment has frequently been expressed in the twentieth century that Western society is somehow disintegrating: as Yeats said, things fall apart. Indeed, so severe was the crisis of liberal culture between the world wars that under the twin burdens of reparation and Depression most Germans were only too willing to trade in political choice for the warrantied dogmas of National Socialism. A Fascist state is thus, in some sense, a community, for it does at least bind its citizens together under a common purpose. Whether that common purpose or the binding required to achieve it are altogether desirable is, of course, another question. But the problem for a communitarian is how one creates communities at a national scale without resorting to coercion. For unless I am a Hitler or a Mussolini, and ready to subsume the welfare of particular persons within the welfare of the mass, then to re-establish commitment, rebuild community, strengthen ligatures, reconstitute the social contract and generally stop things falling apart I still must respect the individual's right of self-determination. In other words I must attempt, as liberalism does, to construct community out of choice.

This leaves me two options. I can ask individuals to act self-lessly, and then hope that enough of them take my advice for society itself to be transformed. Or, steering pragmatically for self-interest, I can advocate in various public policy proposals what the writer on economic communitarianism, Jonathan Boswell, calls "associativeness-in-liberty",[11] arguing that the good society, which is by definition to everyone's benefit, will be realised far more quickly if we all buckle down and co-operate.

Boswell himself puts the case very strongly for the economic advantages of, for instance, a strike-free manufacturing sector. Yet even in the form in which Boswell presents it – and Boswell is no fool – voluntaristic commitment is surely of limited use. To be sure, a novice can bind herself to a religious order by freely-undertaken vows; but if we propose something like this as a model for commitment in general, then we are back with the appeal to selflessness. For every individual who chooses to take final vows there are tens of thousands who don't. The bigger the obligation, the fewer those prepared to see it through.

I use an extreme case to make the point. But the problem is just as real elsewhere. There is a major debate in progress as to whether the social breaches left open by the loss of the traditional geographic community can be filled by non-geographic voluntary associations: the golf club, church, round table, mums-and-toddlers group, local PTA or drama society. Anyone who has been involved with such groups will appreciate their value in widening circles of contact and furnishing grounds for friendship. But because the voluntary base gives members an implicit opt-out clause, and because most groups operate in a highly mobile society where members come and go, their ability to impose obligation is very limited.

This is what makes voluntarism so comfortable, and simultaneously so frail. If Emma at the local Conservative Club has a climbing accident, you will gladly sign a get-well card. You might go to see her in hospital. But when it turns out that she is going to be permanently paralysed from the waist down, you will probably think twice before rushing in with potentially costly offers of help like cooking meals and getting her children to school. Even as a close friend you are likely to feel nervous in the shadow of long-term need. What are you getting yourself into? Where are the boundaries to be drawn? It is not, after all, the responsibility of other players to tend the injured: there are stretcher bearers for that. The game goes on, and you want to keep playing.

You may say I have chosen an extreme case. But the underlying problem is a common one, and it is by no means obvious how voluntary associations in a choice-seeking society are equipped to deal with it. If you are still in the game, if you are one of the strong, you will tend to like voluntary associations precisely because they offer relationships of limited obligation. Such constraints as you feel will usually serve limited purposes related to the function of the group. You will be frowned on by your ballroom dance team if you fail to turn up for the regional heat. But ultimately the others will always respect your right to drop out. You don't have to stay involved.

That being the case, it is not, perhaps, too jaundiced a view of human nature to suggest that voluntarism is most vigorously defended by those whose age and socio-economic status give them most to gain and least to lose from it, and who are apt to project this outlook on to everyone else. Certainly if you get stretchered out – if you suddenly join the weak – obligation starts to look a whole lot more attractive. And we all get stretchered out sooner or later. Having a child, growing old, moving away from kin, giving up your car – any of these will land you with needs a voluntaristic society has little time for because the relationships such a society creates are by and large not ones of mutual responsibility but ones of mutual benefit entered through choice. (This, incidentally, is why the word *community* as bandied about in discussions of prisoner rehabilitation and psychiatric care is almost completely meaningless. The only way most of us care for such people is through the Inland Revenue – by paying professionals to visit them. Threaten to put an AIDS hospice on the average citizen's street and he'll kick up one dickens of a hullabaloo.)

It is important to balance the argument here. In a rarefied way, obligation is respected everywhere in the practice of routine decency and politeness. Every day countless numbers of people go the extra mile, positively inconveniencing themselves to help others. Millions of friends, lovers, and partners have turned their free choice of one another into years of mutual dedication. But the mega-community does not encourage us to see ourselves as obligated to others. It tends to open escape hatches even from legal obligations. To expect the free exercise of choice in itself to generate commitment is to chase a rainbow. Such commitment as we feel toward others is not, in the end, a product of our choice, but rather materialises within us under the spell of particular relationships.

What we seldom pause to think about is that for relationships to weave this spell requires them to be, as it were, potent enough to carry the magic.

An Obituary in *The Times*
Why Relationships Matter

Relationships do not form a major category of social analysis. Legislators passing laws on crime control do not pause to consider what sort of relationships encourage crime or tend to produce criminals. Although pop psychology writers use the word to death, and although most of us would agree that relationships should be "good" rather than "bad" or "difficult", the concept of relationship in itself does not strike us as offering a light through the philosophic darkness.

Yet there are two reasons why relationship – what we could call the R Factor – is central to human life.

One is, rather obviously, that relationships cannot be avoided. In the normal course of events almost everything you do is done in the context of relationships. If you work, you work with or for others; if you eat, you eat what others have made; if you read, you read words written by another, as you are doing now. And relationships endure. If, returning to Yeats for a moment, you decide tomorrow to renounce the world and spend the next thirty years in lofty seclusion cultivating your nine bean rows in your bee-loud glade, far beyond the reach of newspapers and television, you will still in some sense remain in relationship with me – for you have a memory – just as you will remain in relationship with those who educated you, and to the mother you may never have met.

Relationship is one of the base dimensions of existence. In a bizarre way, and without our resorting to seances and ouija boards, relationship even transcends death. We feel we *know* Charlotte Brontë or Thomas Hardy just because they are communicated so vividly in their works. Consequently, if I have died before you read this, the Relational link between us will not be lost. You will still hear my voice, just as you hear, with surprise, your great-grandmother's voice in old love letters you turn up in the attic. We are shaped by relationships, dependent on relationships to the extent that having someone we love removed from us produces the intensely painful withdrawal-reaction of grief.

But there is a second reason why relationships matter. Not only do we live *in* relationships, as surely as we breathe air; we live *for* them. Ask what they value most highly and most people will tell you about their loved ones. Children. Wife. Husband. Parents. So much do we take this for granted that we would think it strange if someone replied, "My Roman coin collection," or "My Porsche." It is likely in fact that the owner of a fancy car will value it not just for its gleaming chrome and stunning acceleration, but for its ability to draw attention and (he hopes) admiration from other people – in other words, for its effect on his relationships. Most material aspirations translate into Relational categories. We use money to express love, to secure influence, respect, a good start in life for the kids, position in a social set, an obituary in *The Times*. Isolated from the Relational money reverts to mere paper and numbers. Friendship without wealth will make a happy man, but wealth without friendship?

Now you might reply – correctly – that much human satisfaction derives from the gratification of the senses: from the aroma of a good wine and the sheer, sweet physical release of the sexual act. Yet this too translates to the Relational. Not many gourmets will eat alone, and not many sexual gourmets will treat their partners as mere objects of lust. In these, as in almost every activity, we wish to be with others, and for those others to treat us with thoughtfulness, respect, and generosity of spirit. Good company belongs no less surely to the definition of wellbeing than adequate nutrition and health care. Indeed we could argue that the Relational takes precedence over the material since it is only through the good ordering of relationships in society that we have food on the shelf and doctors available to cure our ills. To be is to be in relation. "Here," writes Martin Buber, "is an infallible test . . ."

> Imagine yourself in a situation where you are alone, wholly alone on earth, and you are offered one of the two, books or men. I often hear men prizing their solitude, but that is only because there are still men somewhere on the earth even though in the far distance. I knew nothing of books when I came forth from the womb of my mother, and I shall die without books, with another human hand in my own. I do, indeed, close my door at times and surrender myself to a book, but only because I can open the door again and see a human being looking at me.[12]

Implicit in Buber's thought, of course, is the idea that not all relationships are of equal weight. When he opens the door he meets the other person face to face. When he dies, he dies hand in hand with another. While all relationships are of value, there is something especially valuable about encounter relationships, and in particular close relationships.

Almost the first thing my insurance adviser did when he first called was to address me by my first name. He asked me a few personal and professionally irrelevant questions (I am sure he won't mind me telling you this), and must have noted the answers carefully because the next time we met he brought them up as topics of conversation. "How was the holiday in . . . ?" and so on. In return he supplied me with largely unsolicited details about his own life, some of which struck me as information you would normally conceal from a person you didn't know unless you wished to mark it as a confidence.

He is a good man, and I am being rather hard on him. On the other hand I cannot believe that any insurance sales rep worth his salt would be unaware of the dividends the presumption of intimacy is likely to pay in terms of the client's willingness to buy a policy. In the mega-community the stranger is a threat. From the commercial point of view, therefore, a rep has much to gain by giving the impression that he is not a stranger, by breaking as soon as possible into the circle of the client's personal friends.

A clear distinction is recognised here between relationships of encounter and relationships of contingency, and to the sales rep it is the first kind that matters. It matters to the client too; I am certainly not disparaging the smile at the point of sale. At the same time, though, I detect in such Relational transactions not so much encounter itself as the mimicking of encounter for quite different ends. After all, an insurance adviser never phones just to pass the time of day.

Of course I am blowing my own cover here. The fact that this book is written in a conversational style and not with the dry exactitude of a Ph.D. thesis reflects a calculated decision on my part to pack in as much sense of encounter as the written word will hold. Most communicators use the same ploy. On the junk mailshot the marketing manager's name is scrawled in a lively blue, thus giving, however implausibly, the impression that every one of the hundred thousand letters sent out has been personally signed. The advertisement for famine relief uses pictures, not statistics, because an emaciated child staring up from the page will needle the conscience far more effectively than a column of figures about the Somalian drought. The television newscaster never talks as though she is addressing a meeting – she talks intimately, one to one, warning you about disturbing scenes in the next report and wishing you a peaceful weekend. In these and countless other ways the mega-community and its institutions mimic encounter. And in doing so they seem to address a fundamental human need. Anyone who has visited an old people's home will know how television can deputise for real relationships. Mimicry is better than nothing.

But what exactly is it about encounter that makes it worth mimicking?

That encounter relationships are the principle factor in personality formation has been, in some form or other, the received psychiatric wisdom since Karen Horney, G. H. Mead and particularly the American psychiatrist Henry Stack Sullivan overturned the Freudian theory of psycho-sexual determination.[13] Sullivan saw psychological dysfunction as following not from biological factors but from the presence of *anxiety* – by which he meant emotional discomfort – in the individual's closest and particularly her childhood relationships. His work underlies the widely accepted methods of family therapy as well as a good deal of commonsense child-rearing of the a-baby-needs-to-be-loved variety. It would be difficult, therefore, to find any serious opposition to the view that the individual's interpersonal skills, moral awareness, sense of self-esteem and general emotional stability depend in very large measure on his relationships.

We might add other benefits: physical security in old age,

help with the first baby, an informal loan, links established with past and future generations through the receiving and handing down of stories. Such things come only in close, long-term relationships of encounter. Of course the pattern of a person's relationships shifts with time and need. Parents die. Children arrive, or don't arrive. Links with a particular friend or relative may strengthen if he moves near by, or weaken if other interests and relationships intrude. In different circumstances an individual may have a surfeit of available relationships or a dearth of them. Less predictably, he may regard his closest relationships as being with friends and family, or with a person he sees infrequently rather than people he sees all the time.

This relatedness, considered from birth to death and in all its variations, we can call his *Relational Base*. What I mean by this is that the presence of encounter relationships will always be critical in maintaining his wellbeing. How at one with the universe he feels, how well he performs in employment, education and child-raising, how he survives his crises – all these depend on the support he gets from the people close to him.

Finding an adequate visual image for it is difficult. We could imagine scanning the Relational Base in cross-section at a particular moment in time and seeing the individual within a circle of relationships, the encounter relationships arranged near the centre and the contingent ones massed around the periphery. If we scanned it again a few years later we would discover that the number and relative position of encounter relationships had changed, but not their overall closeness to him. The scanning image, however, breaks down in a number of places. It cannot show the individuality and scope of particular relationships. Nor can it show how each meets particular needs, or at how many different levels of intensity they exist in a person's interaction with locality institutions through, for example, postpersons, schoolteachers, librarians and shopkeepers. More importantly, it gives us no way to represent the long-term effects of encounter.

I remember as a child visiting the lady next door to our house in Sevenoaks and being served orange juice in a red glass. Though her rooms are full of memories for me, and she had in her hallway a set of pictures of the Battle of Britain almost guaranteed to impress small boys, it is the drink I recall most vividly. Every time I went there she gave me orange juice in a red glass, even when I was twenty-five. Now in some ways this is a random and unimportant recollection. And yet that lady has contributed to my sense of permanence; she remains, as it were, an active presence in my Relational Base. It is much the same thing, applied this time to immediate family, that we mean by saying someone had a "stable upbringing".

Here the critic may decide that I am just touting family values under a new name and pining, as supporters of family values tend to, for that lost Golden Age when marriages were happy and children did what they were told. I am not, for three reasons.

First, there is little evidence that this Golden Age ever existed, and little agreement anyway on what kind of family it is supposed to have contained. But that is by the by. Second, Relational Base is a fundamentally different concept to family. It is wider, for one thing; and in contrast to family, which is usually understood normatively by its defenders as a certain observable arrangement of kin, Relational Base is partly subjective. I say partly because human beings seem to have at least some Relational needs that are universal. Almost all studies suggest, for instance, that long-term problems follow from a dysfunctional relationship between child and parent. But given similarly happy parental homes, you and I may turn out to have very different Relational needs. I may feel lost without half a dozen good friends within easy reach, whereas you may be happy with one, at the other end of the country. Which leads to the third and most important point.

In any culture, a family is an arrangement of relationships. To that extent it is an instrument, a means. On the one hand it creates the conditions necessary for individuals to have strong Relational Bases, and on the other it brings individuals together within the social structure for particular purposes that usually include security and child-raising. You can justify its existence from the point of view both of the individual and of the society. But it is the relationships that matter, and not the family *per se*. If a family fails to support constructive relationships it is failing in its purpose both from the individual's point of view and from society's.

Clearly families in the West are often dysfunctional. Indeed a good deal of effort was expended by some social critics in the sixties to prove that the Western family, a discredited and oppressive institution, had a label tied to its toe and was on its way to the cooler.[14] This analysis, of course, had a lot to do with the sixties *Zeitgeist*, and in particular with the personal experience of young thinkers in a society that increasingly propagated the values of choice amid institutions still run, for the most part, by the imposing of obligations. The weakness of the abolitionists' case lay in its confusion of the family as an institution (and therefore, in some sense, as a power structure) and the family as a source of encounter relationships. As an institution it can take an enormous variety of forms. However, the Relational instincts and social forces surrounding the process of reproduction seem almost always to anchor it in a nucleus of mother-father-child, and this probably explains why recent attempts to find alternatives to the Western family have either failed outright or pointed to experiments such as the Israeli kibbutzim which, on closer inspection, turn out not to show that families are irrelevant, but to underline the significance of families by operating just like them.

It is, I presume, the essentially proRelational quality of the kin network that leads as discerning a social critic as Germaine Greer to argue that, from a woman's perspective, there is a lot more to be said for the extended family – what she called the Family – than for the ubiquitous "suburban dyad":

For one thing, if the family is to be a female sphere, then it is better for women's sanity and tranquillity that they not be isolated in it, as they are in the nuclear family. The Family offers the paradigm for the female collectivity; it shows us women co-operating to dignify their lives, to lighten each other's labour, and growing in real love and sisterhood, a word we use constantly without any idea of what it is ... Another reason for championing the Family is that it seems a better environment for children ... [15]

Yardsticks
What We Mean by "Good" Relationships

So far we have blithely made a rather important assumption: namely, that it is possible to distinguish, in a rigorous and systematic way, a "good" relationship from a "bad" one. But is the matter really this straightforward?

We have noted that many of the benefits we enjoy are collectively produced. Streets safe for children (even streets, full stop), productive industry and a clean environment can only be achieved by concerted action, more or less as Oxford will win the boat race only if its oarsmen row in rhythm. Ultimately the successful operation of society, including that of the political economy, depends on how well society's component individuals get along.

The network of encounter and contingent relationships binding society together is unimaginably complex. You have to multiply your Relational Base by approximately five billion to achieve something like the whole hum in the circuitry. In a sense nothing exists but those relationships. They are the synapses in the nervous system we call the world. *State, community*, and *company* aren't objects I can look at, but sets of conscious or unconscious agreements by which my links with certain large blocks of strangers in the mega-community are filtered and regulated. That so much of this filtering and regulation is done automatically and without my express consent is one reason why institutions seem so hard to control, and why the political leader's contingent relationship with the electorate (conducted through the ballot box, the polls, and the budget) can compromise his commitment to initiatives as critical as treaties on bio-diversity and global warming.

What possible criteria could we use to decide if any one of these relationships is "good"?

Let me for the time being by-pass the philosophers and theologians, and hit the street. When I use the phrase "good relationship" I generally mean one of two things. With reference to my wife, for instance, good relationship means emotional attachment. I enjoy being in her company, and enjoy her enjoyment of being in my company. I feel concern for her when she is ill, as she feels concern for me when I'm up until two in the morning pushing to make a deadline. We feel upset if we argue, and miss each other when we're apart. And so on and so forth. It is in this sense also – though with less intensity – that I have a "good" relationship with the economist who lives downstairs, with patrons of the local coffee shop, and with the down-and-out who occasionally prevails on me to buy him a salad roll. I feel comfortable around them; we get along.

At the same time I could describe these same relationships as good in wholly functional terms. Somehow or other my wife and I just about manage to keep two careers going and raise children. We share out the duties required to keep a household running smoothly. We manage to bring an adequate variety of experience to our conversation. Similarly, the economist comes up once a month or so to tell me the overspill from my lavatory cistern is dribbling on to his front doormat, and in response I fiddle with the ballcock. The down-and-out presumably enjoys his salad rolls, just as my buying them for him allows me to make a concrete if minute deduction from the sum of the world's suffering. Functionally, these relationships work well. What would happen if my relationships at this personal level were, affectively or functionally, bad instead of good hardly requires elaboration.

These definitions of quality apply with just as much salience to contingency as to encounter, and as powerfully to public life as private. Race hatred is an aggregation of the feelings the individuals of one race have for individuals of another. How quickly the tower block goes up depends not just on its design features, but on how well the people involved in the design and construction process work together. Systems as diverse as aircraft engineering, computer programming, newspaper production and sales cannot operate competitively unless team members work efficiently and without friction – qualities which at the very least require familiarity with accepted codes of behaviour, ability to accept leadership, and willingness to take responsibility.

This brings us to a third definition of "good" in relationships, which is less visible in the mega-community than affection or function but simultaneously far more influential. Referring back to the first chapter, it would not occur to me, for instance, to label my relationship with the Brazilian plantation worker Maria Ferreira as "bad", and yet thanks to the mediation of the world economy there is a real sense in which I, as a consumer and a shareholder, bear a tiny but significant portion of the blame for her poverty. If world trade and investment were organised differently, I might pay 10% more for my chocolate bar, but she would have proper nutrition, proper access to clean water, proper housing, proper health care. Consequently my link with her, such as it is, has a moral dimension. And this implies that a relationship can be judged good or bad not only by how the partners feel and how well their interactions serve a given purpose, but by how they treat one another.

The philosophers and theologians can come back in now. Quite correctly, they will point out that, lifted off the foundation of revealed religion (that is, stripped of its meta-ethical justification), and made subject to the individual's sovereign power of choice, morality can hardly be dropped on to the scene *ex machina* to deliver a single, universal and binding definition of the good. For if a good relationship is good morally we need to reach some sort of consensus on what good means. And yet by what authority do I claim my morality to be better than yours? If I say abortion is not permissible and you disagree, who will judge between us? Of course we could bring every morality we could lay our hands on to a grand international symposium and try to deduce a minimalist definition of the good that everyone could subscribe to. But that would hardly help, since where moral systems agree, as in the prohibition against stealing, they tend to define the offence in different ways, and where the offence is clearly defined, as in the prohibition against a man sleeping with his mother-in-law, the precept is often of limited use in solving such everyday dilemmas as deciding between brands of coffee.

The problem of finding a secure foundation for morality has long been a thorn in the side of liberal political philosophy, and in fact almost did for the entire discipline in the 1930s when logical positivism condemned such long-hallowed terms as "right" and "good" as non-observable and sent them to the guillotine of the verification principle. Nevertheless, that we still use words like right and good long after logical positivism has self-destructed, and that we seem to mean something by them, gives us, I think, reasonable grounds for trusting them. At least in cultures influenced by the Judaeo-Christian tradition (and despite the trend to moral and cultural pluralism), there is still widespread agreement on values like fair play, trustworthiness, honesty, respect for dignity, honour, courtesy, commitment, reliability and altruism: in summary, for the subtle dictum of "doing as you would be done by".

If it isn't exactly a description of Western moral behaviour, this Relational rule of thumb, sometimes referred to as the "reciprocity principle", does at least provide a powerful rallying point. Most of us will agree with it even if we don't apply it, and most of us would like to believe we apply it, at least most of the time. So much so, in fact, that it informs our judgement in an area where morality might be thought least to apply – the marketplace.

Honesty is Cheaper
Markets and Morality

It was Adam Smith who first said that morals were irrelevant to the exchange system.

Not only that, he wrote in 1776, but "By pursuing his own interest, [a person] frequently promotes that of society more effectually than when he really intends to promote it."[16] To show that being selfish is really a way of being responsible is a trick too clever for words. It is the stuff that dreams are made of. But although such a belief has provided the moral justification for many a form of laissez-faire economics, in fact Adam Smith just as sternly preached commitment to obligation. Seventeen years before he published *Wealth of Nations* we find him asserting that "All members of human society stand in need of each other's assistance . . . " and that "where the necessary assistance is reciprocally afforded . . . the society flourishes and is happy."[17]

Given the religious background against which Smith wrote, this combination of ideas perhaps did not, for him, represent as stark a contradiction as it does for us today. But if our intellectual heritage asks us to pick between self-interest and co-operation as motives for economic activity, we will probably pick co-operation, if only because it is hard to see how Robert Maxwell's very enthusiastic pursuit of his own interest benefited the Mirror Group pensioners. The fact that Maxwell got away with it for so long illustrates a major problem. All the legal paraphernalia that we have put in place to buttress obligation – frameworks of constraint like property rights, contracts, safety regulations, policing, courts – cannot guarantee that self-interest will be kept in check.

And yet on the success of those constraints hang not only the flourishing of society but the very sustainability of the economic system.

Distrust in the marketplace carries heavy systemic costs. The less I trust you, the more likely I am to resort to litigation. That is good news for the lawyers, and bad news for the economy. Not only that, but increasing litigiousness in business and the rise in fraud have led to an enormous increase in demand for forensic accounting. Staffing in the forensic department of Peat Marwick, one of London's leading accountancy firms, has jumped from four to thirty-five in the two years since its establishment in 1990.[18] The lesson, surely, is unavoidable: the less that commitment can be counted on in the marketplace, the more resources have to be diverted into keeping everybody straight. And that is a lot of resources. "Honesty," as one famous economist comments drily, "is much cheaper."[19]

Moreover, commerce relies on commitment being in plentiful supply outside its own boundaries. Fairly obviously, a country where property rights are flouted will not attract investment, and one where commitment within families has declined to the extent that provision for the elderly and infirm has to be made from the national exchequer is one where an increasing tax burden will be laid on industry, forcing it to reduce reinvestment and in effect mortgage its future international competitiveness for the sake of financing immediate social needs.

What this demonstrates is that commitment is as real an input to an economic system as technical proficiency or wage bills: it can decide whether an individual company, or ultimately an entire national economy, floats or sinks. But if it is just as real, it is also far more elusive than how well an employee performs and how much you pay her. You cannot secure it through training schemes or investment. Commitment is something you are raised with. It springs from a wider background of belief systems and relationships, and cannot be generated overnight.

Take a very ordinary example. You employ me as a sales

assistant in your hardware store, and suspect, though you can't prove it, that I have had my fingers in the till. Now you can strengthen the constraints on me by tightening your accounting or standing over me while I ring through the purchases. Even if this stops me pilfering, though, it will not make me honest. My honesty, or lack of it, is an aspect of commitment developed, or not developed, within my Relational Base, and probably before I reached adulthood. Certainly dishonesty can be unlearned – why else believe in punishment as rehabilitation? – but the unlearning often takes time, and would require you anyway to gain access to other parts of my Relational Base (home, family, friends, past associates, and so on) which may be influencing my behaviour at work. You would, in effect, have to turn into a social worker.

That commitment, like constraint, is a valuable social resource which the ethos of choice tends not to replenish, constitutes a major weakness in the capital-based economy. Economies are, after all, people in relationship. And if social resources are not cultivated assiduously, as we cultivate energy or agricultural resources, the economy will soon suffer. The question of how we produce good relationships in society is therefore one of immediate, practical, and extreme importance. We cannot take the quality of relationships for granted, or assume that human behaviour will always adapt adequately to the stresses of social change. That is ostrichism. We need to understand what it is about social structures that nurtures or destroys relationships, and put that understanding to use.

Bricks and Chickens
Conclusion

We started this chapter by noting how a human society balances choice and obligation. For various reasons, pre-industrial societies tended to impose strong obligations and allow little choice. In the mega-community obligations become de-emphasised, and choice, expressed in such forms as political freedom, consumer convenience and personal independence, becomes a dominant social value.

We sense in this shift a kind of natural justice. It was because political control in pre-industrial societies was often despotic, and economic power concentrated in the hands of a tiny elite, that in Western thinking the interests of the individual came to be seen as paramount. And we are right to prize a liberal tradition in which the individual enjoys, at least in theory, protection from the too often oppressive designs of the state.

There remains, however, a problem. On almost any reckoning, having three rather than two flavours of cat food to choose from constitutes an expansion of liberty and an (albeit incremental) enrichment of life. But when we apply the same test to, say, driving, or parenting, or contingent relationships with Third World producers, we find that choice can only be increased at the expense of obligation. To regard myself as free to choose which side of the road I drive on is to neglect my obligation to other road users to drive safely. To regard myself as free to change partners in a parental relationship is to neglect my obligation to give my children a stable home. To wish for lower commodity prices in order to extend my financial freedom as a consumer is to ignore my obligation to Third World producers whose livelihoods depend on getting a fair price for their labour.

There is room for debate, of course, over what my obligations are in any one case, and whether the particular extension of choice I have in mind will in fact disrupt them. But the overall problem is a critical one. Obligation in effect holds society together, and yet the mega-community does not cultivate obligation. Under a prevailing ethos of choice the social resource of commitment is gradually depleted. And when commitment wanes, constraint soon follows because people will not long reinforce behaviour in others that they do not regard as binding on themselves. Increasingly, therefore, society is thrown back on structural constraint – litigation, policing – which saddles the business sector with higher overheads and a heavier tax burden, and hamstrings international competitiveness. Meanwhile individuals become far more selective of the kinds of obligation they are willing to recognise and take on. Short-termism and provisionality rule.

This is ultimately what we are referring to when we complain of the decline of "standards" in the West. It is what Ralf Dahrendorf refers to in claiming the task of modern liberalism to be one of "reconstituting the social contract". But how are we to do such a thing? The only rifle in the individualist closet is voluntary association, which assumes that obligation and commitment can be coaxed, like alchemic gold, from their natural opposite – that is, from choice. Granted the social conditions in the mega-community, however, you will no more get an adequate depth of commitment from voluntarism than you will get bricks out of a chicken. Choice does not in any straightforward way provide the answer to its own dilemma.

The only apparent alternative – and it is the one customarily associated with conservative values – is somehow to ensure that obligations are imposed regardless of changes in social structure and social outlook. Clarion calls sound forth from the political establishment. Moral standards must be adhered to; the family must be kept strong. Yet this approach is surely doomed to fail, if only because in a democracy the gathering momentum of choice must eventually find expression in legislation. Indeed in Britain choice has already found its way on to the statute book, not just in overtly liberalising measures like the 1969 Divorce Reform Act, but because the Conservative government during the 1980s leaned strongly to economic liberalism in the form of deregulation.

Again, it is important to emphasise that choice in itself is desirable and necessary. We will solve nothing by eradicating choice, even if that were possible. On the other hand, our ability to generate and maintain and respect obligation needs to be carefully conserved. We need, as it were, to put choice and obligation in separate cages.

The solution to the dilemma, I would argue, lies in the vital connection between obligation, choice, and relationship. After all, it is through our relationships that we first learn to balance our own needs against those of the group. And it is the structure of our relationships that decides both how easily we develop commitments and how susceptible we are to constraints.

Take an example from business. If I deal with you only once, after which I know I will never see you again, I may be strongly tempted to rip you off. If on the other hand I know I am going to be dealing with you regularly over the next five or ten years, I will almost certainly treat you with respect, and the chances are that we will go on to develop a cordial and co-operative relationship. Continuity in the structure of our relationship therefore has a direct bearing on our conduct of it – an effect that game theory has explored with some thoroughness.

And yet it is precisely this kind of structural feature that the mega-community tends to degrade. Many business relationships do not have continuity. Many household relationships do not have continuity. Somewhere in the explosion of the pre-industrial community into the global village, such structural features of relationships have been distended, enfeebled, neglected, lost. There are so many of us. We move so often and so fast. We are scattered over such a large area. With the mega-community, and its billions of slender, contingent relationships, has come a disintegration of the Relational infrastructure on which all human society relies.

Notes

1 "Danes Are Like That", unpublished English manuscript, published in Denmark as "Saadan er Danskerne", (Grevas

Forlag, Aarhus, 1992). Reviewed in *The Economist*, January 25, 1992, p. 48.

2 Peter Willmott and Michael Young, *Family and Class in a London Suburb* (Routledge & Kegan Paul, London, 1960).

3 See Alan Macfarlane, *The Origins of English Individualism: The Family, Property and Social Transition* (Blackwell, Oxford, 1978).

4 Zygmunt Bauman, *Freedom* (University of Minnesota Press, Minneapolis, 1988), ch. 1.

5 See Lenore Weitzman, *The Divorce Revolution* (Free Press, New York, 1985). In Lynn White's summary, "the most significant result of no-fault divorce law may be to eliminate legal support for norms of lifetime obligation and for the expectation that individuals will be rewarded for fulfilling normative roles." See Lynn K. White, "Determinants of Divorce: A Review of Research in the Eighties", *Journal of Marriage and the Family*, no. 52, November 1990, p. 904.

6 See, for example, Kingsley Davis' introduction to his (ed.) *Contemporary Marriage* (Russell Sage, New York, 1985).

7 Andrew Cherlin, *Marriage, Divorce, Remarriage* (Harvard University Press, Cambridge MA, 1981), and Andrew Cherlin and Frank Furstenburg, "The changing European family", in *Journal of Family Issues*, no. 9, 1988, pp. 291–7, both found a positive relationship between divorce and women's participation in the labour force.

8 See Norval D. Glenn, "Continuity versus change, sanguineness versus concern: Views of the American family in the late 1980s", *Journal of Family Issues*, no. 8, pp. 348–54; and Jay Y. Brodbar-Nemzer, "Divorce and group commitment: the case of the Jews", *Journal of Marriage and the Family*, no. 48, pp. 329–40.

9 "Warning on 'granny dumping'", *Independent*, January 10, 1992.

10 Ralf Dahrendorf, *Life Chances* (Weidenfeld & Nicolson, London, 1979), p. 38.

11 Jonathan Boswell, *Community and the Economy: The Theory of Public Co-operation* (Routledge, London, 1990), ch. 2.

12 Martin Buber, *Meetings*, edited with an introduction and bibliography by Maurice Friedman (Open Court Publishing Company, La Salle IL, 1973), p. 61.

13 See Henry Stack Sullivan, *The Interpersonal Theory of Psychiatry*, edited by H. S. Perry and M. L. Gawel (Norton, New York, 1953).

14 See for example R. D. Laing, *The Divided Self* (Penguin, London, 1965), and David Cooper, *The Death of the Family* (Allen Lane, the Penguin Press, London, 1971).

15 Germaine Greer, *Sex and Destiny* (Secker & Warburg, London, 1984), pp. 241–2.

16 Adam Smith, *The Wealth of Nations* (1776), Bk. IV, ch. II.

17 Adam Smith, *The Theory of Moral Sentiments* (1759), Bk. II, ii.3.1.

18 Roger Trapp, "Increasing fraud makes forensics a growth industry", *Independent*, April 28, 1992.

19 Joan Robinson, *Economic Philosophy* (C. A. Watts & Co. Ltd., London, 1962), p. 5.

3

Relational Proximity

Kissogram Culture
The Nature of Relational Proximity

Somebody asked me recently if I knew a certain person, and I replied, "Not really, we don't see one another very often."

In saying this I was attempting to explain the depth of a relationship by referring to the nature of the encounter behind it. Had circumstances brought us together more frequently, I implied, we would know each other better.

Actually I was making the same assumption a father makes in deciding to spend more time with his son: that fuller encounter deepens relationship. It is the same assumption the Smiths make when they say, "It's time we had the Browns round to dinner," and the same one every teenager makes, quite consciously, by going out on a date. Whether the assumption is always true is an important question which we will return to in due course. But the idea that the kind of relationship you can form with another person depends in some way on the kind of encounters you share is unexceptionable, and requires us to define more closely what we understand by encounter.

Encounters differ both in style and intensity. Many encounter relationships are long-term and ongoing. Wife, husband, boyfriend, parents, sister, children, employees, colleagues, friends, neighbours, boss – we see all these regularly, over months, probably over years. But encounter is no less real for being intermittent. My exchange with a hotel porter may last only ten seconds, but even if I never see the man again I have still encountered him. And scattered between such one-off meetings and my repeated interaction with those near the centre of my Relational Base are scores of relationships, with distant friends, irregular business contacts and local tradesmen, which, though not vital to my wellbeing, none the less fulfil a significant function in my life.

Furthermore, I can encounter another person through many different means. Not all encounter is face to face. I can use the car, train, or plane to make a visit. But I can also write. I can phone. I can fax, transfer documents by modem, send videos, flowers and kissograms. All these allow encounter; all of them allow me to "say something" to another person. Even a kissogram tells you I have gone to the trouble and expense of sending it.

It is on such diverse means of encounter, though admittedly not always on kissograms, that central political and economic functions in the mega-community rely. And it is perhaps because they have to rely on them that political and economic functionaries continually wish to improve them. In part they do this by adopting new technology, supplementing the postal system and the phone with the modem and fax. More significantly, however, they recognise the value of the kind of encounter that brings them into immediate, hand-shaking contact. It is only this kind of face-to-face encounter that permits us to use our massive non-verbal vocabulary to communicate, and to engage in anything like a total sense with another person. Thus business deals are customarily prepared through corporate hospitality, thrashed out over a round of golf, and closed after a slap-up meal at the Ritz. In political circles, delegates meet at conventions, ministers at cabinet meetings, Prime Ministers and Presidents at summits. In other words, not only the conduct of our private relationships, but also our whole economic and political life, depends heavily on maintaining what we might call *Relational proximity*.

Let me explain Relational proximity by telling you first what it is not.

It isn't the same as compatibility. There are, I suppose, millions of people in the world whose personalities are compatible with mine in the sense that if I met them we would be likely to form a firm friendship. But I will never meet them. Conversely, the fact that I am Relationally proximate to the man I share an office with doesn't necessarily mean we will get along. You might conclude from this that Relational proximity is another name for geographical proximity. But this isn't true either. The residents of Hvilsager studied by Professor Reddy lived in a high degree of geographical proximity, and yet they hardly knew one another. Conversely, although the distance separating me from my mother in Nairobi reduces our Relational proximity, we are still a lot closer in Relational terms than we would have been a hundred years ago. I can phone, visit, write.

Relational proximity, then, is a description not of the personalities or geographical positions of two individuals, but of the interaction between them. It has at least five dimensions. I will be more Relationally proximate to you if I meet you face to face than if I meet you over the phone or through an intermediary (*directness*). I will be more Relationally proximate to you if I meet you regularly and over an extended period than if I meet you intermittently and short-term (*continuity*). I will be more Relationally proximate to you if I meet you in two or three contexts or roles than if I meet you only in one (*multiplexity*). I will be more Relationally proximate to you if I meet you on an equal footing than if we are separated by an asymmetry of power (*parity*). And I will be more Relationally proximate to you if we have a common purpose than if our interests do not overlap (*commonality*).

How these dimensions of Relational proximity work in practice will be explored in the following sections of this chapter. But two further points should be made here.

First, how much Relational proximity exists in a relationship is often decided by factors external to the relationship itself. Any institution, for instance, will lay out a pattern of Relational proximity between its members. Business and political relationships, and all contingent economic relationships, are set up with a preconceived purpose, and hedged around with legal or contractual constraints defining the role and status of one individual in relation to that of another. In a corporation, then, just as in the armed services, it will be clearly understood who is over me and who is under me, and what my responsibilities are in each direction.

This pattern of Relational proximity will be further defined both by the location of my place of work and by the arrangement of liaisons within and between offices. Usually I will choose to extend the pattern under my own initiative. Our respective firms may require us to attend the same meeting once a week in the City (establishing directness, continuity and commonality), but we may also, for various reasons, agree to keep in touch by phone (increasing directness), and if we get along well I may start playing squash with you on Wednesday evenings or invite you to my house for a dinner party (increasing commonality and introducing multiplexity).

In contrast, Relational proximity outside organisations – among friends and family – is more clearly linked to personal choice. You don't go to the pub on Friday night because your boss tells you to. You have continuity in your relationship with the owner of the local newsagent only because you have decided to stay in the area and to buy your daily paper at his shop. Nevertheless the Relational proximity in your private relationships will often suffer from the spillover effects of your links to an institution. You may have to work the Friday evening shift. If the firm relocates, you may be asked to cancel your subscription at the newsagent and move to another part of the country.

This brings us to the second point. You will see that the loss of encounter in the mega-community in fact results from a loss of Relational proximity. For one thing, the sheer size of the mega-community puts Relational proximity under stress. Like a parting of the seas, contact over long distances is maintained against constant pressure to close it down. Letters are slow. Visits and long-distance phone calls are time-limited and too costly to make with frequency. But distance isn't the only factor at work here. Relational proximity has declined even where people live or work in the same location. Neighbours in Hvilsager don't walk to work together and chat; they leave their houses individually by car, plugged into the mega-community through national radio. Top and middle managers visit different restaurants for lunch. In the average corporation, rates of staff turnover are so high that even if social mixing were the norm most relationships would be temporary – a problem equally entrenched in the public sector.

Taken together, these small breakages in directness, continuity, multiplexity, parity and commonality – breakages between individuals, neighbourhoods and institutions – exact a heavy price from the Western economy. In ordinary parlance, we're not close. And it shows.

Directness
Proximity in Contact

Suppose the unimaginable happened and your cashpoint coughed up ten pounds more than you had asked for. Would you walk straight into the bank and give it back?

Think carefully before you answer. Then imagine the free tenner appearing in the change from your local newsagent. The chances are you will feel more inclined to return the money in the second case than the first. But why? With the bank you might excuse yourself for pocketing the money on the grounds that a national clearing bank can swallow the loss more easily than a local trader, but that is a rationalisation: lifting money you don't own is a morally dubious act no matter who it belongs to, and it is not as though you were going to – as Robin Hood might – turn it over to the Salvation Army. The difference is a Relational one. At the bank you were pushing buttons; in the newsagent you were eyeballing the owner. You had direct contact.

That constraint is bolstered by directness has often been remarked on. The mice play when the cat's away. Directness somehow saddles you with the awareness of responsibility, just as indirectness somehow lets you off the hook. So Zygmunt Bauman formulates the temptation for the consumer: "One cannot desire poverty for others without feeling morally contemptible; but one can desire lower taxes. One cannot desire the prolongation of African famine without hating oneself; but one can rejoice in falling commodity prices."[1] The arithmetic of self-interest works out well as long as you do the sums with your back turned. Thus it has never been the habit of the powerful to set their houses on a ridge overlooking destitution. What the eye doesn't see, the heart won't grieve over.

Equally, what the eye doesn't see may become monstrous in the imagination. Thus the children in Harper Lee's *To Kill a Mockingbird* fashion their unseen neighbour Boo Radley as a nightmare creature:

> Jem gave a reasonable description of Boo: Boo was about six-and-a-half feet tall, judging from his tracks; he dined on raw squirrels and any cats he could catch, that's why his hands were bloodstained – if you ate an animal raw you could never wash the blood off. There was a long jagged scar that ran across his face; what teeth he had were yellow and rotten; his eyes popped, and he drooled most of the time.[2]

If Jem's "reasonable description" proves in the end to be, to say the least, fantastic, we might bear in mind that adult imaginations can conjure horrors from the unknown just as effectively as those of children. During the cold war the Soviets were, from the Western point of view, so many variations on Boo Radley. But Boo Radley finally emerges from his house. The Berlin Wall fell. And when the eye sees, the heart's grief soon follows. Francis of Assisi returned from the cruelties of the Perugian War a changed man; Lord Woolton remained for his whole life haunted by the memory of a starving woman he saw in the slums of Liverpool.

Directness changes you. The immediacy of another's suffering allows no equivocation. To expose yourself to it is to understand, swiftly and acutely, the common frailty of the human race, the there-but-for-the-grace-of-God-go-I of all distinctions in social position and circumstance. To some extent, of course, this effect can be produced through the limited directness of television. But although media images of warfare, injury, malnutrition or disease carry enormous power, they cannot substitute entirely for direct exposure. Society needs cross-cutting linkages to fill it out with encounter, to breach ethnic and class divisions, and to produce among decision-makers and future decision-makers "a more inclusive and vivid sense of 'the community'."[3]

Of course the existence of institutions like embassies, trade delegations, school tours, and sporting events demonstrates how far direct, cross-cutting linkage is already valued in the mega-community. Yet in many key places such linkage is absent. It is no coincidence that Thatcher's Britain, with its gathering undertow of social unrest, should have been one in which the community of government was cut adrift from the nation below, the unions broken, and life peerages and top appointments in the BBC, the Arts Council, the Radio Authority and the Manpower Services Commission given only to people who were, from the Prime Minister's point of view, "one of us". Nor is it a coincidence that we describe some small communities as *insular*, *inward-looking*, *parochial* and *claustrophobic*. Direct linkage between communities is vital at every level. It is the citizens of a twinned town, members of the church sponsoring a missionary, the parents with a son in the Forces, who take a more than normal interest in developments abroad. And although there is obviously a limit to the number of people with whom you can have meaningful direct interaction, there remains an appreciable difference between knowing *only* people of your own kind, who live in your own area, and knowing at least one complete exotic. The fact that I have travelled through India and Africa, that I have friends in these places with whom I exchange letters, gives me specific obligations and loyalties far beyond the territories of the United Kingdom.

It is out of such direct linkage that community at all scales is built. We should not be surprised to find that the troubles of Northern Ireland are largely urban, and that Catholics and Protestants intermixed in smaller settlements where they meet one another frequently and directly are usually inclined to live in peace. In such situations the ability of direct relationships to withstand the political pressures channelled through the mega-community represent civilisation's last bulwark against barbarity and chaos. It is a strong defence. After all, you don't easily shoot someone who's lent you his lawnmower.

Continuity
Proximity Through Time

Just now somebody rang my doorbell: a man with a notebook and a ladder.

"Number sixty-two?" he said.

"Yes," I replied.

"Does Rubber clean your windows?"

"Rubber?"

"A wee baldie fella with glasses and a moustache."

I dimly perceived in this description my regular window cleaner sucking his stub of a cigarette (he's the only person I know who makes a *noise* smoking), the damp, grey remains of a bath towel dangling from the back pocket of his jeans. *Rubber*? How on earth did he get a name like that?

"Yes," I said, "he was here last week."

The man looked crestfallen. "He did your windows?"

"And the two flats overhead. Why, are you drumming up business?"

It occurred to me this man might be an impostor trying to work Rubber's patch while Rubber was down the road – a kind of window-cleaning equivalent of the Cola wars. I felt a sudden flush of loyalty to my old brand.

"How much did he charge you?" the man asked.

"One-fifty."

He tutted and shook his head over the notebook. "Says here, four pounds for sixty-two."

"I don't understand."

"This is Rubber's book."

Had he murdered him?

"I paid one-fifty," I said. "Has Rubber moved away or something?"

"He's on holiday for the week. I'm his assistant." He grinned and shoved the book away. "It's all like this. Can't make head nor tail or it. If you ask me Rubber needs his head examined."

As it turned out, the assistant's difficulties with Rubber centred on directness. Rubber cleans windows in the old town and the assistant covers the estate; they hardly ever meet, with the result that Rubber's cabbalistic scribblings, which no doubt mean plenty to Rubber, convey almost nothing to his assistant. For me the difficulty was one of *continuity*. Because I'd never met the assistant before, I had no way of judging if he was genuine. And if by some misfortune Rubber never returns from wherever he's gone for his holiday it will take a couple of cleans to convince me that the assistant does his job as well as Rubber, and doesn't leave streaks down the glass.

This is a trivial example of a principle with far wider and more complex applications. It takes time for relationships to grow. It also requires a certain frequency and regularity of contact. To say "I haven't known her for long" is to anticipate opinions, capacities, strengths and weaknesses in a person which are obscure to me and may only reveal themselves through events yet to unfold. In his study of neighbouring, therefore, social scientist Philip Abrams puts a statistical seal on what for most of us is a matter of straight observation: that "there are clearly differences between long-term residents and newcomers in terms of contact with neighbours and sort of help exchanged," and that "new settlements, whether working class or middle class, face more severe problems in fostering neighbourhood ties."[4]

It is lack of continuity in relationships, I think, that makes modern visions of community problematic. The oft-lamented breakdown of *Gemeinschaft*, argues Guido Dierickx of the University of Antwerp, in fact "allows us to meet strangers with whom we can develop new, solidary relationships".[5] Michael Ignatieff takes the point further. With the flowering of the great Western cities, "the boulevard, the public park, the museum, the café, the trolley car, street lighting, the subway, the railway, the apartment house . . . created a new possibility for fraternity among strangers in public places."[6] It is the artists and writers, not the politicians, who have given the possibilities of urban belonging its first adequate images: " . . . Seurat's bathers at Neuilly, each couple sitting separately by the water's edge, alone and yet together, sharing civic space in the silence of the painter's eye."[7]

But are Seurat's bathers "alone and yet together", or "together and yet alone"? For there is one togetherness, of the Covent Garden market, sipping coffee in an open café, reading a novel or watching the world and his dog go by; and another of the streets at closing time, of yellow lights in boarding-house rooms, where the word "alone" returns to leaden prominence. We are together, but because we are together with a succession of different people our sense of solidarity with others, and our sense of responsibility for them, remains superficial. Commuters seldom talk on the Underground. Holidaymakers seldom talk to locals in the Costa del Sol unless the locals happen to be changing their bed linen or serving them a drink. When Westerners visit the Third World, notes Bauman, "it is for its safaris and massage parlours, not for its sweatshops".[8]

Only when a relationship develops and matures can it

claim our commitment and yield meaning. Examining the
sense of obligation within families, for instance, Janet Finch
concludes that people "become committed to assist one
another" precisely because family relationships are lifelong
and, in a sense, inescapable:

> I would place considerable emphasis upon the "become".
> Commitments to assist one's kin are not automatically "there",
> ready-made for the fully fledged adult to take on board. They
> develop and change over time; they get reaffirmed through
> reciprocal assistance; they help to establish an individual's
> personal reputation and social identity, which then in turn
> influences the course of future negotiations.[9]

The effects of discontinuity imposed on children through
parental separation and divorce are well documented and
hardly bear repetition here. We might note in passing,
however, that whereas for adults in a failing relationship
separation or divorce is a matter of choice, from the child's
point of view the slanging matches and the resulting total
or partial departure of a parent – events shaking the heart
of the Relational Base – are imposed without her consent
and against her will. Almost inevitably, the adult exercises
freedom of choice at the expense of the child's welfare and
security. That Daddy going is, in the circumstances, better
for the child than Daddy staying merely demonstrates that
so far as the child's Relational Base is concerned the damage
has already been done.

How far this impairs the child's own Relational capacities
(and evidence to this effect isn't hard to find[10]) depends to
a large extent on the continuity of other relationships in her
Relational Base – with the custodial parent, other relatives,
teachers and friends. There is no doubt that a single parent
can raise children well; but there is no doubt either that
in the relatively deprived neighbourhoods which have the
highest incidence of single parenthood she will find herself
severely under-resourced. Further, if, as is sometimes the

case, the role of father is filled by a succession of the mother's transient boyfriends, and disputes are characteristically settled through confrontation and violence, a young person will have scant opportunity to learn commitment and resist the prevailing currents of brutalisation and despair. At the very least, it would seem that the ability to relate to others sensitively, responsibly and peaceably cannot be taken for granted.

The linkage of time and trust in a man's relationship with his window cleaner is replicated almost exactly in commerce – except that in commerce the stakes are higher. "Established in 1891" printed under a company name was once taken as proof of reliability. In the mass advertising age "old" and "good" are no longer assumed to be synonymous; but a pressing need for continuity has become ever more apparent in a company's internal organisation. Rapid staff transfer drags behind it the extensive cost of establishing new Relational linkages and learning new skills. It has been argued, for instance, that a major factor behind the success of the German Bundesbank has been the continuity of policy made possible by its freedom from party political manipulation. In this respect German government institutions contrast strongly with their counterparts in Britain and the United States, where senior civil servants, top regulators and key intermediary personnel in the public sector in general often change jobs more regularly than their equivalents in the private sector.[11]

This kind of discontinuity leads to short-termism. The executive dedicated to a personal career plan will give only a qualified commitment to her company and colleagues; the investor behind the plc is not only shielded by the stock market from direct involvement with the company, but will sell up fast if share prices begin to fall. In neither case is there an assumption of continuity, and consequently everyone goes for the fast buck, shortening financial horizons to one or two years and devaluing the research and investment on which the long-term future of a business depends.

Introduce the expectation of continuity, of course, and you will change behaviour. It is significant, I think, that the only time I have been defrauded by credit card was when I bought a leather coat in Turkey. Not that the Turks are by nature less honest than the people of any other nation; but I suspect the very hospitable owners of a certain leather boutique in Izmir felt able to charge me three times the amount I signed for because they knew they'd never see me again. If I buy my next coat from a shop closer to home I will be treated fairly not just because there are more effective systems of accountability, but because the shop manager, or the company's directors as represented by any outlet in the chain, will cherish my approval. It is only a satisfied customer who comes back for more.

This anticipatory effect of continuity is fundamental to game theory. Thus Axelrod, examining the forces that bear on a self-seeking individual, concludes that

> For co-operation to prove stable, the future must have a sufficiently large shadow. This means that the importance of the next encounter between the same two individuals must be great enough to make defection an unprofitable strategy when the other player is provocable. It requires that the players have a large enough chance of meeting again and that they do not discount the significance of their next meeting too greatly.[12]

For exactly this reason I try not to play loud music at three in the morning when the economist downstairs is marking finals papers.

Multiplexity
Proximity in Multiple Spheres

Because they are role-based, relationships in the mega-community are often one-dimensional.

Rubber is the man who cleans my windows. I've never found out much about him except that he cleans a mean window and charges one-fifty. I find it hard to imagine him sitting in bed in his paisley pyjamas or digging up the weeds in his back garden. To learn more about Rubber I would need to meet him in another context, and talk to the people who relate to him, not as a window cleaner, but as a father or a friend.

Arguably it matters little that I have failed to do this. After all, Rubber is on the periphery of my Relational Base, just as I am on the periphery of his. In a more influential relationship, however, points of communication become important.

For example, one of the more interesting sociological titbits to have been unearthed in the 1980s is that parents with sons are less likely to divorce than parents with daughters.[13] The explanation appears to lie in the degree of the father's involvement: if it's a boy Dad plays soccer with him and messes around in the garden; if it's a girl he leaves her to the dolls' house and goes out to the match. The arrival of the son thus indirectly cements the marriage by opening up a new front of shared interest between husband and wife. The relationship becomes more *multiplex*.

Another way of expressing the same idea is to talk about overlapping spheres of activity. A perennial problem associated with the division of labour is that important relationships – in particular marriages – have to be sustained between people who for much of the time are in different places doing different things. In itself this isn't bad; diversity of experience helps to prevent a relationship going stale. But if the two people involved effectively inhabit different worlds – if, to cite a classic example, the wife never visits the husband's place of work and the husband takes no interest in daily domestic affairs – there can remain, at the end of the day, very little to talk about.

We can apply the same principle to commerce and politics. It is difficult to judge the character of a business contact known to you only through sales pitches or corporate entertainment, just as it is difficult to judge the character of a parliamentary candidate known to you only through an election campaign. In both cases the "person" you see is carefully edited. Only by observing them in other roles and relationships could you truly begin to understand them, or make a sensible judgement as to whether or not they merited trust. The fact that such insights are so hard to obtain in the massive, opaque institutions of the mega-community goes a long way to explaining why Western economies are so prone to fiascos like BCCI and why Western citizens often doubt the good faith of those they have elected to power.

Multiplexity is particularly important in the financial sector. Suppliers of venture capital ask for a high return because they lack confidence in the ability and good character of the client. So it is not simply for a change of air that three hundred venture capital companies have located in California's Silicon Glen. If you make your money by injecting capital into new enterprises you want a thorough knowledge of those you are lending to, and it is only by working in the locality that you will have the chance to meet them in non-business roles and (another aspect of multiplexity) learn what sort of reputation they have by plugging into the local grapevine and talking to those who have dealt with them before.

Parity
Proximity in Levels of Power

Gina King, head of equal opportunities at the Industrial Society, said recently that women who suffer sexual harassment at work are in a no-win situation. If they play up to sexual advances they are flirts; if they join in with the innuendo they are vulgar; if they fight back they are humourless and frigid spoilsports.

"What needs to change," she concludes, "is not us, but our

vulnerability. The position of women has to be strengthened and our confidence raised so we deal with these issues not as a victim but on equal terms."[14]

The expression *equal terms* is apt. It doesn't mean strict equality. Honoured a place as equality holds in the history of Western thought, it is notoriously hard to realise. We have equality before the law, but when we try to apply it more generally the same uncompromising purity that makes it attractive as a political ideal forces us to think twice before committing it to legislation. You may believe that keeping up with the Joneses is a bourgeois preoccupation unworthy of an equal society, but would you really want to live in exactly the same three-bedroom semi the Joneses occupy, wear exactly the same colour of tights as Mrs Jones, and drive exactly the same model of car purchased with exactly the same annual income? Even if such levellings of opportunity really made us equal (and that is doubtful) would they be attractive to us? The answer is surely no. We value our freedoms too much to take equality undiluted.

But more than that, in certain very basic respects human beings are clearly *un*equal. Some are stronger than others, some younger, cleverer; and these distinctions in part underlie the common-or-garden inequalities of the social structure. Children are an obvious example. When I took my two-year-old daughter for a walk this afternoon I made her wear a coat because as an adult I consider my judgement on clothing more informed than hers – in a British December you don't let an infant pit its wits against the weather.

On top of such natural inequalities lie others – of wealth, class, office, and connection – created by the social system and in many cases expressed in hierarchies that define and, within certain bounds, legitimate the power exercised by one individual over another. Hence the lieutenant answers to the captain, the sales rep to the sales manager, and the citizen, via the Inland Revenue, to the state.

I say "within certain bounds" because the existence of

a hierarchy does not legitimate the use of all powers in all circumstances. In a liberal society, legitimacy resides first in the requirement that the choice of whether or not to submit oneself to authority is, as far as possible, freely made, and second in the requirement that obligations to respect and obey authority on the one side are balanced by equivalent obligations on the other to act responsibly and not to overstep the limits set by that particular objective for which the hierarchy has been set up.

For example, a woman's freely undertaken contract with a company gives a senior colleague the right to demand from her a certain number of hours work or the meeting of a given production target. It does not give him the right to make a pass at her. If he does so she has two options. She can accept his abuse of the power differential (perhaps mindful of her career prospects) or she can find ways of consolidating her power against his (by being assertive in her rejection, consulting a superior, threatening resignation, or complaining to an industrial tribunal). It is the latter which Gina King has in mind when she talks about dealing with the issue on equal terms. She is talking about *parity*.

Parity is important in relationships because big power differentials frequently lead to abuse. Surplus power is seldom left to boil away unused, and the use for which it is harnessed nearly always serves the user's interests. It can be confidently predicted that no G-7 leader will dream of donating the full 0.7% of GDP in aid recommended by the UN until mass migration is posing a serious threat to his borders and nations like Brazil and Pakistan have the bomb. It will take more chips than the South was able to bring to the table in Rio in 1992 to get the North seriously interested in global co-operation over poverty. Power, perhaps, doesn't so much corrupt as do away with certain kinds of constraint. You will be tempted to take as many liberties as you can get away with.

By contrast, for there to be parity in society requires a kind of latent balance on the basis of which every member of society has sufficient power against every other. Of course there are a great many channels through which power balances can be maintained, and as the example of sexual harassment implies, not all of them will be deployed in a given situation. You may have theoretical parity, and never invoke it in practice. But to the degree to which parity is realised it becomes a key condition for relating well. Without parity the stronger party will tend to limit meetings with the weaker (the creditor with the debtor, the star with the fan, the lord with the vassal), and their exchanges when meetings do occur will be hampered by the shared awareness of the power gulf between them. They will tend not to see one another as complete human beings. The weaker party will see strength, the stronger party will see weakness.

With parity, such inhibitions are removed. Because the relationship is no longer dominated by a power differential, there are fewer inhibitions to self-disclosure, and a greater likelihood that the individuals concerned will find and cultivate common ground. Parity shortens Relational distance by establishing proximity in levels of power.

There is, of course, a further application of parity where a relationship between two individuals or two groups of individuals defines a relationship between major institutions. The cross-linkages here are numerous and complex, but it is fairly easy to see the concept of parity at work, for instance, in the division of powers between the American executive, legislature and judiciary, and at least the idea of parity behind a multi-Party state where a government is answerable to the electorate. Ripples soon appear on the smooth pond of the British establishment, however, as soon as you look at the too cosy relationships joining Conservative governments to industry and the civil service, and the rather more fractious ones linking local democracy to an increasingly centralised state. But these are issues to which we will return later.

Commonality
Proximity of Purpose

When Bill Clinton, as a newly elected President-in-waiting, mounted the steps of the antebellum Arkansas State House and promised America not a Democratic administration but an administration "open to ... all people who want to solve the problems of this country", he was building *commonality*.

Some values run deeper than Party affiliation, and it is these values, and the purposes attached to them, that the new leader of a democracy customarily invokes to close the rifts opened by the electoral contest. The fight is over, and now the entire population can roll its sleeves up and get down to the more pressing business of ensuring its collective welfare. Working together, building a stronger country, a brighter future, a fairer world. Such are the stock phrases of political oratory.

And the same kind of talk goes on at every level in society. The life of almost any social group will be punctuated by occasions on which one member solemnly reminds the rest of the reasons for their association, of their common purpose. The assembled school is addressed by the head teacher. The sales team gets its pep-talk from the chief rep. At Passover, the father of the family asks his children to recount the significance to the Jewish nation of each element of the sacred meal. At the wedding – at least at the traditional Church of England wedding – the couple are given an amiable lecture on the duties society and the Church append to the estate of marriage.

We use such reminders for two reasons. First, because commonality exerts such a powerful influence on social behaviour. It underlies the whole concept of friendship as an affection realised through the pursuit of common interests. To say of a friendship that "we both like hill walking" or "we both have an interest in theatre" is to identify the root of commonality that binds the partners together. Much the same is true of teamwork, and indeed of any form of voluntary association. The amateur football team embodies a miscellany of purposes – playing, getting exercise, competing, winning, socialising after the match – some of which will be unimportant to particular members but all of which are made possible by joining up. Commonality is, in a sense, implicit in any form of co-operation. It is present very strongly even when the purposes are not ones the individuals involved would choose, which is why emergencies – natural disasters or wars – have such an extraordinarily galvanising effect on those who live through them.

But we remind ourselves of commonality for another reason also: that joint purposes are sometimes forgotten. If I work in a small company where I know both the directors and the details of the business, I am likely to feel "involved" or "part of the team". If on the other hand I work in a department ambiguously placed within a very large organisation, then even if the goals of the department are clearly defined I am liable to feel "lost" or alienated from the organisation's wider aims. I become a "cog in the machine". Indeed it was the tendency of a certain branch of organisational theory to regard the worker as an extension of the machine in the post-war period that to a large degree induced this sort of reaction.

This detachment of the individual from his or her purposive context – this loss of commonality – can occur in many other ways. The loss of commonality occasioned by the departure of teenage children from the family home will often cause the marriage partners to re-evaluate their relationship. Similarly, the loss of commonality has been integral to the reduction of active local communities to dormitory suburbs. Deprived of a function – and hence of joint purpose – a group of individuals will revert to simply that: a group of individuals.

Too Close for Comfort?
Conclusion

I should perhaps make explicit here something which, for the sake of clarity, I have so far only implied: namely, that we can talk about Relational proximity in contingent as well as encounter relationships.

The principle of multiplexity – that in the broad run of things it is better to relate to a person through several roles than a single one – finds a parallel in the idea that one individual will treat another one with more sympathy if he knows something about him, even though they have never met. After all, one of the major problems with these innumerable tiny threads by which we are woven into the mega-community is their inadequacy as bearers of information. What the prospective employer "sees" in the job applicant is a certain number of GCSEs. What the company director knows with most certainty about a shareholder is that she expects a good return on her investment.

Now it is very obviously a futile requirement for everyone in the mega-community to know everything about everyone else. At the same time, however, in institutional relationships particularly, the partial view one individual is given of another encourages us to assume that what is really important about a person is that aspect of him which is, so to speak, visible in the system. Those most affected by this, of course, are the ones on the wrong end of asymmetric power relations: the store clerk trying to get the company to improve its maternity conditions or rest-room facilities; the non-unionised factory worker forced through the operation of a competitive market to work long hours for low pay.

The same kind of extension can be made to the other dimensions of Relational proximity. It makes a difference to company productivity and morale that the boardroom and the shop floor are linked by three layers of middle management and not by seven (in other words, that there is greater directness in company structure). It makes a difference that the workers on the shop floor are unionised, and therefore able to bargain with management as equals (in other words, that there is parity between them). It makes a difference that an investor keeps her money in the same group of companies rather than allowing the shares to be traded freely on the money markets (in other words, that there is continuity of economic contact). And it makes a difference that employees in a retail chain share that chain's commitment to excellence even if they have never met (in other words, that they are bound by commonality).

Here, though, we should return to the objection raised in the first section of this chapter.

We have assumed, and in many instances demonstrated, that Relational proximity produces better relationships. Further, we have suggested that the mega-community continues to function only because its communications networks have preserved a certain amount of Relational proximity within it. And yet the link between Relational proximity and good relating clearly isn't absolute. Two people shipwrecked on a desert island will be Relationally proximate, but that doesn't mean they will get along. A married couple are Relationally proximate, but still one in every three marriages ends in divorce. Is it not true, perhaps, that Relational proximity can put us too close for comfort?

We can begin to answer this question by recalling that Relational proximity is, in the philosopher's jargon, a necessary but not a sufficient condition of good relating. Human beings need to be brought close enough together to make a relationship possible, not crushed against each other in the misplaced belief that maximum exposure will lead to optimal interaction. Of course the degree of closeness, and the degree to which that closeness is enforced by circumstances beyond the individual's control, will both vary. Even in very extreme situations, however, as in the incarceration of the Beirut hostages, Relational proximity provides, in the first instance, a potential, a window of opportunity to interact.

From this perspective it is significant that in many

cases Relational proximity is implicated in marital break-down only through its absence. Typical scenarios for divorce include the absentee husband (lack of continuity), the separation of the partners' social worlds (lack of multiplexity), "growing apart" (lack of commonality), and the isolation of partners from the family members and friends who might otherwise have acted as safety valves for tension (lack of Relational proximity in surrounding relationships). The last is particularly important in the mega-community, not only because mobility breaks up social networks, but because Western culture tends to idealise romantic love and to dream that in the beloved all needs are met and all passions consumed. Patently they are not. Most of us need to be Relationally proximate to other people besides our spouse, and if these supporting relationships are weak, the result may be a loading by each partner on to the other of more roles and expectations than one individual can reasonably be expected to bear. Next stop: implosion.

In general, then, you could say that Relational proximity enables society to meet its essential Relational needs. It does not in itself embody the obligation – if you like, the morality – which is central to the definition of a good relationship. Nor, in the end, does it account for our willingness – our personal commitment – to fulfil those obligations. In these things it is a midwife, not a mother. Obligation and commitment are born from an underlying ethos which is philosophical, arguably metaphysical, in nature. Relational proximity merely keeps in good order the relationships by which obligation and commitment are cultivated, reinforced, and safely transferred from one generation to the next. Unless it safeguards such a mechanism, a society can hardly hope to survive.

The problem in the mega-community, of course, is that the underlying ethos reflects a centrifugal tendency for the individual to pursue his own interests above those of the group. At the sea-bed of the entire Western system, therefore, we find a long-standing tradition of promoting freedom of choice over obligation. At the surface are you and I, with our fragile matrix of relationships. And in the middle? In the middle, linking the two like the substructure of an oil rig, lie the mediating structures and institutions of the political economy. It is to those, and their antiRelational tendencies, that we now turn.

Notes

1 Zygmunt Bauman, *Freedom* (University of Minnesota Press, Minneapolis, 1988), p. 93.

2 Harper Lee, *To Kill a Mockingbird* (Heinemann, London, 1990), p. 19.

3 Jonathan Boswell, *Community and the Economy: The Theory of Public Co-operation* (Routledge, London and New York, 1990), p. 129.

4 Martin Bulmer, *Neighbours: The Work of Philip Abrams* (Cambridge University Press, Cambridge, 1986), p. 83.

5 Guido Dierickx, *Christian Democracy and its Ideological Rivals: An Empirical Comparison in the Low Countries*, a Paper prepared for the ECPR workshop on Christian Democracy, Limerick, 30 March–3 April 1992, p. 11.

6 Michael Ignatieff, *The Needs of Strangers* (Chatto & Windus, The Hogarth Press, London, 1984), p. 140.

7 *ibid.*, p. 140

8 Bauman, *op. cit.*, p. 92.

9 Janet Finch, *Family Obligations and Social Change* (Polity Press, Cambridge, 1989), pp. 241–2.

10 It has been noted, for example, that parental divorce increases the likelihood of divorce for children. See Ellen Greenberg and W. Robert Nay, "The intergenerational transmission of marital instability reconsidered", *Journal of Marriage and the Family*, no. 44, 1982, pp. 335–47, and Sara McLanahan and Larry Bumpass, "Intergenerational consequences of family disruption", *American Journal of Sociology*, no. 94, 1988, pp. 130–52. Reviewing recent research, Lynn K. White writes that "No studies contradict this finding or suggest that the increased

incidence of divorce has reduced the intergenerational inheritance of divorce proneness". See "Determinants of Divorce: A Review of Research in the Eighties", *Journal of Marriage and the Family*, no. 52, 1990, p. 906.

11 Jonathan Boswell, *op. cit.*, p. 100.

12 R. Axelrod, *The Evolution of Co-operation* (Basic Books Inc., New York, 1984), p. 174.

13 S. Philip Morgan, Diane Lye and Gretchen Condran, "Sons, daughters, and the risk of marital disruption: Structural and temporal dimensions", *American Journal of Sociology*, no. 90, pp. 110–29.

14 Reported by Barrie Clement, "Sexual harassment a 'no win situation'", *Independent*, March 25, 1992.

4

In the Land of Giants

The Birth of Loose Capital
Giant Finance

In 1976 William Farley was an investment banker on Wall Street. At 33 years of age he earned a modest $60,000 a year, drove a Buick (American for indifferent success), and cradled a monstrous ambition: to create one of the largest companies in America. To start that epic endeavour cost him, initially, just $25,000. The rest of the $1.7 million he needed to buy out the Californian firm Anaheim Citrus Products, he borrowed. And he went on borrowing. By the time *US News & World Report* featured him in 1987, he owned Chicago's Northwest Industries and was paying off a debt in excess of $1.5 billion.

It takes a particular kind of person to do this and get a buzz from it. "Psychologically," Farley commented, "what separates the entrepreneur from others is internal. You take the risk as opposed to being stuck."[1]

It could be argued, in spite of Farley's subsequent problems in the world recession, that his story illustrates the strength of the capitalist system. After all, here is the American Dream standing in a pair of leather shoes, a nobody who rose to the top because he was the most efficient user of available resources. Nevertheless, remarkable as Farley may be, this kind of success leaves us with some nagging doubts. It is not as though everyone can take the route he did: only so many people can win. At the same time, the hope of winning which his example surely cultivates in others does not encourage the association of success as a concept with the arguably more desirable virtues of hard work and moderation.

More profoundly, the use of a buyout strategy in business in many ways underlines the weakness of the capitalist system as the economic basis of a just society. It seems, when you consider it, extraordinary to have so much loose capital swilling around the money markets that someone like Farley, who by his own admission had little management experience, could get access to it. This is not a criticism of Farley or of any other individual who has discretion in the use of economic power. But if the markets can concentrate economic power so fast, and if economic power can be turned so easily – as it can – into political influence, fighter aircraft or plutonium, the operation of Western, capital-based economics must continually produce disparity. It will rear giants.

You might ask where the phantom billions that fly like lacrosse balls from market to market actually came from.

In fact you will find their earliest traces in such colourful institutions as the United General Sea Box of Borrowtowness. The members of this craft guild, founded in 1634, saved together not for a 10% annual gross rate of interest, but simply, as it were, for a rainy day. This tradition of mutual self-help diversified in the Victorian era to produce the first savings banks, building societies and friendly societies, among them such familiar names as the Foresters and the Odd Fellows. Though their styles and aims differed in detail, these organisations all existed for one reason: the benefit of their members; to raise, as a 1793 Act of Parliament said of the friendly societies, "by voluntary contributions, a stock or fund for the mutual relief and maintenance of all and every member thereof, in old age, sickness, and infirmity, or for the relief of widows and children of deceased members."

A bit like an early insurance policy, you might say. And yet these organisations had a spirit quite distinct from that of a modern insurance company. They were, in the words of the Act, "societies of good fellowship". This meant that in any single organisation a high proportion of the members would be known to each other. They met regularly. According to a Royal Commission of 1874, the Old Amicable Society of Grantham, already over 150 years old, gathered in a public house and allocated five shillings per meeting for the purchase of ale.

It may surprise us today that by the end of the Edwardian era British friendly societies had a total membership of 6.6 million. They were so popular, indeed, that the 1911 National Insurance scheme was modelled on them. The very decision to use an *insurance* scheme to tackle the poverty problem represented a deliberate attempt to extend the spirit of self-help from the skilled workers in the friendly societies to the margin of the unskilled and unemployed. It was not to be thought of as poor relief. Membership might be compulsory, but you paid contributions, not taxes.

Yet National Insurance, an institution by definition removed from local control, could never encourage Relational proximity in the way the friendly societies had, and for this reason it marked a key step in the emergence of the mega-community. It was almost inevitable that in the bid to provide nation-wide unemployment benefit and health care the bonds tying material wellbeing to good fellowship would fall away. This happened even within the self-help organisations. Although memberships of friendly societies continued to rise in the first half of the twentieth century, reaching 8.7 million in 1945, the societies themselves moved away from mutual self-help toward mutual contract insurance.

By now, of course, productivity in the economy had increased, and there was more money around, in more pockets. The would-be investor in 1860 had a good chance of dying before sixty-five, and, if by some mishap she did not, a reasonable expectation of being cared for by her family. Consequently she had little incentive to put money aside for old age. A century later things had changed. Not only was she looking forward to living longer; in a society of growing wealth and accelerating mobility she was less willing – and perhaps less able – to count on family for support. Consequently, large amounts of private money started moving into savings and pensions. The result was that financial institutions – banks, insurance companies, pension funds – suddenly had far greater resources under their control. They became big investors.

Since then we have seen a progressive increase in the efficiency of capital markets. Most significantly, perhaps, the Big Bang in the City of London and similar removals of Exchange controls in foreign markets have combined with the introduction of integrated electronic monitor-dealing services to make international finance approximate more perfectly to the conditions of the mega-community. By the time of the October crash, the Brady Commission noted in 1988, the US and foreign markets had become a single 24-hour market served by 300,000 computer terminals.[2]

The money that now changes screens (it no longer in any strict sense changes *hands*) represents a kind of sonar-echo of the millions of contingent relationships linking company directors to investors. By and large, the money managers who mediate these relationships, rather as telephone operators used to connect callers, equate company size with security. (This is despite the fact that the same principle led to the granting of disastrous and unrepayable loans to Third World governments when huge amounts of oil money poured into the banks in the 1970s.) As a result, large companies receive the lion's share of investment, at lower rates of interest. Size, therefore, confers a structural advantage. Giant firms can borrow more cheaply than smaller ones.[3] They can afford to use expensive and powerful marketing media like national television advertising, which smaller competitors cannot. And they can better exploit the weakness of local loyalties in the mega-community by appealing to national markets. In the Basque region of Spain there is still strong support for Basque institutions. In East Anglia even the building society bearing the region's name functions at the national level.

In short, the bigger you are, the easier it is to get bigger. The result is that business becomes gradually more concentrated, not just in certain sectors but more or less across the board.

This conclusion runs counter to the conventional wisdom on industrial growth. True, Karl Marx advanced a universal theory in his law of capital concentration, arguing that, since only the very strong could weather economic crises, the cycles inherent in the capitalist economy would pick off smaller companies and produce an ever increasing concentration of property and political power. But although this element in Marx's thinking accords quite well with the experience of small companies in recent recessions, it has been criticised not only for an inadequate understanding of the mechanisms behind concentration, but for ignoring the effects of new technology. Thus while steel, shipbuilding and papermaking in Britain have grown more concentrated, causing factory closures and widespread unemployment, other industries based on different technologies have moved into the gap: electrical goods, aircraft, cars, computers.

As long as growth continues, therefore, and as long as technology advances, one might suppose that monopolies and oligopolies will forever be given the runaround by niche-oriented small producers in new sectors. But in fact this is very far from being the case. In as vital an area as food retailing the British market is dominated by just five companies. This isn't only because the largest have more fat for surviving the economic winter of recession. It is because the vaster, cheaper investment capital available to giants enables them to expand predatorially, by takeover. Big-borrowing individuals like Farley are exceptional. The corporations have a natural edge. Competition is a process and not a state. The weak are eliminated; like Wimbledon, business competition has a winner.

You don't have to look far for evidence of concentration. According to the classic work by Siebert Prais, half the manufacturing employment in Britain before World War Two had been in plants with 70 to 750 employees; in 1968 the corresponding range ran from 130 to 1,600 employees. Over the same period the number of smaller plants, employing ten or less, fell from 93,000 to 35,000.[4]

Ironically, it was in the financial sector itself that elimination turned into a bushfire. The proportion of quoted UK shares accounted for by institutional investors (insurance companies, pension funds, investment companies, unit trusts) had already surged from 18% to 40% between 1957 and 1973.[5] In the 1980s, deregulation and the lifting of Exchange barriers set a match to it. Many smaller building societies are being forced to merge to stay viable. The investment scene is dominated by the giants. If you want a measure of the concentration of economic power in Britain, consider that, as I write, over 50% of the money invested in UK pension funds is in the hands of the six largest institutions.[6]

There are other ironies. The money the big guy borrows to buy the little guy out may well be the same money the little guy has been investing in his pension: in other words, you can lose your business to a conglomerate you yourself are an owner of. Tiny particles of your investment, caught up in the flow of loose capital, will also slop up, spill, and congeal into architecture. This is not to deny all value to projects held up with debt finance. The Canary Wharf development in the Docklands provided valuable employment and promised to revitalise London's ill-kept backyard. At the same time, redevelopment conceived and financed on such a massive scale always ran the risk of submerging utility in prestige. It sucked in a disproportionate amount of urban grant money, which in a situation of finite resources meant that equally pressing needs elsewhere in the country went underfunded. And it was unbelievably vulnerable. The massive leverage required to finance Docklands could only have floored the developers in the event of an economic downturn. And in a capital-based economy, downturns do have a habit of turning up.

Big and Beautiful
The Case for Giantism

This analysis of the operation of the capital markets might seem to be leading us inexorably into corporation-bashing and a loud insistence that in almost every respect save, perhaps, the sponsorship of the arts, company size is a liability.

Before examining the Relational difficulties incurred by giantism, however, we might, by way of a prologue, spend a moment considering some of the ways in which size is actually an asset. I am not invoking here Marx's argument that size is an issue of survival in a capitalist economy, but rather wanting to ask to what extent we are justified in casting big companies (as we are apt to do) in the role of spoiler or aggressor, and whether large company structures necessarily trap the individual employee in a mesh of unrewarding and largely functional relationships.

There is, of course, little reason why relationships within any firm have to be unrewarding or function-dominated. Some companies – Marks & Spencer have been a prominent example – go out of their way to optimise working conditions for staff. Not infrequently, the rigorous definition of roles and relationships necessary to reduce personality conflict gives the employee more space and freedom to work. In this way a large company is, perhaps paradoxically, able to accommodate the need for choice felt by its personnel with comparative ease.

By contrast, a number of tensions arise within smaller companies simply because the limited scale of their operation restricts the options from which the employee may choose. This is immediately apparent in career advancement. The smaller company will not be flexible in the kinds of work it can offer, and, therefore, the likelihood is quite high that an employee seeking promotion will not find a position that can make optimal use of her gifts. Also, whereas in the larger company her promotion will seldom affect the promotional chances of her colleagues, a vacancy arising within the smaller company will tend to become a focus of intense and direct competition. Such vacancies are not common. Directors in small companies often occupy the post for life, making promotion to the board almost literally a matter of wearing a dead man's shoes. The only alternative for the ambitious employee, therefore, is to look for a position elsewhere, which may involve changing not only her company but her locality. She will probably not retain her network of contacts (which a relocating manager would certainly hope to do), and will be moving into an alien company culture.

Turning to relations between the company and the community outside, it is true that, partly by virtue of its contribution to the local economy, and partly through its role as a social institution, a large company can set up strong networks of relationships. Indeed the accumulation of economic power gives those who are so inclined among company directors and private owners the opportunity of giving the company a philanthropic function, sponsoring local or national projects or setting up charitable trusts.

Large-scale company organisation, then, clearly has the potential to do much good. By the same token, however, it has the potential to do much harm. And against the background of the capital-based economy there is good reason to expect that, once a company has grown beyond the point where it is able adequately to neutralise restrictions on employee choice, it will increasingly fall foul of a tension between the Relational needs of its staff and the increasing number of contingent relationships that size places between them.

The Muscle Market
How Giantism Works

Look at industrial relations.

It is no accident that the frequency of official strikes in Britain is almost directly proportional to size of plant. When we talk — as we have grown used to doing — of Britain's miserable pre-1980s strike record relative to Germany and the US, we are talking primarily about large plants; for smaller plants Britain's record was comparable or better.

There is surely food for thought here. In so far as they represent a resort to confrontation, strikes measure the state of the relationship between managers and workers more or less as dishes thrown across a kitchen measure the state of a marriage. A Conservative would argue, of course, that whereas the early trade unionists fought to achieve a legitimate degree of parity between the shop floor and the boardroom, by the time their successors were bringing British industry to a standstill in 1973–4 the advantage had swung too far to the union side and stood in need of correction. Yet the question of parity often arises in the first place only because the other dimensions of Relational proximity – directness, continuity, commonality, multiplexity – have fallen into neglect. Top management in a giant seldom has direct contact with the production line, nor will individual managers stay in place long enough to build up trusting relationships even if they make weekly visits to the shop floor. And as for multiplexity, the next time you see a company chairman out boozing with a machine operative you'd better make a wish. (Incidentally, on this last point it must be significant that most of those oh-so-successful Japanese corporate leaders clock in with their workers in the morning and eat in the same canteen.)

By functioning as – so to speak – microcosms of the mega-community, big companies and big plants differ markedly in Relational terms from small companies and small plants. Because they tend to produce little Relational proximity, any obligations between employer and employee will usually be of a purely contractual nature. By contrast, it is hard to imagine a firm that is both small enough to produce Relational proximity and also beset by disputes over wage differentials, new technology or flexible rostering. Not that a small employer doesn't have painful decisions to make – in a sense they are more painful because workers he lays off, and perhaps their families, will be personally known to him.

But that is precisely the point. Where encounter has developed between manager and worker, even if they don't get along, obligation is likely to show itself in the worker's sense of loyalty to the firm, and in the manager's desire to be seen treating him fairly. Stick in a couple more layers of middle management, absorb the independent tin can producer into a tin can corporation, and Relational proximity in the firm will be severely cut back. Not infrequently this supplies the background to a history of troubled industrial relations – the problem cited by the Central Policy Review Staff when they noted in 1975 that "It takes almost twice as many man hours to assemble similar cars using the same or comparable plant and equipment in Britain as it does on the continent."[7]

A corresponding set of problems turns up in relations between firms. It is standard practice in the marketplace for larger companies to bully smaller ones. The manager in a giant would not see it that way; relationships with competitors are not strong enough to foster commitment or constraint, and he will usually think of his actions only as an appropriate response to commercial pressure. It looks different from the other side. This bullying is more than the occasional fisticuffs behind the bike sheds; it is a systematic pressing home of size advantage which permanently restricts the ability of small firms to expand their operations and sales.

Suppose my Amalgamated Cake Company has dominated British cake retailing for twenty years and you start a rival company called, say, Trick or Treat Cakes. Assuming demand is constant our competition will be a zero-sum game: any profit you make will be made at my expense. Once I have identified you as a threat I have a formidable arsenal of bullying techniques at my disposal. If you buy your flour through a subsidiary of the Amalgamated Cake Company, I can restrict your supply; and if you've been advertising on regional television, Amalgamated Cakes can counter by running a more expensive and prestigious series of ads on national television. More crucially, there are numerous tying arrangements by which I can bind independent cake retailers to Amalgamated. I can pay them loyalty bonuses; I can require an exclusivity arrangement whereby the retailer who sells strawberry cheesecakes must agree to sell only Amalgamated cheesecakes, or I can agree to supply my popular line of low-fat super cheesecakes only on condition that the retailer also takes my full range of bakewell tarts and jam sponges – an arrangement called full-line forcing. If all else fails I can afford, for a few months, to drop my prices on cheesecakes to a point where I know I can still survive but you definitely cannot.

In the real world this advantage of the deep pocket is used without compunction. Yet it is not used consistently. The degree of commitment a corporate director feels to his competitors – commitment that might lead him to forgo commercial advantage – varies considerably and has a lot to do with corporate ethos and national culture. In Japan, for example, market leadership has about it a touch of the *noblesse oblige*. When the Japanese equivalent of Safeway or Sainsbury's moves into a new area, all interested parties meet together to discuss how smaller competitors will survive. Some will be given grants to raise efficiency; others will be helped to find alternative employment for their workers.

Companies, and particularly big companies, represent an enormous investment not just in terms of equipment and property, but in human life. A market system that makes this human investment in companies expendable is in many ways pernicious. Because it faces less risk from shareholders, Japanese industry can plan confidently twenty years ahead. By contrast, the British plc is chronically myopic; in constant fear of a raid, management busies itself with maximising short-term profit in order to keep shareholders from selling them out. No one is safe. Even Britain's largest manufacturing company ICI has been targeted for a bid by Lord Hanson.

If there were direct, continuous, multiplex links between shareholders and directors it would be different. There would be an incentive for long-term research and development; industry might take up and benefit from its Relational and environmental responsibilities. So much is this not the case, however, that corporate raiders are now seen as net contributors to the system on the grounds that they concentrate a manager's mind exclusively on the economic.[8]

There are exceptions. It is not impossible for conscientious managers in a plc to give their own stamp to the corporate ethos. Hence in a recent outline of company philosophy from Iceland Frozen Foods plc we find that:

Iceland has a commitment to protect the environment and preserve the quality of life.

We care about the planet, natural resources, family life, fair practices and community issues, and in all Company business give them due consideration.

The cornerstone to our success is, and will continue to be, linking efficiency with a social conscience, and profitability with good business ethics.

One has to say, however, that such acts of statesmanship are rare and, for managers forced by the structure of the plc to keep one eye on the City, conspicuously brave. Short-term financial criteria to measure performance are constantly reducing the freedom of action of the conscientious company chairman – which explains in a nutshell why so many companies are withdrawing bonuses and staff sports facilities and cutting community budgets in order to increase bottomline profits.

Overall it is far easier in the mega-community to go with the flow, to disguise indifferent practice with a big advertising splash that shows you paying your dues. Environment being the flavour of the month, giants are particularly keen to pose as protectors of the planet, doing their bit for conservation. As long as environment appears on promotional rather than technical agendas, "bit" is the right word.

Power Games
Giantism, Government and Regulation

Philosophies like Iceland's are more readily adopted and implemented in private firms and partnerships. Companies that are not plcs, like C&A, which is family owned, or the John Lewis Partnership, have very different performance criteria and thus a different operating ethos. Given that nearly all giants are plcs, however, and given also that the bottlenecked relationship between owners and directors makes it hard for a board to translate its sense of commitment to the environment or social welfare into company policy, there is clearly a need for commitment to be reinforced externally by statute. It is precisely because monopolists and oligopolists exploit power differentials in the market by slowing production and raising prices that Britain needs a Monopolies and Mergers Commission and an Office of Fair Trading.

Did I say *needs*? Actually this idea of needing in the mega-community bears a little examination. We are really saying that when the giants in the marketplace get too big, more spinach must be given to the bureaucratic giant of Whitehall. Similar reasoning turns up elsewhere – to justify UN intervention in regional wars, for instance, and the Trident missile programme – and so long as the good giant stays good there may seem little enough cause to complain. Constraint works even at these high altitudes. But to argue that we *need* one giant to control another is to sidestep a more important question about the desirability of giantism as a general organisational trait.

After all, the thing appears to be self-perpetuating. Why are government contracts usually awarded to large companies? Answers: (1) because large companies can handle government bureaucracy, and (2) because ministers of state prefer to deal with a single big contractor than ten squibs. A giant talks most easily to another giant: giants understand each other. More than that, perhaps, they empathise.

For whatever regulatory functions are shoved between

them, political and business leaders have many interests in common. The minimum kit-bag for the corporate boss will include superior resources to lobby, personal links with government ministers, and the good sense to manure the political soil with a few discreet contributions to Party funds. One can only presume that such high-level clubbing explains the softness of recent MMC and OFT rulings against tied housing in the brewing industry and the differential pricing of cars. It is an unenviable job being a regulator – employed by one giant to rap another giant over the knuckles.

Nor does government exactly dab the corner of its eye with a handkerchief every time it assumes new prerogatives. Recent Conservative governments have consciously reinforced the mega-community's drift toward greater individual choice, and have done so, for the most part, by withdrawing powers from an "overpoliticised" local government arena. Few people, I think, appreciate how significant these transfers of power have been. In the raft of legislation introduced in the 1980s numerous functions were summarily stripped away from local government, and either kept under direct central control (most notably the management of schools under the 1988 Education Reform Act), or re-allocated to extra-democratic bodies like Training and Enterprise Councils, Urban Development Corporations and Housing Associations.

Most damaging in the long run is the undermining of local government's financial independence, first through the uniform business rate (fixed nationally), taking over from locally levied business rates, and secondly through the transformation, via the community charge, of the old locally levied domestic rates into a much smaller local property tax supplemented by a surcharge on VAT. The result is that whereas in 1978–9 local authorities raised an estimated 57% of their own revenue, net of income raised through charges for services,[9] in 1991–2 they were estimated to raise just 18%.[10] In other words, local government is now heavily dependent on central government hand-outs. Generous? Loss of control over funds means loss of control over policy. He who pays the piper calls the tune.

One classic argument for centralising administrative functions is that it increases choice. You may not like a school with 2,000 pupils, but it has more courses on offer than one with 400. Consumer choice has become a watchword – choice of courses, choice of schools, choice of landlords, choice of tumble driers, tenders for refuse collection and street cleaning – and of course the extension of such choices within the economic system is in itself a good thing.

The problem lies in isolating economic choice from its social consequences. As we noted in the second chapter, gains in choice can often be paid for only in losses of obligation. Consequently, the offer to the consumer to have her choices extended will usually have a Relational price tag attached – a price tag to which it should surely be the responsibility of government, if anyone, to draw her attention. So essential is choice to the ethos of the mega-community, however, that on the virtue of extending it the giants of government and business are in complete accord. Regulation hardly gets a look in.

That the extension of choice in the economy may compromise the wider interests of society is an inconvenient fact from which the consumer will need to be shielded by means of some clever public relations work.

You would not guess from the advertising for consumer credit, for instance, that bad debt – the inability to meet credit agreements – fuels a major social problem of the 1990s. The offer is made purely in terms of choice: hundreds of pounds are yours today to spend on whatever you want. Choice also provides the window-dressing for the attendant and less palatable obligations to pay back what you owe. You have a choice of repayment methods, discretion over the period of repayment. Just how little a sales-driven retail sector and a government ideologically committed to financial deregulation are motivated to think of real consumer interests, or even of the preservation of choice beyond the narrow confines of the marketplace, is clear from the woeful lack of support they give to professional debt advice, and to counselling services for those lured by instant consumer choice into lasting social and economic privation.

But there is an even better example than this.

DIY Stores Do It on Sunday
The Myth of Universal Choice

The one thing most of us know about Sunday trading – if only because we have been told so many times – is that the 1950 Shops Act allows us to buy *Playboy* on Sunday morning but not a Bible.

This snippet of information, quoted to death in the media, was selected and pressed into service as part of a co-ordinated campaign to abolish the old law on Sunday trading hours when the Thatcher government brought a bill forward in 1985. Not surprisingly, it is an appeal to our desire for choice. That the choice concerned is one nobody cares about (when did you last want to buy a Bible on Sunday morning?) does not vitiate it. We are being sold choice, pure and unadulterated.

The government's first Sunday trading bill came to grief at its second Reading, and the issue did not hit the news again on the same scale until the food chain Tesco led a run of illegal Sunday opening in the weeks before Christmas 1991. Opponents were quick to point to the principle at issue. To break the provisions of the 1950 Shops Act on the pretext that they were inconsistent and bizarre was none the less to commit a criminal offence. If you denied this you implicitly made all legal provisions hostage to public opinion, and where then the rule of law? The Conservative government – which would no doubt have responded with alacrity had the same argument been put forward by the unions as a reason for disregarding the laws on secondary picketing – nevertheless made no move to intervene, arguing that the matter should be taken up by local authorities.

This wasn't exactly loosing the rottweilers. The average local authority is considerably smaller than a major retailing chain. (B&Q's Sunday sales represent goods to the total value of £168 million, and that is less than 23% of their turnover.[11]) Had a local authority wished to take legal proceedings against a retailer, it would probably have found its local solicitor facing a team of specialist lawyers from the City. In addition it would have run the almost ludicrous risk of legal liability for the retailer's entire lost Sunday revenues should it eventually lose the case – an amount that, at turnovers like B&Q's, would have meant deep cuts in the education budget and extensive job losses. The concomitant risk for the retailer was a maximum £1,000 fine.

In response to these developments the *Financial Times* ran a leader on January 3, 1992 which outlined two of the major arguments for, as the writer put it, liberalising Sunday trading. Stressing that the law-breakers "deserve opprobrium", he nevertheless concluded that the best solution was simply to repeal the law:

> The most immediate argument in favour of repealing the law on Sunday trading is one of convenience for the customer. Most adults now work from Monday to Friday, yet they are compelled to join a scrummage on Saturdays to procure the staff of life. Shops should be free to open on the days of the week which are most convenient for customers.

He went on:

> That Saturday scrummage indicates a second benefit from seven-day trading: more efficient use of capital in retailing. If all shops opened on Sunday, the short-term effect of opening for an extra day would be higher costs. But in the longer term, spreading the shopping currently done in six days over seven will require fewer shops. If retail space is reduced, this should mean lower prices.

There is something odd about this argument. The premise, as you would expect, is the desirability of choice. It is better for the customer to have the option of shopping on Sunday, and better for the shop to have the option of being open on Sunday. Given the premise, and stated in this blunt and absolute fashion, both propositions seem unexceptionable.[12] What the leader writer does not say is that, in the real world, the option of trading on Sunday is better only for *some* customers and *some* shops.

Look at the customer and his scrummage. Having a close friend who faces precisely this difficulty I am far from unsympathetic to the plight of those who work forty hours Monday to Friday and have to collect their entire week's groceries at the weekend. Clearly if every adult were in this position the case for deregulation would be very strong. But just how many adults *are* in this position?

Assume for the sake of argument that the closing of DIY stores and supermarkets on Sunday causes every working adult, including part-timers, a serious problem. Using the figures for 1990, that accounts for approximately six out of every ten people aged twenty or over. The rest (39%) are either retired, unemployed, or in some other way economically inactive, and thus – to pick necessary nits – not *compelled* to "join a scrummage on Saturdays to procure the staff of life". That is not to say they are against Sunday opening. But since the issue is less urgent for them, and since this group – which includes Britain's sizeable elderly population – is the more economically vulnerable, it seems reasonable to make sure that Sunday trading will not have harmful side-effects. And here lies the difficulty.

The leader writer for the *FT* says straight out that "the short-term effect of opening for an extra day would be higher costs". This is a damaging admission. Since higher costs are usually passed on to the consumer, what he is telling us in effect is that, in the short-term, deregulation makes the "staff of life" not only more accessible to the well-off but also more expensive for the poor. He must have felt badly about this because he hastens to add that, in the long-term, Sunday opening "should mean lower prices". But he does not sound very sure. What is more, it appears that if Sunday opening does bring prices down it will be because "in the longer term, spreading the shopping currently done in six days over seven will require fewer shops."

Now this is not fewer as in "fewer cases of typhoid"; it is fewer as in "fewer teeth" or "fewer employment opportunities". It means shops closing not just on Sundays, but for good. I think we can be fairly certain that this casualty list will not include many food and DIY superstores. It is the small traders, not the big ones, who go to the wall under competitive pressure – the ones who cannot sustain a seven-day working week, and whose loans will not stretch to an extra day's salary for an assistant. The ones also – excuse me for laying it on thick – who are most likely to be relied upon by basic-rate pensioners who cannot drag their "staff of life" back from the nearest hypermarket. It is an aspect of convenience conveniently forgotten.

One begins to suspect that the kind of choice uppermost in the minds of retailers who favour Sunday trading is not customer choice in any general sense but the choice some retailers have of dominating others. As Alan Mitchell, editor of *Marketing*, wrote three weeks earlier, "What this is about is monopolisation."[13] He continues:

> No one is crazy enough to believe that grocery sales will rise by 14% just because shops are open 14% longer. Instead, the already squeezed independent sector will lose yet more sales to the multiples and the high street will be further depleted. And the higher costs of seven-day opening will have to be passed on, either in the form of higher prices or lower costs.
>
> Of course, the retailers are only responding to market forces. The problem is that the surest way to create monopolies is to let free markets rip. The strong squeeze out the weak, and use their added strength to squeeze out the less weak, and so on, until there are only two or three giants left.

Here we are pretty smartly brought back to elimination. Mitchell is quite right about the pressure on small traders (he should know): between 1963 and 1983 shops operated by small business closed at the rate of 30 per day, with an estimated job loss close to half a million.[14] Yet if the customer is to retain that important freedom to buy goods from shops outside the major chains it looks as though some kind of restriction on Sunday trading is required. Sunday sustains parity. It also, we might note in passing, sustains directness and continuity in shopworkers' relationships with their families. Of the 2.2 million workers in British retailing and distribution (around a tenth of the UK's total workforce) roughly half are married women, for many of whom regular Sunday working would disrupt the only day of the week when every member of the family can spend unscheduled time together. You could find many who for various reasons (extra pay, shortage of social contacts outside the workplace) would volunteer to work on Sunday. But it is hard to see why shopworkers in general should be enthusiastic about seven-day work rotas when people in other professions want their weekends left whole. Try asking your dentist to work on Sunday. Try asking yourself.

It is because the supremacy of choice as a value is largely taken for granted in the mega-community that the non-economic functions of retailing (what it achieves by reducing its activities to a minimum for one day a week) are so easily ignored. For the place of Sunday in Britain has to do primarily with obligations, not choices. It is a means of protecting Relational proximity within social groups, including the family, and a way of realising society's responsibility to its weaker members. Remove the constraint of statutory controls on Sunday trading hours, and another support for good relationships in society is cut away. Now you can argue over the importance of Sunday relative to other factors promoting commitment and obligation, but that is not my concern here. My point is simply that Sunday trading illustrates the tendency of political and economic power blocks in the mega-community to co-operate in projects of dubious benefit to society as a whole.

The saddest thing about it is how uncritically a liberal press supports them. Indeed the *FT* leader positively eggs them on:

> The government fears that reform would suffer the fate of an earlier attempt to liberalise shop hours, which was wrecked in 1986 by an alliance of sabbatarians and the shopworkers' unions. But a quick bill could be passed through parliament before the special interest groups had set their word processors to work.

This is lurid writing, to say the least. (Was Mrs Thatcher's government really brought to its only parliamentary defeat by *sabbatarians*? Where are these people?) But then it has a clear function; for it is only by creating in the public mind an image of the opponents of Sunday trading as a coalition of unreliable Lefties and religious headcases that you can get away with the frankly extraordinary incitement to the government to put a "quick bill" into law before the electorate has had a chance to contest it. That and, of course, by bewailing the sorry mess we've been left in by the previous legislation. "What cannot be allowed," he concludes, "is for the present confusion over the law – and the law-breaking which goes with it – to continue." He might as well have started in on Bibles and pornography.

In fact, he did.

Are You Really Necessary?
Giantism and the Individual

Most of us have come up against that irritating phenomenon called the unexpected bank charge.

To take a real example, suppose you discovered your bank had started to charge you £12 for handling overseas drafts. You might not object in principle to paying them for a service; but I think you would feel annoyed at having to pay them

£12 for something the bank over the road would do for £1, particularly if you used the service regularly.

The question is what you do about it. It is you against the bank – hardly a fair match. According to A. O. Hirschman,[15] you could exercise your right of *exit* by transferring your account to another bank – but that would mean a lot of fiddling around with direct debit forms and letters to British Gas. Alternatively, you could use your *voice*; in other words, write to the bank's chairman and give him a piece of your mind. Company chairmen, however, usually divert letters like this to a complaints department, who will send back a form reply telling you ever so politely what regrettable and unavoidable circumstances have forced the bank to this position, and thanking you for taking the trouble to write. (This is now pretty standard stuff in the mimicking of encounter. Someone wrote to the *Independent Magazine* recently to say he'd complained to British Airways and received back, not compensation, but thanks for giving them the opportunity to apologise.[16])

Naturally things would be different if you could rally a hundred thousand account holders with the same grievance. But it would take a momentous effort to contact them all, and would cost you a lot more than you are paying the bank. In the end, the bank remains impervious to your individual efforts to call it to account. You have no direct, continuous links with people inside it. Your relationships with them are entirely contingent. Not only are you powerless to change their policy, you don't even know, really, what they are doing. The bank's operations are as obscure to you as the bank's central personnel, hidden behind the tinted glass walls of their City tower block.

In fact very few institutions in the mega-community, public or private, are what we could call inherently transparent. Day-to-day exposure to public scrutiny occurs most often in the retail and service sectors. You can see the hairdresser's salon, as you can see the quality of the finished cut. In a fruit shop you can pick up the avocados and squeeze them. Very soon in the mega-community, however, we come to thresholds information fails to cross. In a fast-food franchise you will often glimpse the chef at work, but go to a conventional restaurant, and you will have to take the good order and cleanliness of the kitchen entirely on trust.

Larger organisations than restaurants are opaque not only because parts of them are physically hidden from view, but because their structures and operations are often highly complex. When I buy a drug for headaches I am not able first of all to inspect the drug company's factory, and if I could, observing the manufacture of so many buttony white tablets would tell me nothing about their effectiveness, or their possible side-effects, or the dubious methods the company might be employing to market its wares in Ghana. This suggests that the media in the mega-community is characterised as much by locks as canals, as much by points of stoppage as by fields of dissemination. Direct surveillance of the drug company's operations can only be carried out by statutory bodies, pressure groups or the media's consumer sleuths. No method is foolproof. And the information asymmetry between management and customer — which in effect is a power asymmetry — precludes constraint and opens up a wide margin for abuse.

A fairly well-known illustration of this is the government's recent sale of the Rover group to British Aerospace. Evidently it did not strike Lord Young as dishonest to clinch his sale of Rover to a reluctant BAe by using unpublicised sweeteners. Yet these were substantial. BAe were able to defer payment of the £150 million asking price (thus saving themselves £22 million in interest), and also received a government subsidy of £11 million toward the cost of buying out Rover's remaining private shareholders. The subsidy required Lord Young to keep even the House of Commons in the dark. As he wrote to BAe Chairman Roland Smith on July 12, 1988, " . . . since a grant of above £10m . . . requires affirmative resolution (and thus debate) in the House, it seems there are two choices: a) to cap the BAe grant at £9.5m and b) to set the ceiling at £13.5m and for you to accept the greater risk of challenging and thus repayment being required."[17] Repayment was indeed required – by the European Commission – of £44.4 million.

In the Rover affair the free press more or less fulfilled its role as a countervailing power. Somebody leaked a Whitehall memo to the *Guardian*, and the *Guardian* published it. Following up other stories, however, the press has run into direct intimidation. As Anthony Sampson admits,

> Most journalists have been constrained from reporting or criticising the excesses of the financial boom, by pressures from owners, advertisers, and above all libel lawyers. The Maxwell scandal embarrassed more than anyone the journalists, including this one, who could not reveal beforehand that he was a crook.[18]

What this tells us, ironically, is that the media itself has become a giant. If big business can only be regulated by big government, it is equally true that big government can only be balanced by big media, big political opposition and, despite dwindling membership, big unions. The problem is that, being a giant, the media becomes a member of the giants' club.

One way of imagining the power structure of the mega-community is as a kind of *ménage à trois* between the media, business and government. Each relies on, influences and contains the others. Although in some areas media personnel hold a tactical advantage (the television news editor decides, for instance, whether or not to include a given item in the programme), the media as a whole tends to be financially dependent, and this makes it susceptible to leverage from both the political and the corporate sectors.

If you believe in the editorial independence of the national broadsheets, you may be interested to know that a friend of mine, who worked in the advertising department of a major daily, customarily offered editorial cover to any new client bringing an account of over £50,000, and that the danger of a big client withdrawing an account was a constant factor in deciding editorial policy. In light of this, it is surely not coincidental that the national press, which is strongly pro-Sunday trading, also carries large amounts of advertising for the DIYs.

No giant, then, is completely independent. Each influences and is influenced by the others, with the result that in the media, as much as in business or government, the individual finds herself on the wrong end of a power differential. As a member of a minority group you can be as invisible to the television cameras as you are in the corridors of Westminster. You can lobby. But even if you succeed in using the media to gain political attention – which you may not – your success will come at a cost: lobbying, as the supporters of the Beirut hostages discovered, is arduous, expensive and time-consuming. The individual's voice simply does not carry to the level of national government. He is not tall enough. It is only the giants who can make themselves heard. Hardly surprising, then, that large companies have a strong vested interest in keeping political decision-making at a high level, for this is where their lobbying power is strongest. Hardly surprising, either, that the biggest multinational corporations generally support moves to European integration. Who else could be represented as effectively – who else could be represented at all – in Brussels?

The Big Sleep
Conclusion

There are a lot of people in the mega-community. Yet there are relatively few major institutions. That means that major institutions are very major indeed, and the people at the top of them endowed with large amounts of discretionary power. In theory there is no autocratic rule; governments can be voted out by the electorate, and corporate bosses brought to heel by their shareholders. If you ask, though, how the individual exercises power as a voter or a shareholder, there are really only two answers. She contributes her tiny grain of sand to the pile, as an individual in a mass society, or she seeks the patronage of an institution. Balancing of power in the mega-community, therefore, becomes increasingly a matter of balancing one very large institution against another very large institution – media against government, government against business – all the while hoping that they don't find common cause and gang up against you.

Perhaps the most worrying aspect of all this is the dramatic change that technology has made to the task of social control. In the mega-community technology advances rapidly in the name of convenience. But the further data and information systems (EFTPOS, electronic banking, credit schemes, social security) are developed for the sake of efficiency, the greater the degree of *de facto* power major institutions, and particularly government, have over the person in the street.

With the 1980s behind us it is a little *passé* to be making comparisons between British society and Orwell's *1984*. If you have read the novel, however, you will have noted that the only thing separating the world of *1984* from the National Socialist and Stalinist regimes of the 1930s is the all-seeing eye of the telescreen through which the state maintained its tireless watch over its citizens. Telescreens over the mantelpiece in Kensington? Perhaps not. But for a ruling authority to be able simultaneously to freeze the accounts of whole sections of the population no longer seems implausible. Indeed it is the sheer credibility of controlling individuals through their dependence on the ubiquitous financial institutions of the mega-community that today makes Margaret Atwood's *The Handmaid's Tale* a far more terrifying vision of the future than *1984*.

At the very least the strength and the will to hold the powerful accountable for their actions can only become more crucial. Yet conditions in the mega-community often push us in the opposite direction. The individual finds it is easier to acquiesce, to try and believe that the people at the top know what they are doing and have his best interests at heart. This being the case, it is remarkable how lightly we use the word *democracy*. We talk about getting democracy in place as though a country without a democratic tradition could adopt a new political system as easily as we pull on a new pair of trousers. That democracy cannot assuage animosities, that societies unused to it can shake it off again like a skin-graft, and that in fact for all practical purposes it may barely exist in the political system that bears its name, are small-print complications most of us don't bother to look into. We have little desire to rule ourselves. So long as there's pizza in the oven and a good movie on TV, liberty, fraternity and equality can go take a jump.

Notes

1 "The Buyout Man", *US News & World Report*, January 26, 1987.
2 For a fuller exposition of the role of telecommunications in the financial markets, and particularly of the part played by Reuters, see Jeremy Tunstall and Michael Palmer, *Media Moguls* (Routledge, London, 1991), pp. 45ff.
3 In Japan the discrimination of capital markets against small firms results in small businesses paying at least 50% higher rates than large corporations. See M. Gibbs, *Industrial Policy in More Developed Economies* (National Economic Development Office, Discussion Paper no. 7, 1980).
4 Siebert Prais, *The Evolution of Giant Firms in Britain* (CUP, Cambridge, UK, 1976), p. 51.
5 *ibid.*, p. 120.
6 See *Pensions Management*, July 1992, published by Financial Times Business Enterprises plc, London.
7 Central Policy Review Staff, *The Future of the British Car Industry* (HMSO, London, 1975), p. 79.
8 Anthony Sampson, "The Anatomy of Britain 1992", *Independent on Sunday*, March 29, 1992.
9 *Finance, General and Rating Statistics, 1978–9* (CIPFA, London, July 1978).

10 *Councillor's Guide to Local Government Finance*, 92nd ed. (CIPFA, London, July 1992).

11 Submissions to the European Court in *Torfaen BC v B&Q plc, Case 145/88 [1990]* 1 All ER 129. Quoted by Paul Diamond, "Dishonourable Defences: The Use of Injunctions and the EEC Treaty – Case Study of the Shops Act 1950", *The Modern Law Review*, vol. 54, January 1, 1991.

12 It is for this reason that polls sponsored by the Sunday trading lobby tend to phrase questions about Sunday trading in ways that suggest benefits to the customer. Even so, when MORI, on behalf of the National Consumer Council, asked in March 1988 "Are you in favour of Sunday trading?" more than a third of respondents said no.

13 Alan Mitchell, "Retailers: on the road to monopoly", *Marketing*, December 11, 1991.

14 John Dawson, *Small Firms in Retailing: Terminal Illness or Just a Cold?* Paper presented at a conference on the Problems Facing Small and Medium-Sized Enterprises, at Glasgow, November 1983, and London, December 1983.

15 See A. O. Hirschman, *Exit, Voice, and Loyalty* (Harvard University Press, Cambridge MA, 1970).

16 *Independent Magazine*, July 4, 1992.

17 Quoted in "More sweeteners than light", *The Economist*, June 23, 1990.

18 Anthony Sampson, *op. cit.*

5

Liquid Demographics

Choice on a Map
Mobility

I'm often asked where I come from. (One way or another, we do a lot of *coming from* in the West today.) If I'm away from home I usually answer "Cambridge", because that is where I live. But I am not "from" Cambridge in the sense that I was born there. If I rewound the video of my life it would whisk me back from Cambridge to Tanzania, Kenya, the United States, India, and finally to Sevenoaks in Kent where I spent my early childhood. Even Sevenoaks, however, is only a stop along the way. For from here my roots spread in all kinds of directions. On my father's side the line runs back to Hamburg, where I still have family connections, although my direct forebears left in the 1850s. On my mother's it can be traced to a great-great grandfather, owner of a Florentine bank whose collapse, I am told, ultimately provoked his suicide.

Like most moderns, I think of my roots as a kind of trans-generational pontoon that joins the places I come from to the place I am. I could draw them as a crooked bifurcating pattern over the atlas. They are, in a sense, routes as well as roots; not one place, but strings of places, linked by my own occupancy and that of my ancestors.

Now one notion implicit in the concept of *place* is that individuals somehow take on the ambience of the landscapes in which they are raised, making it possible to identify them as forest people, plains people, river people, islanders, urbanites.

But clearly there is more to a place than its physical features, or what the Chinese would call its *feng shui*, its spiritual configuration. Your workplace is a certain arrangement of rooms in a certain building on a certain street; but it is also, and perhaps much more, the group of people you meet there. Place therefore denotes social and not just spatial location. You sit at the vice-president's desk, but you are also vice-president; you live in a palace, but you are also queen; you have a British address, but you are also a British citizen. Your place, in other words, is a place in the social and not just the physical environment, to which is attached a particular pattern of obligations.

This link between physical and social place in terms of specific residential location is now relatively weak. In most pre-industrial societies, major life-decisions about your marriage, residence and employment were made – and usually not by you – on the basis of the limited options offered in the local community: social and spatial confinement went hand in hand. So intimate was this link between place and obligation, in fact, that the word *place* itself often has a social connotation. We say "It's not my place to intervene," that "I'm well placed," or, less happily, "I know my place."

Of course it's at the point where place takes on a meaning close to that of "estate" (a description not just of where you live but of your proper position in the social order) that an individualistic culture stands up and asks for its money back. For clearly this definition of place smells of oppression. It feels like a prison, and prisons are to be busted. Such sentiments have become fairly common in the West, and the protagonist in Jeanette Winterson's *Oranges Are Not The Only Fruit*, whose quest for sexual self-realisation ultimately forces her to leave her home town, provides a contemporary symbol for it. In the mega-community the answer to oppression is to hit the road. If obligation finds its spatial expression in place, choice finds it in mobility. Mobility is choice drawn on a map.

As you would expect in a culture dominated by choice, the

map is well used. The recent study of executive career paths conducted by Nicholson and West suggests that mobility is now embedded in the role-expectations of business managers.[1] The normal pattern of advancement is now spiralist: "a progressive ascent of specialists of different skills through a series of higher positions in one or more hierarchical structures, and the concomitant residential mobility through a number of communities during the ascent."[2] Such freedoms are not to be sniffed at – indeed with a mobile background like mine I would be a hypocrite to start sniffing. And yet if we examine current social attitudes we will find that mobility enjoy; rather less unanimous support than choice. For example, Nicholson and West's survey showed that role expectations of mobility are characteristically a *male* phenomenon: far more women than men are concerned with "location", and having "a job which fits in well with my life outside work".[3] This is not, I think, to be explained by that tidy theory that women like to arrange the skins on the cave floor while men prefer to run after things and throw spears at them. You only have to flick on the TV and watch the commercials (advertising being the most sycophantic art-form and thus the most accurate barometer of social aspiration) to see that images of independence and liberation are outnumbered, irrespective of gender, by images of homecoming, security and communality. The man going into the bar is hailed by a troupe of hearty friends. The lone bachelor who runs out of milk in the morning, and has to leave his modish warehouse flat to draw cash from an ATM, is none the less shown in community: as he steps out on the street the newspaper vendor grins and waves.

Such images appeal to our ineradicable need to be loved, included, celebrated; to belong; to possess, in fact, a Relational Base that links us not only to family but to friends, colleagues and neighbours. Without that sense of belonging, without a place to which we can return from our wanderings, we are simply lost. As Shakespeare's Lear discovers, beyond place – the royal court and the kingship he barters away for his daughters' false love – there lies only the heath, which is no place at all. It does not allow even sanity.

We see such displacement almost daily: the refugees fleeing from war or drought or both, torn from their places and thrown on to the heaths, the in-between areas, the no-man's-lands, the roads and the camps. Probably, like me, you watch it and feel thankful it's not you. And yet in a way it is you. In the mega-community we have turned displacement into a way of life.

Stories of Joe Goth
The Displaced Society

If my family had been more careful about keeping diaries I might well find my lines on the atlas extending a couple of pages east into central Asia, and then running by goodness knows what contortions across the Caucasus or the Iranian Plateau to Mesopotamia. For in his mobility the modern really is just a barbarian in T-shirt and sneakers: Joe Goth the Salesperson migrates, as Joe Goth the Tribesperson migrated before him, out of a simple desire to eat.

There are some obvious differences. Joe Goth the Salesperson desires things (fridges, cars, weekends off) that never crossed Joe Goth the Tribesperson's mind, and gets them in ways (ceremonies involving bits of paper and plastic cards) that Joe Goth the Tribesperson would have deemed passing wondrous and strange. But that is incidental. A second and more important difference is implied in the term *tribe*. For Joe Goth the Tribesperson travelled in a gang. How the gang was organised, and how small gangs were grouped into larger gangs, are questions we can safely leave aside. What concerns us here is that as long as peoples moved *as peoples*, with their cultures and Relational networks in tow, in a very real sense they took their places with them.

Clearly it is hard to know how Joe Goth the Tribesperson

conceptualised place, or how significant a part in his conceptualisation was played by the physical environment he could not pack up and take away. Also, it might be argued, what appears from a distance to have been a leisurely five-hundred-year stroll across the steppes was, close up, a matter of being figuratively poked in the back and on occasion not so figuratively slaughtered by Joe Visigoth and his mates in the tribe behind – hardly conditions conducive to the continuity of relationships or the preservation of a sense of place.

Be that as it may, modern mobility is a wholly different phenomenon. The scale of it is really quite staggering. US Census returns for 1983 indicate that 17% of the population – that is something approaching 40 million people – moved house in the year 1980–1 alone.[4] Comparable figures for Britain show that in 1981–2 around 800,000 people moved between regions, a figure that rose to over a million by the height of the housing boom in 1988.[5] In 1986, 2.4 million people in employment in the UK reported a change of address during the year, and between spring 1986 and spring 1987, address changes were registered by between 12% and 13% of all residents in East Anglia, the South-west, Greater London and the rest of the South-east.[6]

Not all these moves were long-distance. Yet many were. And in neither country could those who moved be described as mobile in the way Joe Goth the Tribesperson was mobile. These weren't *peoples* carrying their places with them from one location to the next. They were *people* – individuals and their immediate families – leaving their places behind. The so-called drift of population across the British Isles is in fact only the net product of a vast number of individual and small-group moves in every direction. Looked at from above, Western mobility is less a blowing of sand than a ceaseless electron dance.

It is seldom understood how far this movement is a function of the mobility of capital. A fundamental dictum of neo-classical economics is that the market ensures a perfect allocation of resources to needs. This means much what Norman Tebbit meant by his celebrated remark about the unemployed and their bicycles. For in neo-classical economics labour is a resource, just like capital or coal. What matters is not that it's happy (what could that mean for a resource?) but only that there's enough of it in the right place when required. To use the official euphemism: people should be free to move where the labour market offers them the highest wage. Since capital resources in a largely deregulated world market can zip from one side of the planet to the other almost instantaneously, and since ultimately it is capital investment that pays wages, the onus will always be on the worker to catch up with the money. He will have to pedal fast.[7]

In many cases, of course, the company itself will present him with the bike. Although much movement in Britain between 1971 and 1986 resulted from private decisions (notably of the retired and the upwardly mobile) to shift from metropolitan centres to the more congenial surroundings of smaller towns and villages, a large and growing number of migrants were moved by their employers, either because the firm relocated, or because, in the received wisdom of big organisations, "Relocation of staff is increasingly seen as an integral part of company manpower policy."[8] Dr Tony Munton, research fellow for the Medical Research Council, estimated recently that around 250,000 senior managers and their families are moved annually by UK employers.[9]

For many readers this catch of having to move an indefinite distance sideways to climb just one level up in the professional hierarchy will be a matter of raw experience. Less well known, perhaps, is the degree to which mobility is enforced as a *modus operandi* in the public sector services.

Despite the recommendations for longer postings made by the Gaffrey Report in 1987,[10] for instance, it remains common for young Service personnel, and (since many of them are married) for their families, to be uprooted every other year – one unavoidable consequence of which is the sending of army, navy and air force children to boarding school. In the NHS, still the largest non-military employer in the Western world, managers face much the same difficulties with mobility as they would in the private sector, while doctors at training grades (and in the tradition of hospital medicine all doctors below the status of consultant are at training grades) are often obliged to find a new job every six months.[11] A similar critique could be made of the system of overseas postings in the Foreign Office.

Now of course the whole point of moving personnel is to broaden professional experience, and this is a perfectly legitimate aim. Furthermore it can be argued – and I would agree – that job mobility in its social and spatial dimensions is an important source of cross-cutting encounter: the bringing together of individuals who under other circumstances might never have met. That being the case, it might seem odd that our experience of mobility is in many ways such a negative one.

Or perhaps not. For after all, bearing in mind Alvin Toffler's maxim that "change carries a physiological price tag with it . . . the more radical the change, the steeper the price,"[12] the average move turns out to be a pretty stressful affair all round. Of course you will maintain links with old neighbours, friends and wider family – to varying degrees, depending on factors like geographical distance and sociability – but you don't take these people with you. They aren't there to make cups of tea and amuse the children while you fiddle with the central heating and wonder where you packed the sheets and towels. If the move has covered any distance, not only the physical surroundings but a range of key relationships – with colleagues, neighbours, members of sports or social groups – will disappear, leaving your Relational Base in need of replenishment. For whatever building you move into will stand, for you, in a Relationally undeveloped plot, bare to the horizon.

Naturally I am over-egging the pudding a bit here. In one way you cannot avoid bringing your place with you. In fact in the mega-community your place is designed to be packed up in tea chests and stuffed into a removal van. That is what you create when you nail your pictures on the walls and set out your furniture: *your place*. And if you have a family, your place will come complete with your most precious relationships, a bit shaken up maybe, but unbroken, and not in essence much different from Joe Goth the Tribesperson's relationships except in one respect: that they are very few. You and your spouse. You and your dog. You.

Here Today, Gone Tomorrow
Transit Camps and Suburban Nomadism

Place, then, is now the individual home. It is also the nation within which those homes move. Yet the more the mega-community polarises place in this way, the less relevant the word becomes as a description of regions and localities. In the closing moments of Peter Shaffer's play *Equus*, the psychiatrist Richard Dysart reflects that rational science, having exorcised the capacity for worship, passion and pain, will in return give his patient only " . . . Normal places for his ecstasy – multi-lane highways driven through the guts of cities, extinguishing Place altogether, even the idea of Place!"[13]

The same idea has found expression repeatedly since the 1950s in nearly all the arts. In the mega-community the tendency is for culture to be levelled. Minority cultures are drawn upwards and diluted. Indeed the awareness of this process has been one of the principal motives for expanding local and ethnic television programming during the 1980s, and for efforts to preserve in common usage national languages like Gaelic and Welsh. But such efforts have to be made under the onslaught of the wider culture. Satellite and cable have begun to make television international, multiplying choice, and yet simultaneously restricting it because television companies reliant on advertising revenue will always bow to market forces by screening what is most popular and therefore most commercially viable. Malls, high streets, motorway service stations and hotels have fallen under the control of relatively few big chains, making it increasingly difficult to know, just from your surroundings, what part of the country you're in.

One reason why ideas of place are so weak is that the economic and mass communications networks holding the mega-community together do not, in most instances, require to know much about your place except your telephone number or post code. The other and more significant reason is simply mobility. Modern cities and their environs are littered with *transit camps*. I use this term to describe what social researchers tend to call middle-class neighbourhoods – although in a situation of increasing affluence and shifting employment structures "middle class" must be used with some latitude. In transit camps, average income and owner-occupancy are relatively high, unemployment is relatively low, and the dominant characteristic is transience. They feel like big hotels. Indeed if you compared a group of people from such a place with a group of people staying at a hotel, the groups would be equally devoid of function. Most neighbours in a transit camp are separated by stays too short, plots too large, and, not infrequently, conventions too strong to allow neighbourly interaction. Streets that were once forums, public spaces linking houses together and thus contexts of encounter, are now highways, preserves for the car, firebreaks between houses.

We must be careful not to argue by caricature, and there are certainly wide variations in the degree of encounter different neighbourhoods encourage or allow. Nevertheless the conclusions drawn by a MORI poll for the Henley Centre at the end of 1989 illustrate how easily encounter disappears, even in a situation of geographical proximity, when land ownership patterns, transport technology, architecture and behaviour all reflect and reinforce the values of choice. Of those surveyed fewer than three in ten said they had a lot in common with their neighbours; more than half nodded or said hello when they met neighbours in the street, but most shunned proper conversations. According to the Centre's associate director, Michael Willmott, most respondents resented neighbours knowing too much about their business: "With most people looking further afield for their friendships, neighbourly chats over the fence are nowadays more likely to be combative discussions about loud stereos or next door's barking dog." Most significant, perhaps, was the division of attitude by age, older people by and large still considering good relationships with neighbours important, but more than 70% of under-35s viewing them as "irrelevant".[14]

In the mega-community, neighbour relations are conducted very much on an "I'm okay – you're okay" basis. We don't want involvement with people we haven't chosen to live near (we choose the house and the "area", not the neighbours). We expect politeness and civility and fair play, but this is about as far as obligation goes. On the other hand, as we noted in the second chapter, the emergence of the mega-community has not been accompanied by any perceptible shift in our Relational needs, and so, as mobility progressively softens the idea of place, we compensate, trying to beef up our Relational Bases by creating encounter out of choice. A classic expression of this is the computer dating agency, which offers you the prospect of a direct, parity-based, and (who knows?) perhaps continuous relationship with a person whose vital characteristics are yours to select, but who your restricted movements within the mega-community would almost certainly prevent you meeting by chance. In a similar way members of the mega-community seek to create encounter not on the basis of shared space, but of shared interests (the bridge club, the pub, the amateur dramatics society, the local RNLI branch) and shared needs (mums and toddlers groups, women's support groups, slimmers' clubs).

Maybe we should not be surprised that an influential strand in communitarian thinking has abandoned the notion of place altogether and declared, in effect, that if ideas like *belonging* or *association* are to have any meaning at all in the mega-community they will have to be founded on voluntarism and not on territory.

The principal objection to this we have noted already. Rewarding and useful as voluntary association is, there are difficulties with the argument that relationships entered into on a purely voluntary basis can be relied on to provide the sort of caring support the majority of us will need at some time, for example, because of illness or old age. Human nature simply isn't like that. There is too little expectation of future continuity in relationships, too little depth of obligation, too little substance to commitment and constraint. Things opted into are too easily opted out of.

But one reason why difficult relationships are opted out of – though no doubt unwillingly and by degrees – is the cost of sustaining encounter over distance. The further away your elderly father lives, the greater the sacrifice of time and money required to visit him. It is easier to write a letter; easier still just to phone. At least, easier for you as a wage-earner. The mere fact that communications systems are services that have to be bought means they discriminate against those who can least afford them. Food for thought when the Post Office and BT are virtual monopolies. A person on a basic pension really does count stamps.

We arrive, then, at a paradox. Our systems of communication – telephone cables, satellites, airlines, roads and railways – are Relational lifelines. They allow a degree of Relational proximity between individuals who are geographically separated. Indeed, that is why we depend on them. At the same time, however, they establish conditions in which relatively low degrees of Relational proximity become the norm. And this is problematic. Neither the post nor the phone can substitute fully for face-to-face encounter, even if the encounter is intermittent. Nor can intermittent encounter, however direct, substitute fully for encounter that is regular and frequent. Distance deprives you of the most intimate and practical means to give and receive love. You can call your elderly father for a chat, or send a cheque in the post, but you can't hug him unless you make a visit. And even being there to hug him twice a year won't help him do the housecleaning or mow the lawn.

Ultimately, belonging and association cannot be isolated from their spatial context. Geographical proximity facilitates relational proximity – though, of course, it is by no means guaranteed to produce it. Indeed this is the rationale behind the modern search for "community" and the urbanite's flight to the countryside.

The village in many parts of Britain could be seen as a front line of the mega-community, a location where "locals", people whose families may have lived there for generations, rub shoulders with an insurgent group of "incomers". Whether the incomers find the community they are looking for is another question. Certainly in Relational terms it is difficult to "join" a local community if your roots are elsewhere, which is why incomers tend to retain this title even if they have been in the village since childhood. The tendency is rather the reverse: for the locals gradually to lose their affiliations with the village and merge into the mega-community. At which point the village ceases to be a place in the Relational sense, and becomes instead another transit camp, with prettily restored old buildings and a history everyone is vaguely interested in but no one can precisely remember.

Sitting in the Doldrums
Detention Areas

Not all British homes are in transit camps, however. Many are in *detention areas*.

Ironically, what distinguishes the *detention area* is the extreme difficulty most of its residents face in moving out. It is a product of mobility, and yet its chief characteristic is immobility. The population has been corralled into it, or perhaps left behind in it, while the outflow of capital has depleted employment opportunities, reduced average incomes, and let the property go to the dogs. It tends therefore to accumulate the classic dysfunctions of poverty: dilapidation, violence, drug-trafficking, prostitution.

Such areas – they are not places in the sense I have implied – are to be found not only in the decaying inner city, but in the housing estates and high-rises planners received awards for in the 1960s and residents later learned to curse.

In many cases, the Relational problems of the notorious post-war housing scheme arise because planners often set out with the deliberate intention of constructing living environments consistent with conditions in the mega-community. It is significant, for instance, that residents integrated far more readily in Crawley, with its seven self-contained communities, than they did in Milton Keynes, which was designed only to give individuals maximum choice between service centres. At a finer scale inadequate thought was given to the effects of architectural design on the way people relate to one another. The high-rise is so Relationally debilitating because its transformation of the "street" into vertical space makes residents invisible to one another unless they happen to meet in the unconducive environment of the stairwell or lift. Doing odd jobs around the front garden gives you a good excuse to chat with passers-by. What excuse do you have for loitering outside your door on Landing 19?

Unlike the ethnic enclaves of the cities of late-nineteenth-century America, and unlike even the Victorian tenements in Britain where families could be jammed in two to a room and forty to a stairway, detention areas often do not bring their residents together. In part this reflects the relatively low levels of encounter achieved between neighbours in most urban environments; in part the society-wide replacement of obligations based on common identity with an ethos of individual choice; in part the lack of neighbourhood function; in part, finally, the fact that transience persists even inside detention areas through mobility within and between them. Although, particularly in community groups, a sense of common grievance may strengthen commitment, the influence of voluntarism is limited simply because so many individuals in the neighbourhood – typically the young – choose to exclude themselves. In addition, the manifest lack of parity in relations between those in the area and those outside it tends to ignite in xenophobia, aggression, and white-on-black and black-on-white racism – narrowings of commitment which further reduce cross-boundary encounter, and not infrequently lead to the establishment of Harlem-style no-go areas where gang violence, street crime and sexual abuse are rife, and where the community, such as it is, has no effective control.

For an affluent society, the tendency of capital mobility to produce and extend detention areas will ultimately constitute a threat to the social order. In the novel that became in many ways a definitive symbol of 1980s America, *The Bonfire of the Vanities*, Tom Wolfe puts in the mind of a fictional Jewish mayor of New York what must surely be the ultimate nightmare of the rich in a divided society – that the poor will overwhelm them through sheer weight of numbers:

" . . . And Queens! Jackson Heights, Elmhurst, Hollis, Jamaica, Ozone Park – whose is it? Do you know? And where does that leave Ridgewood, Bayside, and Forest Hills? Have you ever thought about that! And Staten Island! Do you Saturday do-it-yourselfers really think you're snug in your little rug? You don't think the future knows how to cross a *bridge*? And you, you Wasp charity-ballers sitting on your mounds of inherited money up in your co-ops with the twelve-foot ceilings and the two wings, one for you and one for the help, do you really think you're impregnable? And you German-Jewish financiers who have finally made it into the same buildings, the better to insulate yourselves from the *shtetl* hordes, do you really think you're insulated from the *Third World*?" [15]

What "insulated" might mean in practice – a south Manhattan

screened off behind a hi-tech military cordon – had already been explored in Paul Theroux's *O-Zone*. Wolfe's use of the term "Third World" is a reminder that cosmopolitan New York only reproduces in microcosm a global mal-distribution of wealth, and a danger of migratory invasions of a wholly different order. That civil war, economic failure and natural disaster could trigger an insurgence of the hapless poor into Western Europe's tidy back garden is a possibility now taken very seriously indeed by EC policy-makers – indeed we have already seen a practice run in the collapse of Yugoslavia. When entire nations become detention areas and systems of food distribution break down, it seems reasonable to assume that, out of desperation, people will move, as people always have, towards the centres of wealth.

The Quantum Household
Displacement at Home

One aspect of displacement I have so far set aside. It is arguably the most important, for whether displacement affects you through transience or detention it will do so most profoundly in your closest relationships, and in almost every case this will mean *family*.

Critics in the late 1960s and early 1970s, who tended to regard the family as an instrument of oppression, either forecast its imminent demise or recommended its abolition. For better or worse, however, and for richer, for poorer, the family has survived. Since human beings have an apparently irresistible urge to turn themselves into what Germaine Greer calls copulating couples, it is arguable that the family is a lot more durable than its critics believed. "In the *Götterdämmerung* which over-wise science and over-foolish statesmanship are preparing for us," Ralph Linton wrote in 1949, "the last man will spend his last hours searching for his wife and child."[16]

But the family has survived in an altered form. And exactly

as you would expect in the mega-community, the reforms
that carved the modern family out of its older versions were
prompted not only by the desire for social justice, but in
deference to individual choice. In Ronald Fletcher's words,

> The modern family as we know it . . . is founded on the basis
> of free personal choice by partners of equal status, and the
> expected basis of it is that of personal affection (not legal
> constraint). Responsible, planned parenthood is firmly expected
> of it, casual and irresponsible parenthood is condemned. Within
> it children enjoy a high status and much parental and social
> concern. Dogmatic parental (chiefly paternal) authority has been
> superseded by reciprocal discussion and sensitivity to the needs
> of all the members of the family, when decisions are made . . .
> Finally, a *chosen* degree of involvement between the family and
> its wider kindred has replaced the earlier *necessitous* dependence
> and constraint.[17]

As Fletcher points out, in these and many other respects
the modern family is a marked improvement on what went
before. As he also points out, however, the dominance of
choice in family life has its drawbacks.

The democratisation of the family – the tendency to see
relationships within it as ones of contract, where members
reserve the right to pull out if certain conditions aren't met
– is also a loosening of the family into a less cohesive unit.
If freedom of choice is my dominant value I am more likely
to contemplate ending a relationship if it goes wrong, and
less likely to be deterred by social constraint, because in the
mega-community, while it is generally still seen as wrong to
shirk your responsibilities, it is just as strongly affirmed that
the individual should not be inconvenienced or "tied down"
against his will.

Individual choice has also transformed the family's function in wider society. Families in low income countries,
though extremely varied in form, are nearly always more
coherent in both time and space than their counterparts in the
West; they are communities of kin within which leadership

is handed down, and which, like the Montagues and the Capulets, have a kind of monolithic presence, never ceasing to exist. This is chiefly because they are economic as well as social institutions, and indeed this has been the pattern in most known societies in history. Macfarlane writes of the early Eastern European peasantry that "Exclusive, individual ownership with the possibility of disposing of the rights in an object was absent. This explains to a very considerable extent the identification of farm and family; the household was the basic unit of production and consumption because it was also the basic unit of ownership."[18]

Clearly for most of us conditions have changed dramatically. It can be argued that the modern family retains the traditional functions relating to the personal welfare of its members (providing food and shelter, for example), and even − so far as things like child-raising, education and the claiming of welfare are concerned − that government regulation has made these functions more specific. At the same time, as sociologist Talcott Parsons pointed out,

> the family has become, on the "macroscopic" levels, almost completely functionless. It does not itself, except here and there, engage in much economic production; it is not a significant unit in the political power system; it is not a major direct agency of integration in the larger society. Its individual members participate in all these functions, but they do so "as individuals" not in their roles as family members.[19]

It is significant that Parsons himself links this functional shift not to choice *per se*, but to mobility. The transformation has been fundamentally a spatial one. Since 1945 the proportion of people sharing a home with relatives has fallen with the increase in housing stock. Also, the tendency to split inheritances more or less equally between children, as well as liability for death duties, generally means that the family home is sold and the territorial focus of family life lost. Mobility has tended to separate the generations. So although studies of Dagenham and Banbury indicate that kinship networks made up of parents, children and siblings "can form in a generation",[20] in a society of transit camps and detention areas the spatial stability required for this to occur can hardly be taken for granted. Generally in the mega-community stability is achieved and encounter secured only with difficulty, and the result is that the wider family tends to shatter.

In plain sociology-speak, we have witnessed the transformation of the extended kin-group into a completely new phenomenon called the isolated nuclear family. That is usually what we mean now when we use the word "family". It is what we see driving around with suitcases on the roofrack and sharing a table for four in the hamburger joint. That hallowed unit – mum, dad, kids – is no longer part of a wider whole. It is a social quark, a subatomic particle that materialises in courtship, whizzes through marriage and child-rearing, and dissolves in divorce or old age. It comes together, divides, and vanishes. And its seclusion puts a double pressure on its members. First, they are often geographically isolated from wider kin. Second, they are often living among strangers. It is in these two facts that the phrase "the death of the family" begins to have meaning.

Breaking Up is Hard to Do?
The Lone-parent Family

Forgive me for being a shock-and-horror bore if I quote the much-abused estimates that 40% of British marriages solemnised in 1987, and two-thirds of all first time marriages in the United States, will end in divorce.[21] Such figures are notoriously hard to interpret, and too often and indiscriminately used to announce the end-of-civilisation-as-we-know-it. On the political Right, where family obligation has traditionally been stressed to prevent unwelcome social responsibilities being unloaded on to the state, a favoured method of solving the divorce problem is simply to make it more difficult. But divorce really isn't the problem.

The problem is that once, so to speak, the honeymoon is over in a marriage, the most powerful reason the mega-community can offer the partners to stay together is that it remains in their individual best interests to do so. This isn't easy. So deeply assimilated is the prerogative of choice, so much do husbands and wives invest in this one central relationship, so great are the emotional fulfilments sought in it, and so intense and pressurised are the conditions displacement creates in the home, that the marriage relationship seems from the start almost doomed to go wrong. It is hardly surprising that half the people contemplating marriage in England and Wales now "try out" their partners before taking their plunge down the aisle. Nor is it surprising that increasing numbers appear to have settled for cohabitation and ditched marriage altogether. There is even evidence that cohabitation is developing its own characteristic forms – as when cohabitees retain separate households in what the Dutch call "living apart together" – so establishing itself not merely as a surrogate but as a distinct and full-blown alternative to marriage.

Certainly this is the view put forward in a recent report on marriage in Europe.[22] If, as the report claims, a central reason for the decline of marriage is a "reduced willingness to sacrifice opportunities for individual growth and development", then even if you argue that cohabitees split up because the kind of people who move in together are also the kind of people who don't mind moving out, you will have to concede that the replacement of marriage with cohabitation is likely to produce higher rates of relationship dissolution. Which, of course, is what you would expect of unions entered into with the aim of preserving individual choice. And the result? As the report goes on, "in countries with high rates of relationship dissolution, a substantial proportion of children will be brought up by mothers alone for much of their childhood. If this trend continues the only indissoluble relationship will be between mothers and their children." In other words, the isolated nuclear family may not after all be the indivisible social unit. Below it lies an even newer form: the lone-parent family.

Here we are teetering on the brink of a bitter debate. The bare facts of the matter are that lone-parent families have become increasingly common in the last three decades. As a proportion of all families, they rose from 8% to 14% in the UK (1971–87) and from 9% to over 20% in the US (1960–85).[23] As with divorce, interpretation is difficult, particularly in the United States where the rise of the single parent family has been increasingly politicised, being greeted by the conservatives as an aberrance and an indicator of social disorganisation, and by the feminists as a legitimate family form consistent with the emerging economic independence of women.

There is no reason, of course, why a lone-parent family should be less loving and nurturing than a conventional one. It may often be more so. At the same time, however, lone-parent families face considerable problems. The one best researched and most commented on is the financial. Since the vast majority of lone parents are women, lone-parenthood has been cited as a major contributor to the feminisation of poverty. A survey commissioned by the Department of Social Security and published in mid-1991 showed that 94% of lone-parent families in Britain relied on the state for most of their income, either through income support or family credit. Of those, 60% described themselves as "hard pressed".[24] Research in the United States suggests that roughly one out of two single mothers lives below the poverty line, as compared with one in ten married couples with children.[25] They receive lower hourly wages, and work fewer hours than married fathers. During any given year between 30% and 40% report no earnings at all.

It is important to remember, however, that while divorce, separation and bereavement have financial consequences they are in themselves *Relational* events, not financial ones. Child development specialists have been arguing for some time that divorce, irrespective of its financial consequences, interrupts primary bonds between parents and children, and may therefore interfere with children's normal development and socialisation.[26] Since it has been found recently that less than half of the eleven- to sixteen-year-old children with divorced parents in the United States had seen their fathers during the past year,[27] there is good reason to believe that divorce disrupts continuity in the child's Relational Base. The lone parent appears to be less available to help adolescent children with homework or to supervise their social activities,[28] leaving them more susceptible to peer pressure.[29]

There is little serious disagreement on either side of the Atlantic about the long-term effects of lone-parenthood on children. The body of research is too large even to summarise, but conclusions reached by social scientists in the United States include the following. Children from lone-parent families are more likely to drop out of high school than children from two-parent families.[30] They have lower earnings in adulthood, and are more likely to be poor.[31] They are more likely to marry early and have children early, both in and out of wedlock,[32] more likely to divorce and become lone-parents themselves,[33] more likely to commit delinquent acts and engage in the use of drugs and alcohol.[34] These effects were found to be consistent across a large number of racial and ethnic groups. There is no evidence to suggest that the experience is less unsettling in adolescence than in early childhood.

In Britain, at a 1991 seminar organised jointly by the Joseph Rowntree Trust and the Institute of Economic Affairs, similar conclusions were reached by Professor A. H. Halsey of Nuffield College, Oxford:

Such children, on the evidence available, tend to die earlier, to have more illness, to do less well at school, to exist at a lower level of nutrition, comfort and conviviality, to suffer more unemployment, to be more prone to deviance and crime, and finally to repeat the cycle of unstable parenting from which they have themselves been formed as relatively unsuccessful social personalities.[35]

What this means is still a matter for debate. Professor Halsey "shudders for the next generation". Such politically incorrect terms as "unstable parenting" and "unsuccessful social personalities" sound strange tripping from the tongue of a socialist academic. As you might anticipate, Professor Halsey blames "hedonistic, egocentric, individualistic" attitudes fostered under Thatcherism. But a Right-winger could make exactly the same speech, only blaming the problem instead on permissiveness and the collapse of moral standards. In this respect Professor Halsey buys into what is more recognisably a Conservative critique in arguing (against Neil Kinnock's assertion that the government should support the family whatever its structure) that the proper ideal of government policy should be traditional marriage.

From the Relational standpoint, of course, the isolated nuclear family (which the phrase "traditional marriage" now implies) is almost as vulnerable as the lone-parent family. However hard the adults try to protect their children in such institutions – and many of them try very hard indeed – they will always be struggling to compensate for the decline of encounter and commitment in the society around them. If, as the feminist commentators claim, the under-performance of children in lone-parent families reflects existing preconditions in the people concerned, and not the influence of lone-parenthood itself, that is, I think, all the more reason to be worried.

Lunch is for Losers
Displacement in the Corporate Ethos

One of the annoying things economists have discovered about

human beings in the last fifty years is that they don't behave predictably.

Economics yearns toward the Newtonian; it would like to have financial systems reduced to a set of coloured buttons with labels like *tax*, *interest rates*, *inflation*, *wages*, *investment* and so on, and a little booklet that tells the financial mandarins which ones to press in which order to keep the economy on a steady upward path. The reason the economy doesn't behave like this, and why the gurus that governments listen to, like Keynes and Friedman, have ended up with egg on their faces, is of course that the economy isn't a Newtonian system at all: it is Relational.

What you have really got out there behind your big sign saying ECONOMY is a lot of people making individual and collective decisions about buying, selling and saving, for reasons the economist can only guess at. To describe the stock markets as "confident" or "nervous" is a way of saying how far down the money managers are chewing their nails. You really don't know what the effect of pressing any button will be. There was a time when economists thought you did, and politicians believed them. Now even the politicians know better. Not that they'd say so in public, of course – you don't get elected by promising you will be a better guesser than the Opposition.

This obsession about making economics into a science explains a good deal of woolly thinking about human behaviour, of which the economic view of mobility is a good example. Since capital by definition has no "place", it makes perfect scientific sense to have free markets for capital. But people (which is what we mean by labour) can't be treated as a kind of oil you circulate around the economic engine to keep it running. Move them too much, and they will get displaced. And displacement means inefficiency, loss of production, reduced returns to the employer, and significant increases in social overheads (such as welfare benefits) to society as a whole.

It is remarkable how unwilling corporate bosses are to

recognise this. Dr Tony Munton has recently been advocating the use of psychologists and counsellors to help relocating managers cope with the stresses of transition. He has run up against a lunch-is-for-losers mentality in which need equals weakness and goal-attainment becomes a function of machismo. Thus: "When I ran the idea of counselling past one British entrepreneur, he replied, 'We don't want any of that crap here.' That is the typical response of executives to these kinds of policies."[36]

If they recognise the problem at all, they tend to throw money at it. A survey conducted among subscribers to IRS Employment Trends in 1989, to record improvements made to relocation policies in the previous two years, found that "improvement" was consistently interpreted as the increasing of *financial* incentives. Only Allied Dunbar and TSB had introduced information provisions, and only Optical Fibres and BUPA had begun to take account of the myriad issues involved in moving a family. This in spite of the fact that relocation can be shown to have clear negative consequences for managerial performance. Munton's figures are as good as any: eighteen months after moving, a third of managers and more than a third of managers' partners were losing sleep, feeling less confident, displaying symptoms of anxiety and irritability.[37]

Perhaps the strongest argument against mobility as company policy is the fact that a lot of managers plain refuse to go. A survey of twelve hundred job-hunting executives at the prime mobility age of twenty-five to thirty-five found that two out of three had discounted otherwise suitable jobs because they were located in the wrong part of the country.[38] And when NEC moved from Motherwell to Milton Keynes after 1985 it found that business priorities conflicted with the needs of employees and that key members of staff would not be persuaded to move if their families were distressed.[39]

From the company's point of view, of course, which is generally the scientific-economic point of view, refusniks are "constraints on mobility".[40] Yet, as Munton says,

The people are the single most important investment any employer can make and it can cost around £250,000 for an employer to relocate a manager. They will take great pains over the movement of a £250,000 machine ... But they won't do that for their manager and his or her family.[41]

The ripples of the mobility culture spread far beyond the troubles experienced by relocaters. The more frequently a manager moves within or between companies the more likely he is to look for short-term payoffs. After all, there is little incentive to lay foundations for company profitability ten years down the road if you are going to leave in eighteen months. Long-term research and development, therefore, will tend to be neglected for the sake of gains that can be realised before the manager moves on. Furthermore, relationships of trust and loyalty are difficult to develop if no one can be sure where they will be living or working next year. Not only that, but it becomes extremely difficult to identify and trace the person responsible for a bad decision five years ago, and thus also extremely difficult either to hold him to account or to prevent him doing further damage through incompetence in his present position. As McKean points out, "Rapid change of conditions, associates, acquaintances, or locations makes tradition or ethical codes less effective because rapid change ... reduces the perceived gains from customs and honesty, makes them less certain, and/or attenuates the enforcement mechanism."[42]

In what may turn out to be one of the twentieth century's most important works of theoretical economics, Fred Hirsch advances a similar argument for business relationships in general.[43] Since friendship has a clear *economic* content, Hirsch argues, the time-pressure that leads inevitably to a general decrease in friendliness and to inefficient "piecemeal transactions" should be considered a diseconomy. In other words, because displacement produces temporariness and a reduction in friendship, it has an overall social and therefore an economic cost. It is Relational pollution.

Free to Move, Unfree to Stay
Conclusion

All too often, of course, the costs can stay hidden. We don't think of them as costs because we accept mobility as inevitable. And in a sense we are right: in the operation of capital-based economies mobility *is* inevitable. In so far as it caters for our need to choose, it is even good – after all, half of the relocated managers Tony Munton interviewed said they loved moving and would have got bored staying in the same place. But in our Western fear of being held down, restricted, oppressed, we perhaps fail to notice the irony in all this. For in shaking free of a political economy that limits the freedom to move, we have embraced one that limits the freedom to stay still and put down roots. Since the other of our two fundamental needs – obligation – is so intimately connected with place, that would seem to be a serious disadvantage. Indeed in our desire to rediscover community we implicitly acknowledge that. We sense our displacement.

Then how did we get displaced? Certainly we never chose it. At no stage was the economic system behind it proposed as a bill and debated in parliament. To that extent it is extra-democratic. One could argue, not too cynically, that displacement is a form of social control maintained, or at least allowed to proceed, by those whose position in the political and economic power hierarchy renders them least vulnerable to its effects. At any rate, coming in the broad sweep of social change, displacement has helped to induce, in society at large, a kind of amnesia. We find it hard to imagine that things have ever been different. We find it hard to articulate clearly what sort of balance we are trying to achieve between choice and obligation, or even to find a language in which such a question can adequately be addressed. Home may be where the heart is – but where is the heart?

Notes

1 N. Nicholson and M. West, *Managerial Job Change: Men and Women in Transition* (CUP, Cambridge, 1988).

2 W. Watson, "Society, mobility and social class in industrial communities", in M. Gluckman (ed.), *Closed Systems and Open Minds* (Oliver & Boyd, London, 1964), p. 147.

3 N. Nicholson and M. West, *op. cit.*, p. 41.

4 See P. Voydanoff, *Work and Family Life*, Family Studies Texts Series (Sage Publications, California, 1987).

5 See D. Coleman and J. Salt, *The British Population* (OUP, Oxford, 1992), p. 415.

6 See "Labour mobility: evidence from the Labour Force Survey", *Employment Gazette*, August 1991, pp. 437–52.

7 It is a measure of the entrenchment of mobility in the British way of life that the largest single category of moves is described, not as "economic", but as "social". This indicates, first, that many moves are undertaken for proRelational reasons – that is, to establish or restore Relational links – and, second, that mobility takes place in a setting where such links are perpetually being lost.

8 "Regional recruitment problems and skill shortages", *Relocation News*, no. 6, Spring 1988, p. 10.

9 See article by Judy Jones, "Executives 'left to cope with stress when firms move'", *Independent*, October 18, 1991.

10 Col. M. Gaffrey, *The Army Wives Study, Part 2 – The Way Ahead*, MOD, April 1987.

11 F. R. Elliott, "Professional and Family Conflicts in Hospital Medicine", *Social Science & Medicine*, vol 13a, 1979.

12 Alvin Toffler, *Future Shock* (Bodley Head, London, 1970), p. 296.

13 Peter Shaffer, *Equus* (Penguin Books, London, 1973), p. 108.

14 See Virginia Matthews, "Shun thy neighbour is the modern way", *Daily Telegraph*, December 18, 1989.

15 Tom Wolfe, *The Bonfire of the Vanities* (Bantam Books, New York, 1988), p. 7.

16 From Ralph Linton, "The Natural History of the Family", in *The Family: Its Function and Destiny*, ed. Ruth Nanda Anshen, 1949. Quoted by Ronald Fletcher, *The Shaking of the Foundations* (Routledge, London, 1988), flyleaf.

17 Ronald Fletcher, *op. cit.*, pp. 176–7.

18 Alan Macfarlane, *The Origins of English Individualism* (Blackwell, Oxford, 1978), p. 21.

19 Talcott Parsons, "The Family in Urban-Industrial America: 1", in Michael Anderson, *The Sociology of the Family* (1971), pp. 56–7.

20 Stacey *et al.* (1975), quoted in Peter Willmott, *Social Networks, Social Care, and Public Policy* (PSI, 1986), p. 20.

21 See J. Haskey, "Current prospects for the proportion of marriages ending in divorce", *Population Trends*, no. 55, HMSO, London, 1989, and Teresa Castro Martin and Larry Bumpass, "Recent trends in marital disruption", *Demography*, 3, no. 26, pp. 37–51.

22 Duncan Dormer, *The Relationship Revolution*, One Plus One: Marriage and Partnership Research, Central Middlesex Hospital, 1992.

23 See Office of Population Censuses and Surveys, quoted in *Social Trends 20* (HMSO, London, 1990), and US Bureau of the Census, 1960, 1961, 1988.

24 Liz Hunt, "Most lone parents 'hard up'", *Independent*, June 10, 1991.

25 Irwin Garfinkel and Sara McLanahan, *Single Mothers and Their Children: A New American Dilemma* (Urban Institute Press, Washington DC, 1986).

26 See Robert Hess and Kathleen Camara, "Post-divorce family relationships as mediating factors in the consequences of divorce for children", *Journal of Social Issues*, no. 35, pp. 79–96.

27 Frank Furstenberg, Philip Morgan, and Paul Allison, "Paternal participation and children's wellbeing after marital disruption", *American Sociological Review*, no. 52, 1986, pp. 695–701.

28 Sara McLanahan, *et al.*, "The role of mother-only families in reproducing poverty" (Paper presented to the Conference on Poverty and Children, Lawrence, Kansas, June 20–2, 1988).

29 Laurence Steinberg, "Single parent, step-parents, and the

susceptibility of adolescents to antisocial peer pressure", *Child Development*, no. 58, 1987, pp. 269–75.

30 Sheila Krein and Andrea Beller, "Educational attainment of children from single-parent families: Differences by exposure, gender and race", *Demography*, no. 25, 1988, pp. 221–4.

31 Mary Corcoran *et al.*, "Intergenerational transmission of education, income and earnings", 1987 (unpublished ms., Institute of Public Policy Studies, University of Michigan, Ann Arbor).

32 Allan Abrahamse *et al.*, "Single teenage mothers: Spotting susceptible adolescents in advance" (Paper presented at the annual meetings of the Population Association of America, Chicago, 1987.)

33 Sara McLanahan and Larry Bumpass, "Intergenerational consequences of family disruption", *American Journal of Sociology*, no. 94, 1988, pp. 130–52.

34 Ross Matsueda and Karen Heimer, "Race, family structure and delinquency: A test of differential association and social control theories", *American Sociological Review*, no. 52, 1987, pp. 826–40.

35 Nicholas Wood, "Professor 'shudders for next generation'", *The Times*, July 3, 1991.

36 Judy Jones, *op. cit.*

37 Peter Pallot, "Company moves can break up families", *Daily Telegraph*, October 18, 1991.

38 D. E. Guest and R. Williams, "How home affects work", in *New Society*, no. 537, January 18, 1973.

39 R. Giddy, "Moving into the South-east", in *Moving Experiences*, vol. II, Price Waterhouse and the CBI Employee Relocation Council, January 11, 1989.

40 *Relocating managers and professional staff*, Institute of Manpower Studies, 1988.

41 Judy Jones, *op cit.*

42 R. N. McKean, "Economics of Trust, Altruism and Corporate Responsibility", in E. S. Phelps (ed.), *Altruism, Morality and Economic Theory* (Russell Sage Foundation, New York, 1975), p. 35.

43 Fred Hirsch, *The Social Limits to Growth* (Routledge & Kegan Paul, London, 1977), pp. 77–80.

6

Trapped in the Fairground

The Fairground Economy
Consumerism and Manipulation

There is a long tradition among media analysts of seeing advertising as manipulation.

Roughly since the publication of Vance Packard's *Hidden Persuaders* the popular image of the advertiser has been of the psychologist turned to crime: someone whose skill in the surgery of the mind is bent entirely to the problem of making you buy a certain brand of cologne, jeans or cola. Most frightening of all to the fragrant jean-clad cola-drinker was the thought of an advertiser being able to subvert choice; that the brands he fondly believed he'd selected himself had in fact been selected for him by grey men meeting in bunkers a hundred feet below their corporate HQs; that, in short, he could be made to do something *against his will*.

It was all a bit paranoid. True, something you might call coercion survived in the social systems of the West even as late as the 1960s, but that had to do with the way you earned your money, not the way you spent it.

In the early phases of industrialisation (that is, more or less until World War Two), the individual's chief contribution to the economy was as a producer. Whether he spent his ungenerous earnings on groceries or booze mattered little, except in so far as too much boozing might reduce his productivity, and this the surrounding culture strongly discouraged. In particular, there went with the emphasis on labour as an economic input a corresponding regard for work as a social virtue: not only your financial security, but also your status and self-esteem depended on having a positive attitude to work. Diligence, application and enterprise won respect; sloth, in Britain, put you in danger of the workhouse. But whether you laboured of your own volition or because laziness or misfortune cast you on the stern mercy of the Poor Law, it was work that socialised you, work that taught you self-discipline and obedience to authority, work that supplied the plainest explanation of what life meant. After all, you spent a great deal of your time working.

You will still hear people in the 1990s talking about the "dignity" of work; but it is rare, I think, for anyone to mean by this that working in itself has more value than the things that go with it – income, social contacts, the enjoyment of what you do. We consider ourselves lucky now to be able to retire early, and if a job doesn't pay us substantially more than we'd get on benefit we feel little joy in taking it.

We haven't just grown lazy. The economy itself has changed. Motivating a person to produce has become less urgent than motivating her to consume. To put it crudely, the work ethic has given way to the pleasure principle, the necessity of earning to survive to the opportunity of spending to satisfy. Economists now look to changes in levels of retail sales as a key indicator of upturns and downturns in the economy. Politicians try to persuade the public that the economy has turned the corner so that the public will go out and resume their consumer spending. Choice rules. We live in a fairground economy.

The great advantage, of course, is that a fairground is the sort of place everyone wants to go to. In contrast to the world of production, where elimination quickly puts paid to competition in the drive toward monopoly, the world of consumption celebrates competition and harnesses it. Between producers, competition incurs a social cost. But between consumers it becomes largely symbolic, and therefore harmless. Seeing my clapped-out Volkswagen Beetle parked next to your spanking new BMW may make me feel envious or humiliated, but it won't ruin me. In fact I may utter under my breath a secret vow that one day I'm going to show the world what I'm made of and bring home a Rolls.

In the fairground economy, therefore, the utility-value of the merchandise (how well it serves its purpose) is absorbed into a sign-value in which "purpose" no longer has to do with performance, but with status. I compete to have a *better* car, a *better* body, a *better* management technique than yours. Consequently cookery ascends into aesthetics. Sex turns into the art of giving and receiving pleasure, of which reproduction is in most cases definitely not the desired outcome. And buying allows entry into what Daniel Boorstin calls *consumption communities*.[1] You belong to that group of people who have fitted double-glazing, gone for a holiday in the Caribbean, use a certain brand of deodorant. In the mega-community, where it is impossible to encounter more than a handful of others, the goods, services and experiences you consume – job, clothing, hairstyle, tastes, physique – become tokens of status and belonging, symbols from which you construct and project your identity.

In other words, what you consume begins to define what you are. Far from being a hidden persuader, then, advertising is left with the happy task of inviting us to do what we really want to do already: make ourselves feel good. Of course there is an ineradicable minimum of pain involved in feeling good, in so far as pleasure has its price (after all it is only because we pay for the rides that the fairground remains a going concern). One very important role of advertising, therefore, is to administer the morphine.

If the price is low enough relative to the quality of the product you may actually be quoted a figure; if it is too high you will be assured (amid subliminal throat clearings and shifty sideways glances) that it's "cheaper than you think" or available at "a surprisingly low cost". Usually the question of money isn't broached at all. The one thing you definitely don't see in television commercials (except those advertising financial services) is a man signing a cheque. The suppression of cost considerations is essential to the logic of purchase. So too is the attempt to convince you that you are showing symptoms of precisely that disease the product sets out to cure. This "therapeutic ethos" covers a lot more than headaches and spots. You have an imperfectly mown lawn. You are eating badly, your breath smells, you have germs lurking in the recesses of your bathroom. Once your disease is diagnosed, the purchase of the product is supremely rational – in fact there may be a hundred satisfied customers or a man in a white lab coat (equals scientist) right there on the screen to tell you so.

Consumerism is all-embracing. Even your escapes are planned, scripted, marketed. You rent a video for Saturday night, join a sports centre, go on safaris, weekends in Paris, fortnights on Crete. You might say that in its economic dimension the mega-community is nothing less than an institutionalised escape where work will be put for ever at the right hand of leisure. There is no need to leave the fairground. Indeed the gates are locked from the outside. But who cares? For it is in the fairground economy of consumerism that the divergent interests of individual and society – those oil-and-water needs of choice and obligation – come closest to being reconciled.

What I mean by this can be understood most easily by picturing yourself in one of the West's quintessential creations: the shopping mall. A mall is advertising in three dimensions, the high street in a greenhouse, an urban paradise sumptuously fusing the natural and the artificial into forms that soothe and caress. It is not a place of assembly. It has no commercially wasteful open spaces, no inscriptions reminding you of the virtues of fellowship. You approach it as an individual, at most with two or three friends or members of your immediate family. Yet the structure is designed to accommodate huge numbers, and in North America will characteristically be surrounded by a wide foreshore of tarmac where patrons can leave their cars.

Inside you are very much in company. You may even feel a background camaraderie, arising from the crowd's sense of common purpose. Most people will take a lost child to an attendant, stop to help if somebody faints.

Yet in the end, the mall, like the fairground economy in general, exists to facilitate choice, not obligation. You choose between shops, restaurants, and goods. You choose when to arrive and when to leave. If you have enough imagination you can criticise the management for not extending your choice further by providing more toilets or a room to change babies. But the genius of the system is this: in the fairground economy choice and obligation are turned into the same thing. We keep the economy moving through the indulgence of our natural desire for pleasure.[2] This is one spoon of medicine, and sugar by the ladleful. Across a broad swathe of our experience we can believe that obligation, for all intents and purposes, has ceased to exist.

Ultimately it is consumerism that makes the Western mega-community viable. The universality of the desire to enjoy yourself provides a remarkably effective source of social stability. You don't have to force anyone to have fun. That is why advertising works. It is also why the Western mega-community, in its variety of forms, differs markedly from Communist mega-communities, which rested on the unreliable assumption that individuals can be made to respond to obligations imposed on them by a centralised political power.

If, like the authorities in Orwell's *1984*, you could find enough cameras and microphones and enough functionaries to watch and listen, you might just succeed in making the mega-community work through coercion. It is perhaps because the necessary technologies were too expensive in the real world that the Soviet bloc has now exchanged a mega-community built on force for one that employs the subtler and far superior method of seduction. Both in the end perform the same function – to conform individual behaviour to the needs of the system, and hence to benefit those who have greatest discretion in the use of power. The difference is that consumerism achieves this conditioning with the full consent of the victim.

Lolling and Slopping
Television as Competition

In Relational terms the fairground economy is a lot less secure than it looks from Westminster or Whitehall.

It is all very well to use the extension of choice as a way of "buying" the obligation you need to run the economy. But there are more obligations in the social structure than those underlying the market, and for many of them, notably those contained in the family and the neighbourhood, the extension of choice brings more damage than liberation. That being the case, a society that tends not only to promote choice indiscriminately, but also to socialise its members into choice-seeking behaviour, may expect to run into trouble.

The very extensive literature on moral development and the transmission of values[3] assumes what has in fact always been true: that the grounds of obligation – moral sentiment and Relational skill – are bestowed on the young person principally in her first five years of life and within the primary group of the family. A shift in the focus of socialisation away from the primary group and toward the dispersed networks of media and economy represents, therefore, a weakening of the crucial checks and balances by which obligation in the social structure is preserved.

It is here that we find a vituperative exchange going on about the effects of television.

An in-house study published by the BBC in 1959 (when broadcasting hours were limited and only 40% of British adults had televisions at home) concluded, with an almost audible sigh of relief, that "The outstanding result of the enquiry has been the fact that it has uncovered hardly any evidence to support the large and sweeping generalisations often made as to the effects of television upon family life and social habits."[4] Some American critics, however, have their fingers on the panic button. "Television," one claimed recently, "is destroying America ... What I find particularly appropriate," he continues, comparing television to the Odyssean Cyclops, "is that, first, the Cyclops imprisons these men in darkness, and that, second, he beats their brains out before he devours them. It doesn't take much imagination to apply this to the effects of TV on us and our children."[5]

Indeed not. And bereft as they would be if they had to exchange their telly for a vase of flowers, most people seem to agree. Thus Roald Dahl on children's viewing:

> In almost every house we've been,
> We've watched them gaping at the screen.
> They loll and slop and lounge about,
> And stare until their eyes pop out.
> (Last week in someone's place we saw
> A dozen eyeballs on the floor.)
> They sit and stare and stare and sit
> Until they're hypnotized by it,
> Until they're absolutely drunk
> With all that shocking ghastly junk ...[6]

But if the stupefying effects of the television set have become something of a running joke in Western culture, the question of what television does or doesn't do — whether it broadens your mind or gives you square eyes and turns your brain into a walnut — remains important because television represents the media's foremost influence on socialisation.

The average British home has two TV sets, which on average the occupants will spend twenty-five hours per week watching.[7] An estimated five million have virtually no other leisure activity.[8] In anyone's language that's a lot of time to spend relating to a TV set; more, by roughly 5,000%, than most men spend talking to their wives.[9] None of which means you suffer for it, of course. But this elbowing-in of television on the individual's Relational Base has two distinct implications.

The first is that time devoted to watching TV is time diverted from personal interaction. You might object that viewing isn't necessarily antiRelational since whole families will sometimes settle down in front of the TV together. That is true. There is no doubt that television can generate shared experience and pleasure and, to that extent, contribute to, rather than detract from, relationships between viewers. There are some important qualifications to this, however.

If you examine television's effect on behaviour you will find that most shared viewing is parallel, not interactive. Once you start to talk you have ceased to watch the TV, and if the TV is on you tend not to talk. Presumably the two million Britons who reputedly make love in front of the television[10] don't do it in the middle of their favourite programme. The BBC could say what it liked about the effects of TV; as early as 1951 Maccoby had shown that school children did not talk while viewing,[11] an observation corroborated twenty years later when Walters and Stone asked respondents how much they talked while the TV was on, and found that 52% reported no conversation at all.[12]

This is all assuming that the viewers are in the same room. But are they? Watching TV is in the end an individual activity engaged in by individuals. You don't need other people. Their presence can enhance or spoil your enjoyment, according to circumstance; but you don't need them. One in five seven-year-olds now has a television set in the bedroom.[13] But even if he didn't, would you sit down and watch cartoons with him? Do you watch the rugby with your husband? The answer is probably no – tastes differ, which is why it's so hard to make a completely popular choice when you go to the video shop.

It may be a wistful misconception that in those strangely elusive good old days the family would gather around the piano on a Sunday night and sing (mine never did). Nevertheless there remains a qualitative difference between households where members do a lot of things together, and households where obligation has loosened to the degree that each person has his own schedule and the home functions predominantly as a time-shared dormitory and canteen.

Television, then, belongs to a broad selection of freely chosen activities – others might be guides, or the golf club – each of which is capable of enriching relationships outside the home, but which collectively tend to impoverish relationships inside the home because household members have to consult their diaries before they can do things together. It can be defended as a source of companionship for the lonely, and rightly so. Yet it is this same deftness at substituting for a social life that makes television a disincentive for seeking encounter. We watch TV instead of going out. We watch TV instead of inviting friends in. We watch TV instead of talking. On this score it is telling that a conference the BBC and IBA sponsored in 1980 to explore television's role in supporting family life saw it not just as a positive resource for interaction, but as a way for members of a troubled family to stay apart.[14] It is not surprising, perhaps, that Linder blames such material preoccupations as television, which make ever growing demands on a fixed supply of time, for increasing loneliness and neglect in the upbringing of children.[15]

The Bed Next Door
Television as Educator

The second implication of the rise of television has to do not with what it prevents, but with what it does.

The role of the television medium in shaping our culture is too large a study to précis here. Television has narrowed our attention span, made us addicts of the moving image. Far more than newsprint, it has encouraged us to see politics as story, a real-life soap where conflicts are clothed in opposing personalities and actions rise and fall. Television transforms entertainment into extravaganza and tragedy into spectacle.

(Stunning, just how closely those missile tracking shots from the Gulf War resembled those on video combat games; stunning, too, how the use of a Gulf War logo on television news gave Operation Desert Storm a corporate image.) Television levels culture like a gale. It moves entertainment and ideas faster than cars move people. Just as mobility makes places more alike, so television tends to standardise taste and experience. It encourages social uniformity.

This being so, it is predictable that opinion about the norms conveyed by television should be deeply divided. There is, I think, a real problem with television as regards the preserving of obligation. First, the much-vaunted principle of value-neutrality, designed to prevent any single moral viewpoint gaining a monopoly in programme output, by its very nature expresses the ethos of choice. In the mega-community it could hardly be otherwise without turning broadcasting into an instrument of propaganda. Nevertheless, to present in a completely disinterested fashion disputes about the legitimacy of conflicting claims to obligation (gay as opposed to straight, Left as opposed to Right, Christian as opposed to secular humanist) is to say, with the very considerable authority of the centralised media, that obligation in general is something you *choose*. Of course most viewers and broadcasters recognise certain overarching obligations to the extent that they agree programme output should be subject to moral censorship. But in the mega-community even this must be negotiable. As we noted in an earlier chapter, if choice is your central value then, ultimately, on what grounds, apart from majority vote, do you discriminate against the bad? How do you even define the bad?

Exactly this dilemma was highlighted at a recent convention of the Royal Television Society, where a mock schedule was circulated showing the kind of programming in 1993 that could result from the auction of ITV.[16] The new ITV was anticipated to have looser responsibilities in the area of public service broadcasting. It would still be required to put out a "sufficient amount" of high quality programmes, but the 1990 Broadcasting Act did not stipulate that, for instance, documentaries be screened in primetime slots. Reflecting a commercial environment where ITV will for the first time face direct competition for viewers and advertising, from Channel 4, Channel 5, cable, satellite and video, the mock schedule pushed ITV's current flagship *News at Ten* to 11.30 p.m., leaving weekday evenings free for a four-hour run of light entertainment. Where the *News at Ten* used to be, on Tuesdays and Wednesdays, a new show moves in, teasingly titled *The Bed Next Door*.

This blunt intrusion of market forces places television under much the same pressure as retailing. Primetime – television's shop window – is decorated with the TV "products" most in demand. The convenience of the individual consumer is taken as blanket justification both for extending selling hours (there was little discussion, for example, about whether we needed breakfast television, or what unwanted side-effects it might produce), and for the screening of what some would regard as offensive material, on the grounds that you are complying with regulatory standards by screening it after the 9 p.m. watershed, and that, anyway, those who object are free to change channel or switch off. It is up to the consumer to choose.

The net result of all this is that television's ability to preserve the idea of obligation is greatly impaired. Arguably this wouldn't matter if television were a minority interest like grand opera or poetry reading. But it's not; television is possibly the major socialising force of the mega-community. And it will only increase in importance. If parents perceive the streets as unsafe, they will be the more motivated to keep children indoors, and as every parent knows, the temptation to pacify restless children by turning on the TV is very strong. Not only that, but the prevailing trend toward increasing personal autonomy will tend to devolve choice about television viewing to the child herself. It must be legitimate, therefore, to ask what sort of socialisation TV effects.

The literature here is very extensive, and concentrates particularly on the screen portrayal of violence and sex. Although the point has been vigorously debated on the former, recent studies have tended to corroborate the conclusions reached by the American Commission on the Causes and Prevention of Violence:

> The preponderance of the available research evidence strongly suggests that violence in television programmes can and does have adverse effects upon audiences – particularly child audiences . . . Television enters powerfully into the learning process of children and teaches them a set of moral and social values about violence which are inconsistent with the standards of a civilised society . . .[17]

On either issue, the debate is too often reduced in the public mind to a contest between blue-rinse moralists and the supposedly libertarian directors of television drama. In fact the problem arises just as strongly in news coverage, and follows from the pervasiveness of television as a medium. The presence of the television in the home breaks down almost every barrier between the child and society. The mega-community sleeps in the living room. Not only dramatised sexuality and aggression, therefore, but the full cruelty and confusion of the real world are available to anyone – child or adult – who cares to press the switch. The child will see injured civilians being carried away from a mortar blast. She will see the blood of a Loyalist murder victim spread over the pavement. She will see children like her, hungry, traumatised, separated from parents, interned, dying.

Clearly, how she reacts will depend on a great variety of factors. Children are not made of glass. But the fact that parents often feel a desire to "protect" them from such images indicates, I think, a disjunction between the Relational needs of the child and the almost total inability of television to distinguish children from adults. Certainly as far as advertising is concerned the distinction is wilfully ignored.

Children are targeted with sophisticated advertising for toys, just as they are targeted for drugs in many playgrounds. Like everyone else in the mega-community, they are regarded first and foremost as individuals, with discretion in the use of economic power. And children certainly have such discretion, either through their own earnings from paper rounds, or through their increasingly generous allowances in pocket money, or through the pressure they can bring to bear on the parental purse.

Of course there is a certain irony in this. Childhood, wrung from the grip of commerce in the nineteenth century, has been reinvaded by it in the twentieth. Saved from economic participation as a producer, the child is plunged back in as a consumer. It is, after all, the child who best likes the fairground.

Stretchers in the Fairground
The Social Costs of Consumerism

A fairground economy needs to advertise. To maximise returns, it is necessary to maximise sales, which cannot be done effectively without the use of advertising to persuade the potential customer that he or she wants the product.

We have already noted that in an effort to build some sort of relationship with the consumer, advertisers set out to mimic encounter. In fact the treatment of the consumer as an individual, rather than as a member of a client group, has become the latest new wave in the advertising industry. In 1990 Quaker Oats cut marketing spending by $33 million in one quarter, with the aim of developing one-to-one contact with end-users as a means of building relationships and thus brand-loyalty. Catalogue companies have been playing this game for some time, addressing customers by name and affecting a breezy manner as they lay out their wares: competitions, draws, prizes, membership cards, special offers. "Being market-driven will no longer be enough," according to analysts Rapp and Collins. "The new leaders will be relationship-driven."[18]

Whether he stresses markets or relationships, however, the advertiser works within the tight constraints imposed on him by the mega-community. "Relationship-driven" doesn't signify a change in attitude toward you so much as an improved capability in his software: he becomes a better mimic. As before, his aim is to guide you gently through your flirtation with the goods to the full consummation of purchase. As before, it is *de rigueur* in the commercials for the purchaser to emerge from his consummation smiling, as though the buying itself, the securing of possession, were itself climactic.

Such messages, whispered incessantly through commercial breaks and the pages of glossy magazines, together convey another, deeper message, a meta-message, whose successful transmission is the single essential foundation of all advertising. It says, *You deserve to enjoy yourself.* For it is not enough in the fairground economy for the advertiser to sit like a red devil on the consumer's shoulder. He cannot afford to wrest each indulgence of desire from a nervous conscience. The consumer must be given moral permission to enjoy himself.

In this conscious attempt to transform social values, advertising really is manipulative. Under some guise or another (and it is often under the guise of advancement toward the good society) it encourages us in the cultivation of appetite, not just by allowing those tantalising smells to waft out of the kitchen, but by saying, in effect, that it is right to be hungry. Materialism is not, as we sometimes think, simply an individual moral vice; it is part of our socialisation into the mega-community. The system relies on it. The self-regarding objectives of individuals must be enlisted for the sales effort, because the advertiser has so few other motivations to work on. "Consumer advertising," as Fred Hirsch says, "comprises a persistent series of invitations and imperatives to the individual to look after himself and his immediate family; self-interest becomes the social norm, even the duty."[19] The fairground economy could not, by definition, survive in a society of nuns.

This isn't a pitch for asceticism. No moral opprobrium attaches to enjoyment *per se*. Furthermore it is true both that individuals often seek to enjoy themselves in unselfish ways, and that at least some products advertised (family holidays, for instance) provide genuine opportunities for building relationships. But the net influence of advertising on the social structure is to weaken obligation and commitment, not to strengthen them. The advertiser invites me to extend my choices, not my responsibilities. That I want an investment plan for my wife's sake as well as my own matters to him only in as much as it provides another motive for me to spend. Outside the area in which my commitment moves me to make commercial choices there is little reason for the economy to be bothered with it.

Does this matter? In a confined sense, perhaps not. Advertising does not bear sole responsibility for preserving obligation and commitment in society, and it is, anyway, almost by definition engaged in the business of publicising options. To that extent you might argue that it has its place, and is socially neutral. On the other hand, there is every reason to believe that the incursion of the ethos of choice into economic behaviour – which advertising explicitly encourages – has socially undesirable effects.

Debt is a cogent example of this. In little more than a decade the advertising industry has turned borrowing into a virtue. By the early 1980s you no longer had to slink in to see your bank manager, ashamed of your need for a loan. The bank was out looking for custom. The terminology changed. Risking your house for the sake of ready cash became *loan security*; taking out a second mortgage became *equity release*; best of all, by a bold inversion, debt itself turned into *credit*. Who would have paid for dinner by debt card or bought a new car on a debt agreement? Yet going into debt to obtain consumer goods, anathema just a few years before, was suddenly the smart thing to do.

In the thirteen years since the passing of the first Finance Act in Mrs Thatcher's administration, British consumers have pushed their collective debt, excluding mortgages, from £10 billion to £50 billion. Yet outside the roughly forty specialist advice centres and the CAB, little serious attention is paid to the social costs when debt turns bad. That your inability to keep up with repayments may easily result in chronic anxiety, isolation and marital breakdown is of no consequence to the creditor. Not generally because he is mean, but because your relationship with him is contingent. He doesn't know you. He's never met you. He can conduct a harassment campaign without a twinge of conscience because he has never visited your home or been introduced to your wife or husband or children. And anyway he probably has enough heartaches of his own without listening to yours.

It is paradoxical that, in a system where so much has been invested to remove the stigma from borrowing, the inability to service debts remains an acute form of social disgrace. Society will see your falling behind on repayments as evidence, not of a fault in the system, but of bad luck, or more likely, ineptitude. The debtor isn't a victim, but a flawed consumer, stripped of rank for incompetence with cash. He sinks to the level of the constitutionally poor – the long-term unemployed, the elderly on state pensions – and becomes invisible. He registers in the media only as the subject for a worthy documentary. In the fairground economy he is an onlooker, the person who can't afford a ride, the person on the wrong side of the Have/Have-not divide which is one of the most elemental in the mega-community.

And yet, locked in the fairground, he is content for his social value to be measured on the scale of consumption. Like nearly all the poor he swallows whole a philosophy that undervalues and condemns him, and does not resent it. Why not? Because everybody wants a ride. As Zygmunt Bauman points out, "Consumers are not enemies of the poor, they are patterns of the good life, examples one tries to emulate to the best of one's ability. What the poor are after is a better hand, not a different card game."[20]

Bauman sees the supreme image of consumer society in the Abbey of Thélème, with whose construction François Rabelais ended his satirical masterpiece *Gargantua*. Thélème, where wealth is a virtue, pleasure life's purpose and amusement an art, is separated from the society that supports it by immensely thick walls. No one inside the abbey goes out. No one wants to. No one needs to. It is, of course, an apt analogy for the divisions of the consumer world – foyer from service entrance, market from sweatshop, winner from loser. But the image of the wall speaks also and more profoundly of the loss of encounter. Whatever balance consumerism strikes between choice and obligation is struck only for the insiders. For the rest – for the disadvantaged and for the growing mass of permanently poor now dubbed the underclass – no balance is possible, because the mega-community not only deprives them, as it does everyone else, of the resources derived from obligation, but also strips from them the opportunity for choice. It should perhaps not surprise us that the underclass (in Britain estimated to number 4 million in 1986[21]) occupies the zones of social and spatial immobility – the detention areas. Nor that, being penniless in the fairground, members of the underclass are more prone to crime and more subject to coercive methods of social control.

Two Pages of Fiction
Can the Fairground Survive?

After the upheavals of the Great War and the Depression a new orthodoxy took hold among the economic theorists. They believed the roller-coaster of boom and bust could be levelled out by the application of strict scientific planning. It was a heady notion, inspired by the Soviets' apparently successful fusion of socialism and technocracy ("I have been over into the future," said the writer Lincoln Steffens in 1919, "and it works"), and its opponents quickly found themselves in a minority. Ludwig von Mises' famous attempt to show that, contrary to popular thinking, "economic calculation is impossible in a socialist society"[22] was comprehensively trounced in 1936 by Oskar Lange. "Professor Mises' contention," wrote Lange, "is based on a confusion concerning the nature of prices."[23]

As it turned out, however, the confusion belonged to Lange. Looking back on the debate, Mises' one-time protégé, Friedrich von Hayek, argues that Lange's paper contained "two pages of fiction" regarding the plausibility of planning.[24] Lange, said Hayek, tripped up in his assumption that a few administrators in a central planning agency could obtain as detailed a knowledge of demand, prices and resources as producers possess collectively through the market. For Lange to hold that "The administrators of a socialist economy will have exactly the same knowledge, or lack of knowledge, of the production functions as the capitalist entrepreneurs have," was, to Hayek, "an assertion so absurd that it is difficult to understand how an intelligent person could ever honestly make it . . . a sheer impossibility which only a miracle could realise." This did not bode well for centralised planning. "Persistence on this course," Hayek concluded gloomily in 1935, "must lead to economic decay."[25]

Fifty years on, history has proved Hayek's point. The Soviet empire has collapsed, not under the pressure of the Western military threat, but through an inherent contradiction in its own economic structure. Over the long-haul, despite the determined efforts of Brezhnev to revive it and the desperate shots in the arm from American cybernetics, Gosplan proved unworkable. And it proved unworkable substantially for the reasons Hayek outlined before World War Two.

The demise of planning has left capital-based economies top dog. Indeed many have seen in the collapse of the Eastern bloc a direct vindication of capitalism. Capitalism "works"; state socialism does not. The salvation of the new ex-Communist republics, it is widely believed, lies in submission to the disciplines of the market. There is even a certain poetic justice here, in as much as Reaganomics and Thatcherism – arguably the most extreme expressions of capitalism practised in the modern era – embody in large measure the theories developed by the school of one Friedrich von Hayek.

The mega-community as developed in the West, then, is gradually fastening its grip at the global scale. As we look to the future, we generally do so within a conceptual framework the mega-community lays out for us. Our political ideals revolve around the liberty of the individual (choice incarnated as democracy). Our economic ideals revolve around the priority of consumer choice founded on continuing economic growth – indeed we regard the capital-based economy's "wealth-producing capacity" as its chief legitimation.[26] That in practice these do not always square with our social ideals – with the longing for justice, association, and some sort of equality – should perhaps ring a warning bell at the back of our minds. For to be sustainable, a political economy must surely serve felt needs; and while we are right to value the extensions of choice which the mega-community makes possible in our political and economic affairs, we also know that choice in itself cannot complete us as human beings.

This dilemma has been formulated in various ways. From the socialist perspective it is a matter, if not of who owns the means of production, then at least of how wealth is distributed in society, and, in its most dilute form, of the need to make the market "social" – that is, to divert a larger proportion of government spending into the public sector. To the moralists – and I include the environmental lobby here – the critical problem lies in the motivation of the individual, particularly of those individuals who occupy key decision-making positions and can thus give expression to claimed public sentiments on issues ranging from abortion to oil spillage and the culling of seals. A third group, broadly identified as communitarian, sees the weakness of post-industrial society as impersonalism, and proposes a return to more intimate communities and smaller units of production.

There are many more. Nor are the ones I have described mutually exclusive; indeed it would be surprising if they were, since each, through its particular critique of Western culture, seeks to restore the one countervailing need of obligation. But how far does the loss of obligation matter in practice? It is, after all, something we can soak up indefinitely, just another social change to which, grumbling as usual, we will sooner or later adapt and settle down? Or are the prophets who claim that the Western political economy will usher in a golden age just writing us another two pages of fiction?

There are three areas, I think, in which the decline of obligation will prove critical.

First, and perhaps most obviously, there is the threat to the economic base. The medium to long-term effect of Relational breakdown can only be to impair performance and raise costs. The loss of trust within the exchange system has already imposed a substantial fiscal drag in the form of litigation, and in different ways displacement, limited commitment and short financial horizons reinforce this. At the same time, the mega-community accumulates massive social overheads in the form of policing, health care and social security, all of which have to be paid for out of the national budget. In Britain the problem is exacerbated by the changing age-structure of the population. We have a higher proportion of older people. They are living longer. And translated into economic terms that means a substantially increased expenditure on health care and pensions.

In a free-choosing society, therefore, and without a high rate of economic growth, a government will find unwelcome choices forced upon it. To stay solvent it will have to reduce its per capita expenditure on social needs, or finance them by increasing the tax burden on the private sector. It is in many ways an impossible choice. If business has to shoulder a higher tax rate, it will become even more vulnerable to international (and therefore uncontrollable) competition.[27]

Given the close links between the giants of industry and government, therefore, and also since the mega-community characteristically operates on the principle of protecting the economy first, a government would be likely as a first option to shed its social responsibilities by cutting welfare allocations and putting welfare functions out to tender. Indeed the Conservative government has already started doing this.

The effect is slow and cumulative. One would predict on the basis of present trends a widening gap between the productivity of the Japanese labour force and that of the UK. Japan has industrialised recently and rapidly, and it will take several decades (though arguably fewer than it took in the West) for the mega-community to eat into Japan's Relational fabric and for its effects to become visible in the social indicators. By contrast, northern European countries like Britain are suffering the Relational fallout from two centuries of industrialisation. They are on the downwave, and this is an ominous outlook both externally, in terms of competitiveness on the world market, and internally, in terms of political stability. For if social overheads in the West continue to rise, the strategy of privatising welfare will only buy time. A country can only go so far down the road of expenditure-capping before it risks unrest, as the poor look for means other than the ballot-box to right their grievances.

Second, then, there is a threat to democracy. More than any other polity, and paradoxically in view of the fact that it gives political expression to individual choice, democracy rests upon the commitment of the citizen to fulfil certain obligations to the state. Where the political economy does not foster such commitment, and where individuals have been encouraged to regard the acquisition and possession of material wealth as a high priority, the population will be likely to protect its financial interests even at the expense of its political freedoms. Such fears may be premature in the Britain of the 1990s. But our long traditions do not make us immune to this well-charted descent into totalitarianism.

We have no real idea what would happen to British society in the event of an enduring fiscal crisis. And meanwhile it is certainly true – indeed who hasn't experienced it? – that as time goes on one takes more care over security, not less.

Third, there is the threat to the environment.

We are apt to think of environmental issues as a product of self-interested business leadership and insufficient political will. But the flouting of obligation which lies behind environmental abuse reflects specific losses of Relational proximity: executives who live a thousand miles from the fishing communities endangered by an oil spill; shareholders too far removed from company operations to regard them as anything other than a potential source of profit. The dependence of local farmers on contingent relationships mediated through the market largely explains the persistence of environmentally harmful practices like deforestation. The lack of parity-based, cross-cutting linkage in relationships between polluters and populations puts the onus on specialist surveillance/pressure groups like Greenpeace to make industrial practice transparent to the individuals it most affects. At another level, and as the 1992 Earth Summit showed only too plainly, concerted action on the potentially lethal problems of global warming and declining bio-diversity – not to mention that grim heritage from the cold war, nuclear proliferation – requires at the local, regional, national and supranational levels a substructure of relationships strong enough to carry mutual commitment, trust and good faith. Without such relationships, environmental treaties aren't worth the paper they're written on.

Decline and Fall
Conclusion

If we don't resent the mega-community, that is probably because it has brought us many benefits. After all, there is nothing wrong with individualism *per se*, nothing shameful in the assertion of individual rights over the claims of the group. More than that, individualism became a valuable corrective to social, political and economic structures that were all too often blatantly oppressive. In the end, the fact that it found its way into the heart of the mega-community may be a trick of history, for other industrial soiceities – notably those of the former Eastern bloc – have existed on the basis of very limited degrees of personal freedom.

But having become the core sentiments of the mega-community, individualism and the ethos of choice seem, almost as a matter of course, to undermine the obligations which give individual life its meaning and society its cohesion. The mechanisms by which this occurs have been examined in the last three chapters. We have seen that the mega-community's top-down power structures create conditions in which contingently related individuals enjoy more or less equal rights under the law, yet find themselves able to influence only with great difficulty the tiny elites who control the political and economic power blocs. They suffer displacement, not just as relocators, but through the transformation of neighbourhoods into the low-encounter environments I have called transit camps and detention areas. Finally, as participants in a consumer, fairground economy, they find themselves conditioned into behaviour patterns that vitiate challenges to the power structure, yet at the same time meet the needs not of the person, but of a choice-driven economy.

To talk about the "ethos of choice" is in part to address a moral issue, and it is certainly true that the widespread loss of religious conviction and moral absolutism in the West has been one factor behind the decline of obligation. But that is not the whole story. Obligation itself may have moral or religious roots, but our ability to recognise obligations and to feel obligated depends heavily on certain qualities being present in our relationships – qualities to which I have given the collective title "Relational proximity".

Relational proximity creates society. At least minimal amounts of directness, continuity, multiplexity, parity and commonality must be present in relationships, and particularly in key institutional relationships, if society is to remain coherent and functional. It is the ability of transport and telecommunications to create and maintain Relational proximity which has allowed Western societies to merge into what I have called the mega-community. But although the mega-community continues to refine its communications systems, in most other ways it undermines Relational proximity, and the result is that, like obligation, Relational proximity is becoming a scarce resource. Unlike obligation, however, Relational proximity is tangible. It is capable of being manipulated and structured, both by individuals and by policy-makers. And if that is true, there must be a possibility of so shaping and defining relationships – at both the personal and the institutional level – that obligation and choice are kept in balance. We must be able to create a Relational society.

Notes

1   Daniel Boorstin, *The Americans – The Democratic Experience* (Random House, New York, 1973).
2   For a broader and very incisive development of this argument, see Zygmunt Bauman, *Freedom* (University of Minnesota Press, Minneapolis, 1988), ch. 4.
3   For a comprehensive bibliography see J. Leming, *Foundations of Moral Education* (Greenwood Press, Westport CT, 1983).
4   W. A. Belson, *Television and the Family: An Effects Study* (BBC Audience Research Department, 1959), p. 127.
5   Larry Woiwode, "TV: The Cyclops that eats books", *AFA Journal*, April 1992, p. 5.
6   Roald Dahl, "The Television Song", from *Charlie and the Chocolate Factory* (Puffin Books, Penguin Books, Harmondsworth, Middlesex, 1973), p. 121.
7   Broadcasting Audience Research Board and British Broadcasting Corporation, quoted in *Social Trends*, no. 20, HMSO, London, 1990.

8 Data from a 1991 NOP survey commissioned by the *Radio Times*. Intriguingly, according to this study, one in eight people claims to spend ten hours a week "doing nothing". See "Television heads list of leisure activities", *Independent*, April 2, 1991.

9 Deborah Tannen, for example, recalls her husband justifying his lack of communication with her on the grounds that "studies have shown that married couples who live together spend less than half an hour a week talking to each other . . . " See Deborah Tannen, *You Just Don't Understand* (Virago Press, London, 1992), p. 24.

10 "Television heads list of leisure activities", *Independent*, April 2, 1991.

11 E. E. Maccoby, "Television: Its Impact on School Children", *Public Opinion Quarterly*, vol. 15, 1951.

12 J. K. Walters and V. A. Stone, "Television and Family Communication", *Journal of Broadcasting*, vol. 15, 1971.

13 See Vivienne Cato et al., *The Teaching of Initial Literacy*, National Foundation for Educational Research, 1992.

14 See R. Rogers (ed.), *Television and the family: Papers from a conference conducted in London, March 1980*, UK Associations for the International Year of the Child and University of London Department of Extra-Mural Studies, London, 1980.

15 See S. B. Linder, *The Harried Leisure Class* (Columbia University Press, New York, 1970).

16 Maggie Brown, "Come on down with ITV", *Independent*, September 5, 1991.

17 Quoted in A. Quicke, *Tomorrow's Television* (Lion, Berkhampstead, 1976). One of the better-known studies, which suggests a link between television violence and child behaviour, is T. M. Williams (ed.), *The Impact of Television: A Natural Experiment in Three Communities* (Academic Press, Orlando, 1986).

18 A. Rapp and T. Collins, *The Great Marketing Turnaround: The Age of the Individual and How to Profit From It* (Prentice Hall, New Jersey, 1990), p. 155.

19 Fred Hirsch, *The Social Limits to Growth* (Routledge & Kegan Paul, London, 1977), p. 82.

20 Zygmunt Bauman, *op. cit.*, p. 93.

21 David Smith, *Understanding the Underclass* (Policy Studies Institute, 1992).

22 *Archiv für Sozialwissenschaft und Sozialpolitik*, vol. XLVII, no. 1, April 1920. Translated with additions in Ludvig von Mises, *Socialism* (Jonathan Cape, London, 1936). See particularly Section I, chapter 2.

23 Oskar Lange, "On the economic theory of socialism, I", *Review of Economic Studies*, vol. IV, no. 1, October 1936.

24 Friedrich von Hayek, "Two Pages of Fiction: The Impossibility of Socialist Calculation", *Economic Affairs*, April 1982.

25 Friedrich von Hayek (ed.), *Collectivist Economic Planning: Critical Studies in the Possibilities of Socialism* (George Routledge & Sons, London, 1935), p. 242.

26 Paul Johnson, "The Capitalism & Morality Debate," *First Things*, March 1990, p. 18.

27 In 1983 the European Parliament commissioned Professors James Ball and Michel Albert to report on European recovery. One of the arguments to emerge in the report was that heavier taxation would reduce investment in industry, which in turn would make European industry less competitive in world markets.

7

Between There and Here

Futurewatch
Toward a Relational Society

Our culture looks obsessively forward. We are future-watchers. We strain our eyes at a temporal horizon over which lies, according to our point of view, a tumbling into new dark ages or the turnstiles of an earthly paradise. In using the phrase Relational society, however, we have moved beyond prediction. We are no longer second-guessing tomorrow's history, but changing today's. To say that a Relational society would be better than the one we have is, of course, an ambitious claim, and can be recognised only if, as I have argued, human beings need to be understood in their inherent relatedness, and not merely as individuals clubbing into collectives or as collectives broken into constituent parts. For if that is true – if the good of both the individual and the group rest on the quality of interpersonal relationships – two very important points surely follow. One, the ability to nurture general (and not specifically economic) wellbeing is the proper yardstick by which to judge the success of our political-economic system.[1] And two, the creation of a Relational society is the proper object of social policy.

What is a Relational society? The words suggest a static social order conceived in abstract purity and fostered on the real world by unpersonable zealots. And yet the notion is highly fluid. We could define it as a society that organises itself around the changing inputs of climate, technology and raw materials, with the conscious aim of preserving both choice and obligation, and of promoting quality of relationship in the same way as other social philosophies have promoted liberty or solidarity. It is not another applicant for that widely advertised vacancy of the political middle-ground. It has no corollary in current Party politics at all. Because it implies a definition of human flourishing, and deals in attributes all members of society share, it operates far more at the level of a constitution. Indeed a constitution, expressing as it does the essential framework of relations within a society, would be its natural form.

Such consensual forms of organisation do not emerge from thin air, nor does their authority rest on the opinion of those who draft and sign them. "We, the people of the United States", begins the preamble to the US Constitution. That the finished document owed much to the genius of Thomas Jefferson is beside the point: it voiced the sentiments of the people and received their free endorsement. By the same token, if a parliament ever writes a Relational constitution, the origins of its mandate will lie in the present revival of interest in relationships, for which this book attempts to lay out a systematic foundation. We are becoming, by stages, more Relationally conscious.

What is most astounding is that this revival did not begin sooner. We assume, wrongly, that skill in relating comes to us automatically, by social osmosis, without the need for conscious participation in the learning process. And yet our key economic and political institutions rely on relationships. Relationships carry vast potentials for joy and sorrow. They can bring us sustenance, and tax our stamina to the last penny. Most important, perhaps, our socialisation into the mega-community through the media, which limits our opportunity to develop personal Relational skills, at the same time confronts us with more varied and unpredictable situations in which to relate.

Much contemporary interest in relating revolves around the problem of how to do it better. Even this very basic approach, however, blows open some crucial questions. For one thing, how do you measure improvements in something as mercurial and subtly nuanced as a human relationship? There can be no sample set of "good" relationships to which every marriage or casual acquaintance must seek to approximate. No two relationships are the same, because no pair of individuals is the same. Within the bounds of morality – what we earlier called the reciprocity principle – "good" relationships will be found to take as many forms as there are ways to arrange clothes in a suitcase.

An often under-rated source of diversity here may turn out to be the differing Relational styles of women and men. A friend who went on vacation recently took with him his wife, his children, and a heap of scientific journals. Evidently he expected his wife to build the sandcastles; for him the holiday was chiefly an opportunity to catch up on work. Now, the least complicated interpretation of this little cameo is one of preoccupation leading to neglect, and there may indeed by no more to say on the matter. On the other hand, it may also be the footnote to a now substantial literature which argues, against the feminist tendency to underplay gender differences, that men and women do on average communicate in different ways.[2] Men, for example, are less likely to disclose personal information about themselves than are women; are less likely to punctuate their listening with encouraging prompts like "Mmm", "Uh-huh" and "That's interesting." Deborah Tannen's recent work comes closest to developing a systematic theory of gender and communication, with the suggestion that men, in general, communicate in order to establish their position in a hierarchy, while women, in general, communicate in order to make connections.[3]

If there is, as Tannen maintains, such a thing as "gender-lect", this would seem to imply that, for whatever reason, a woman will usually be better equipped to act Relationally than a man. At the same time it is equally true that Relational action does not constitute a threat to masculinity: the Relational is a function of humanity, not of a specific gender, and applicable in all spheres, not only that of home and family. Men and women who succeed in politics and commerce do so through Relational skills, for even in the mega-community, and despite their many weaknesses, political Parties and plcs remain team-organisations. They are not slave galleys. They compete as groups, and their competition is bounded and defined by larger social structures (parliamentary systems, markets) which they co-operate to preserve.

This may explain why the deluge of material now available from popular and academic sources on interpersonal communication is directed at both sexes.[4] The broad conclusion of the literature is that relating improves with study, though Steve Duck perhaps overstates the case slightly when he says that "Poor conduct, like poor health, poor diet or bad exercise programmes, can be treated . . . "[5] Either way, however, my concern in this chapter is not with the art of Relational self-improvement but with the institutional structures that stifle the art's potential. For what the communication theorists largely neglect, and what this book has sought to draw attention to, is the extent to which good relating depends on the contexts in which relating takes place.

Living Relationism
Strategies for the Relational Lifestyle

FATHER SENTENCED TO DINNERS (Topsfield, Mass.) Oct. 25. The father of a 16-year-old accused shoplifter is serving a 30-day sentence – of dinners at home. A Salem district judge, Samuel E. Zoll, ordered the father of a Masconomet Regional High School student to be home between 5 and 7 p.m. every night. Their names were not released because a juvenile was involved. Judge Zoll said the father should "be at home for a meal where he could sit down and talk with the family."[6]

A good deal could be said about "living Relationally". My

object here is not to give a kind of monastic rule, but to suggest just three areas in which Relationism might make a significant difference in the way we do things.

Social eating. In every culture food has social significance. When almost every individual is involved in some aspect of food production, food can actually define social relations. The taro, or sweet potato, regarded by the Melanesian Wamira of Papua and New Guinea as having a quasi-human genealogy, represents both in symbolic and functional terms what I have called obligation. The Wamiran term for eating together contains a root meaning "to grow", whereas the term for eating separately derives from the word for "beggar".[7]

There is a certain irony in the comparison with the West, where most of us have grown nothing tougher than a plate of cress, and where eating has become, to a far greater extent than elsewhere, a private activity. I am not referring to the many people who for one reason or another live alone and so are forced to eat alone. In the West, food in general has little relevance to status (except perhaps in the symbolic value attributed to certain foods like caviar or port, or to the actions of throwing a party or paying a restaurant bill). Also, within the domestic group food is seldom, except on special occasions, viewed as a means of social contact. Not infrequently Mum or Dad cooks dinner and the rest of the family eat it in front of the television.

And yet food clearly still offers vast potential for the nurturing of encounter. When we talk about working breakfasts, having lunch together, going out for a drink, we are thinking primarily not of the food itself but of the encounters that accompany its consumption. Food preparation can be a shared activity. Eating and drinking can provide time for relaxed interaction and the building of relationships – something the French, by and large, understand better than the British. Time, really, is the key issue. Meal times have to be given priority and space. They cannot be taken in shifts by family members on the run to another engagement – an effort has to be made by everyone to be home simultaneously. And this Relational use of leisure time in the household clearly applies to more than meals. In different ways, evenings, Saturdays and Sundays and holidays all provide opportunities to balance private and voluntary pursuits with activities that involve every household member – in other words to foster commonality and directness in the home. Whether you read scientific journals on the beach or build sandcastles with your children is, Relationally, an important issue. It tests your priorities. The parent who has no time for his children teaches them to have no time for him.

Teledieting. One obstacle to encouraging Relational proximity in the household is the fact that the mega-community creates so many apparently worthy yet conflicting demands. There is always something else do do. Work you've brought home. Cooking. The lawn. Squash. Most frequently, perhaps, television.

Television is both friend and enemy. It can introduce multiplexity into our contingent relationships, and, if quality programming survives in the commercial 1990s in rather poorer health than it once enjoyed, we can still agree with screenwriter Alan Plater that television is "a unique and extraordinary medium wherein to celebrate the diversity of the human spirit".[8] Certainly television of every kind provides stimulus for conversation and to that extent could be called Relational. Yet it also keeps us from having friends in, limits interaction in the home, makes us less accustomed to relax through conversation, becomes too easy to switch on and too hard to switch off. Probably we just plain watch too much of it. Most of us could use a little *teledieting* – deliberately restricting our viewing to, say, an hour a day, and exercising greater discrimination about what we see. It is astounding how much extra time the teleslim citizen has.

Rootedness. Both social eating and teledieting – which centre around the protection of time for relating – presuppose that you have people to relate to. But again, this cannot be taken for granted. In a mobile society there may be a high turnover even in your primary relationships – those with family and close friends. To a large extent we replenish our Relational Bases naturally, seeking new contacts to replace those we have lost, but it's not always easy. The average relocator takes several years to get established in a new neighbourhood. Worse, the mobility culture is changing the rules by which neighbours relate. I remember once asking my wife if it was worth getting to know the new people who had just moved in two hundred yards down the road. We decided it wasn't, because they would probably only stay for a couple of years before moving on, and in fact this was exactly what happened. The significant point looking back, however, is not that displacement could make relating difficult, but that the mobility culture, with its expectation of displacement, removed the incentive to relate at all.

It is here that rootedness becomes important. There remains in the end an indissoluble link between encounter and place. Transport and communications stretch the link but they cannot break it: you can only live so far away from someone before the level of encounter in the relationship has to be traded against the cost of conducting it. Clearly, though, you don't have to live in the same town as another person to experience Relational proximity. When we talk about roots, we are talking in terms not just of locality, but of region. Your roots can be in Cornwall, not just in Penzance; in the Highlands, not just in Fort William.

Even so, the decision to put down roots can be painful. It means planning your career not with a view to maximising your chances of promotion, but giving yourself and your household locational stability. It means loyalty to one place with its people and institutions. It means accepting the obligations that arise through continuity, commonality, and directness. For place on its various interlocking scales is largely a function of people and their relationships. If the place is convivial it sustains Relational proximity. This is why the neighbourhoods we describe as "warm" or "friendly" tend to be those where the layout of public space, the methods of transport used, and the arrangement of personal timetabling enable those who live there to be Relationally proximate. Such features of the Relational infrastructure are not created overnight. If it is to be created at all, one requirement must be that the majority of residents choose to stay rather than move on, to settle in a single nexus of relationships rather than shift from one place to another, belonging to none. It requires swimming against the tide.

"The Government Should Do Something . . . "
The Limits of Intervention

If your company is relocating you will be forced to choose between your place and your employment. You go and continue working, or you stay and stop working. Clearly, then, your efforts to live Relationally can easily be defeated by forces beyond your control. Not that, in an abstract sense and within certain legal restraints, you aren't free to do as you like; but the mega-community does not resource your freedom to put down roots, and in choices of this nature resources are likely to be determinative.

A similar argument, of course, applies to other decisions. Whether or not you can have a day at home on Sunday with your husband and children, if you are a shopworker, will depend on whether there are laws which prevent the shop you work in from opening on a Sunday. The extent to which you will use consumer credit will depend on what rules govern its advertising and whether there are minimum deposits or other safeguards required before loans are made available. All these things are regulated by national laws and are the subject of politics.

For individuals in the mega-community to think Relationally, then, isn't enough: Relational thinking must also take hold among those with the power to determine the options of others. In particular, relationships need to become an issue of public policy.

It is important to clarify at this point what can and what cannot be achieved for relationships by means of government intervention. Pressure for legislation on relationships has, after all, been applied for some time by the various proponents of so-called "family policy". I say "so-called" because conceptions of the family, and of what family policy ought to do, differ widely according to your viewpoint. Given that this is so, however, and given also that the idea of family and the idea of Relational proximity are not synonymous, we can identify a number of policy initiatives which, if the government chose to implement them, would be seen by many as beneficial to relationships. For brevity's sake I will examine only the three most prominent ones: (1) increasing levels of government spending on Relational problems, (2) improving sex education, and (3) reforming the law on divorce.

A great deal of stress in relationships could be relieved by boosting the social security budget. No benefit is index-linked, and there has in particular been a massive transfer of resources away from those raising children. Carers remain largely neglected, and yet there are enormous gains to be made in the carer's Relational stability simply by financing holidays and home helps. Extra allocations to the housing budget would give greater continuity of relationship to many now living in temporary accommodation, and cut the number of homeless – estimated at 172,000 in 1990, with a further 760,000 "hidden homeless" (Shelter estimate, 1991), and 300,000 who are six months or more in mortgage arrears and therefore in danger of repossession (Council of Mortgage Lenders, 1992).[9] Not least, if child care were subsidised, the mothers who find the company of small children socially isolating would be free to work and so relieve financial pressure and develop more fulfilling relationships outside the home.

But the spending option has a number of disadvantages. Most obvious is the limitation on funding. Only so much can be squeezed out of the taxpayers for a national budget, and only so much of a national budget can be allocated to social purposes. Perhaps more controversially, it is arguable that, in any case, increases in government spending only make the problem worse.

Part of the rationale behind Britain's long history of social legislation has been that poverty should act as an incentive to self-help. In one sense, the Victorian poorhouse was as much a deterrent as it was a safety-net. It aimed to keep family and community support networks strong in order to prevent the poor becoming a burden to the state. Although the poorhouses have gone, the government retains a direct interest in cultivating obligation and commitment in the family. However, the economic forces set up in the mega-community, which ironically all post-war governments in Britain have given free rein to, are precisely the ones that undermine obligation and lead us to conceptualise society not as a network of families and localities but as a mass of individuals. To the extent that members of the population think of themselves as individuals, as choice-maximisers, it becomes very easy for them to discard or reformulate their mutual obligations, and to avoid, if they can, entanglement in socially costly relationships. Young people today are less likely to regard it as a duty to care for their ageing parents, and the retired, by the same token, take pride in maintaining their independence.

Against this background, increased government provision will easily be seen as relieving family and community of an onerous and inconvenient responsibility. If the government provides more money for bringing up children, the household becomes more self-sufficient, and the tendency will be for the sense of obligation on the part of relatives to be attenuated; if disability benefit is increased, the tendency will be for the friends and neighbours of a disabled person to do less to help. Encounter relationships between relatives and neighbours are incrementally replaced by contingent relationships mediated through the welfare system.

Of course this isn't an argument against welfare; far from it. For one thing the Relational issues in government spending are rarely distinct. The personal social services run by the local authority may provide help to the family carer in the form of a home-help who subsequently becomes a close friend of the family. Financial support thus turns Relational. Nevertheless it is apparent that we have to take account of the antiRelational as well as the proRelational effects of increasing government spending. Evidence from international comparisons between Western societies and low income societies, as well as historical analysis of trends within the West, suggest that greater government welfare spending is highly correlated with a weakening of support from locality and extended family networks. The line of causality runs in both directions: the decline of informal support necessitates higher spending, but in many cases that same spending tends to reinforce the decline and add to the problem it is meant to solve.

A second interventionist policy initiative is sex education. There has been a strong lobby for teenage advice on abortion and for more explicit teaching in schools on the use of condoms. There is a clear Relational argument to be made in favour of this. The creation of another human being is no light matter. It has consequences for the parents, and particularly for the mother, whether the pregnancy is terminated or goes full-term. Assuming the latter, the teenage mother who conceives unintentionally is far more likely to become a lone parent and suffer financial hardship – both of which will involve Relational costs for the child.

The problem is that another Relational case – and perhaps a stronger one – can be made on the other side. It is difficult to recommend that schoolchildren use condoms without communicating a meta-message to the effect that casual sex between schoolchildren is acceptable. You could argue, of course, that this whole argument is about whether or not to close the stable door, and in practice it may well be true that discouraging casual sex between schoolchildren is a lost cause. Nevertheless, realistically we have to take account of the evidence linking, for example, sexual activity before marriage to higher rates of divorce.[10] In other words, against the short-term Relational benefit of reducing rates of unwanted pregnancy we have to weigh the long-term Relational cost of implicitly allowing commitment in sexual relations to be eroded.

The third policy initiative – tougher divorce laws to prevent relationship breakdown – suffers from the same ambiguity.

There is some sense in the argument that, especially where children are involved, society should insist on a longer interval between the official breakdown of a marriage and its formal dissolution. Five years after a divorce, advocates of this approach will tell you, 40% of divorcees say they would have preferred to stay married.[11] There is also some sense in the argument that a society where divorce is easy is one where marriage becomes increasingly difficult – in other words, that the institutionalisation of choice in the current divorce law weakens anticipation of the relationship continuing, and deprives commitment of any meaningful legal dimension. "Marriage inherently is a relationship which needs continual servicing, review, tolerance, compromise and occasional overhaul rather than easy escape routes."[12]

On the other hand one gains little Relationally by binding people into relationships which have, for all intents and purposes, gone irrevocably wrong, and if the legal demands made of those entering into holy matrimony are too stern, many more of them will ditch the formalities and simply cohabit, further reinforcing the trend toward provisionality, and further diminishing the chances that a child will grow up with a strong Relational Base.

In the delicate business of preserving marriage, then, a tough law on divorce is a very blunt instrument indeed. As with government spending and sex education, its effects on the way people actually relate are ambivalent.

If we want to improve relationships we will have to do more than throw money around, plead with teenage boys to wear condoms, and tie legal string around unglued marriages. We will have to confront the social and economic forces that make relationships hard to sustain and make us think in terms of choice rather than obligation.

Just how powerful these forces are can be seen by comparing Western social institutions with those in more proRelational cultures. With characteristic acerbity, Germaine Greer observes that "In the end the modern nuclear parents get what they deserve, a long, barren and meaningless old age, made worse because of their inability to relate to their own peer group."[13] Yet we barely comprehend the alternatives:

> Because very few of us who have been brought up in the unending parent–child confrontation still really like our parents, we imagine that the extended family is simply a proliferation of negative attitudes. If we see twenty Parsees taking up a table at a Chinese restaurant to fête some ancient female of their clan, we expect there to be an atmosphere of constraint . . . In fact, the old lady is seated at the centre of the table, with her favourite grandchildren and great-grandchildren around her, and every joke and every piece of showing off is staged to her and for her. She is the pivot of the social group, surrounded by a circle of admiring faces . . . There is never so much as a hint of boredom or annoyance; indeed the hilarity at the table makes the rest of us feel downright gloomy by contrast.[14].

What we are glimpsing here is a culture in which obligations are celebrated and fulfilled, and where, within the familial group, Relational proximity – directness, continuity, multiplexity and commonality, though arguably not parity – is stronger than it is in the West. Greer, for one, is quick to note the potential of such an extended family network for enabling women to fulfil themselves as both wives and mothers and as working professionals. Of course Relational proximity among women – what she calls "sisterhood in action" – is won at a price. There are duties as well as freedoms, obligations as well as choices. Nevertheless, in Greer's view the obligation involved for women in membership of a wider family is a price worth paying.

Getting to There From Here
Conclusion

It is difficult for the individual to live Relationally when government policy in general discourages the development of strong relationships. But if changes in government policy are restricted to areas in which Relational breakdown is already in evidence – if, in other words, they amount to a containment exercise – they will have little prospect of success. Policy revision must address itself to causes, not effects. Again, there are some options open here.

First, you can change employment practice. Although the government has little direct influence over the private sector, it could require every company quoted on the Stock Exchange to produce a Relational audit. This could be conducted by an external agency at the firm's expense, and cover a range of issues, including home–work conflicts, staff mobility and Relational dysfunctions arising from loss of parity within the organisation. The concept of environmental auditing is becoming well established. The Chartered Association of Certified Accountants recently introduced Environmental Reporting awards to encourage companies to seek exellence in this area. The case for Relational auditing is at least as strong and could follow similar procedures. The results would be published in the company's annual report.

Second, you can require the government to set its own house in order. Public sector mobility could be reduced by changing training and career paths in the medical profession, adjusting personnel policy in the Foreign Office, and, in the armed forces, by reorganising home base staffing distribution and placement procedures. Similarly with the tensions between home and work. The current provision that junior doctors work a maximum of eighty-four hours per week (except in emergencies) often means in practice that they work in excess of one hundred hours, with a consequent stress not only on patient care but on their relationships with wives, husbands, children, and the wider family.

Third, you could take more seriously the need to educate people in relating. It may be true, as the adage says, that social skills are caught not taught, and that many aspects of relating, being dependent on good role modelling, are not readily learned in the classroom. But if a deteriorating home environment gives many children a weak Relational Base, and if, as is the case in Britain, relationships are not generally regarded as the proper domain of analysis and technique, there must be a strong case for bringing teaching on relationships into school curricula and adult education programmes. Indeed the National Family Trust has recently begun to produce course material covering much of the basic ground.

At best, however, initiatives of this kind have limited aims and limited effects. Neither employment policy nor education in relationships addresses the Relational crisis at its most fundamental level, which is the level of prevailing ethos and institutional structure. Just how much education would you need, for instance, to counter the impact of TV soaps on a viewer's understanding of sexuality? You are, in effect, asking people to act proRelationally in a largely antiRelational system: that is, a system in which choice has become dominant at the expense of obligation, and in which institutional structures constrain or erode Relational proximity. In the end, Relationism forces us to challenge not only our behaviour, public spending priorities and social policy, but the whole way our society is organised. A Relational society demands a Relational economy and a Relational democracy.

Notes

1 GDP is an unreliable measure of wellbeing. To give an extreme example, if every mother in Britain went out to work as a childminder, and employed another mother to look after her children, the GDP would jump dramatically just because

childminding is recorded as an economic activity. No one, however, would be better off financially. Arguably no one would be better off Relationally either. A comprehensive index of wellbeing, therefore, would have to measure not only improvements to the material standard of living but also reductions in Relational dysfunction as recorded in, for instance, rates of crime, some forms of mental disorder, divorce, separation, illegitimacy, and the loneliness of the elderly.

2 See, for example, S. M. Jouard, *The Transparent Self* (Van Nostrand, Princeton, 1971); Ted L. Huston and Richard D. Ashmore, "Women and Men in Personal Relationships", in R. D. Ashmore and F. K. Delboca, *The Social Psychology of Male–Female Relationships* (Academic Press, Orlando, Florida, 1986); S. Duck, *Friends for Life* (Harvester Wheatsheaf, Hemel Hempstead, 1991); and J. A. Hall, *Non-verbal Sex-differences* (Johns Hopkins University Press, Baltimore, 1984), pp. 141 ff.

3 Deborah Tannen, *You Just Don't Understand* (Virago Press, London, 1992).

4 Although the literature is too extensive to list here, the following references may be of interest to readers. C. R. Berger and J. J. Bradac ("Language and social knowledge – uncertainty in interpersonal relations", *Social Psychology of Language*, no. 2, Edward Arnold, London, 1982) examine the particular role of language in uncertainty reduction. Various attempts have been made to develop more comprehensive models: P. Feingold, "Toward a paradigm of effective communication: an empirical study of perceived communicative effectiveness", Ph.D., Purdue University, Indiana, 1976; R. Hart and D. M. Burks, "Rhetorical sensitivity and social interaction", *Speech Monographs*, no. 39, 1972, pp. 75–91; and R. B. Adler, C. B. Rosenfeld and N. Towne, *Interplay – The Process of Interpersonal Communication* (Holt, Rinehart and Winston, New York, 1986). Adler *et al.* draw attention to the neglect of listening, and this skill is further examined in L. Barker, *Listening Behaviour* (Prentice Hall, Engelwood Cliffs, New Jersey, 1971). K. Dindia and L. A. Baxter, "Strategies for maintaining and repairing marital relationships", *Journal of Social and Personal Relations*, no. 4, 1987, pp. 143–58, deal with communication in particular Relational settings, including

ceremony and shared time. Finally, a number of studies have concentrated on the role of self-disclosure in communication. E. M. Waring and G. J. Chelune, "Marital intimacy and self-disclosure", *Journal of Clinical Psychology*, no. 39, 1983, pp. 183–90; P. C. Cozby, "Self-disclosure: a literature review", *Psychological Bulletin*, no. 79, 1973, pp. 73–91; and M. R. Leary, P. A. Rogers, R. W. Canfield and C. Coe, "Boredom in personal encounters: antecedents and social implications", *Journal of Personality and Social Psychology*, no. 51, 1981, pp. 958–75. Among other things, Leary *et al.* note that boring communicators are egocentric, make banal comments, don't offer information, and don't value other contributors to the conversation.

5 Steve Duck, *op. cit.*, p. 191.

6 *New York Times*, October 26, 1975, quoted in I. D. Glick, J. F. Clarkin and D. R. Kessler, *Marital and Family Therapy* (Grune Stratton, Orlando, 1987).

7 M. Kahn, *Always Hungry, Never Greedy* (CUP, Cambridge, 1986), pp. 134–5.

8 Alan Plater, "The outcome is more dramatic than the act", *Independent*, November 11, 1992.

9 Figures cited from Jubilee Policy Group, *Who Cares for the Homeless*, Cambridge, December 1992, ch. 2.

10 See, for example, J. R. Kahn and K. A. London, "Pre-marital sex and the risk of divorce", *Journal of Marriage and the Family*, vol. 53, no. 4, November 1991, pp. 845–55.

11 See Gwynn Davis and Mervyn Murch, *Grounds for Divorce* (Clarendon Press, Oxford, 1988), p. 59.

12 *Families and the Nation: Safeguarding our Social Ecology*, National Campaign for the Family, London, February 1992, p. 9.

13 Germaine Greer, *Sex and Destiny* (Secker & Warburg, London, 1984), p. 253.

14 *ibid.*, p. 241.

8

The Relational Market Economy

Foundations
Economics as Relationship

Well, now I have jumped off the deep end. The next two chapters are, from my point of view, the hardest to write, for I have to demonstrate to you, in the relatively few pages most thinking people would wish to devote to political economics and social theory, that Relationism is a conceptual framework as complete and as robust in policy terms as capitalism or socialism – indeed that it is more complete, and more robust, and that the foundation I am able to build in the rest of this book is solid enough for terms like Relational Market Economics, Relational Democracy and Relational Justice to become the weightier items of intellectual baggage we take with us into the next century.

I say "solid enough" because I am not presenting a policy blueprint precise to the last detail, any more than I am trying to pass off a narrow concern with the environment or economic policy in the guise of a general social vision. What follows is rather an indication of the directions Relational thinking takes you when you apply it to the organisation of society and its institutions. The first topic I will deal with is economics, and this prompts me to make an apology. Dealing with economics, even Relational economics, requires the use of a certain amount of technical language. Dealing with economics at sufficient length to prove that Relationism generates a comprehensive and coherent policy direction, but also with sufficient brevity to keep the reader awake, is tantamount to squaring a linguistic circle. I will do my best.

We can begin with the simple observation that economics is a Relational concern with Relational implications.

We are often told, for example, that inflation reduces the value of savings. But there is more to this than percentages. Because wages are far more likely to be index-linked than earnings-related pensions, the net consequence of inflation is a transfer of wealth from those on fixed incomes (the pensioners and the unemployed) to those in full-time employment. Inflation makes the poor poorer not only in real terms but relative to the rest of society. The transaction is Relational.

A similar transfer will occur between generations through the accumulation of public debt. When the government finances current needs by increasing the Public Sector Borrowing Requirement (PSBR) it effectively allows living standards to be raised for taxpayers today at the expense of taxpayers tomorrow. For it is tomorrow's taxpayers who will have to pay the borrowed money back, with interest: there is an intergenerational transfer of wealth. This is why, in William Gladstone's estimation, "An excess in the public expenditure beyond the legitimate wants of the country is not only a pecuniary waste but a great political and, above all, a great moral evil."[1]

Not all policies are this clear cut from a Relational standpoint. Devaluation makes British goods cheaper overseas. But this helps only those companies and individuals in Britain who make their money through exports. Those dependent on imports suffer because their devalued money buys less from foreign suppliers. In a similar way, a rise in interest rates will hurt mortgage-holders and companies using debt finance far more than it will hurt home-renters, those using equity finance, and those who are debt-free.

What is true of economic variables, of course, is equally true of economic institutions, and most significantly of the market. We noted earlier how Adam Smith taught us to see the market in nonRelational terms: as a mechanism by which individual self-interest inadvertently and inexorably promotes the interest of society as a whole. He argued, in effect, that the need for obligation (society's interest) was met by the general exercise of individual choice (self-interest), and managed to avoid a head-on collision between the two by assuming – not unreasonably at the time – that economic decision-makers would display high degrees of commitment and constraint, and thus behave, for the most part, in proRelational ways.

Clearly, however, the emergence of the mega-community in the two centuries following the publication of *The Wealth of Nations* has undermined this assumption from two sides. First, commitment and constraint are considerably weaker in the West today than they were in Adam Smith's time: Adam Smith did not reckon on Robert Maxwell. Second, the market itself has been expanded, stretched and depersonalised. Price monitors and telephones give an international market just as much Relational proximity as it needs to perform its highly restricted function, and no more.

In contrast, a Relational Market Economy aims to ensure, as far as possible, that markets of all types – between producers and consumers, producers and suppliers, employers and workforce – are based on high levels of Relational proximity. That being so, we can make four initial observations about the way the system operates.

First, a Relational Market Economy accommodates competition.

Of course we must distinguish the positive function of competition in the marketplace from the bludgeoning use made of it by corporate giants. Competition between companies is not necessarily antiRelational; it is clearly beneficial from the perspective of the buyer, who gets a cheaper or better product or service as a result of it, and it has general proRelational benefits for competing companies, especially where they are geographically close. By raising the quality of the product, or by reducing costs, companies encourage each other to innovate, to search for improved ways of operating, to seek alternative resources and types of raw material. This constant "prodding" by a competitor can be a valuable means to achieving excellence and international competitiveness – an issue we will return to later in the chapter.

Second, a Relational Market Economy seeks sustainable economic growth.

Growth undergirds material standards of living. It compensates for the dilution of overall wealth produced by the constant increase in world population. And it makes possible a closing of the gap between rich and poor. A more equitable distribution of wealth is, after all, far more readily accomplished by channelling new wealth to the disadvantaged than it is by holding a pistol to the heads of the Haves and asking them to transfer existing wealth to the Have-nots. From a Relational point of view, however, neither growth nor improved living standards are ends in themselves. Rather the ultimate purpose of growth is *wellbeing* – a concept that covers both the material and the Relational, and suggests not only that development is a more comprehensive aim than growth, but also that the particular material aims of the development process (including food, health, education and housing) have significance beyond their benefit to the individual.

Third, a Relational Market Economy affirms the necessity of the private ownership of property.

The Marxist and socialist models based on collective ownership have been shown to work at best badly, and at worst disastrously. This is mainly because state ownership deprives the worker of incentives. John Greenwood, the Chairman and Chief Economist of G. T. Management (Asia) Limited, makes the point succinctly:

> Concerning the incentive to work, the Russians often say: "Under Communism we pretended to work, and the government pretended to pay us." Concerning the incentive to maintain assets in good condition, they say: "What everybody owns, nobody owns." Or, in the same vein, "In a Communist system, who will get up in the night and tend the sick cow?"[2]

In contrast, "private" ownership is usually taken to mean

ownership by individuals, with the implication that the worker is motivated to benefit himself and perhaps his immediate dependants. If the worker happens to be a prominent landowner, industrialist or fund manager the disadvantages of this incentive to individual gain are fairly apparent. It can too easily become an invitation to greed, a recipe for exploitation, and a mandate for environmental destruction in the pursuit of growth.

Private ownership does not have to be defined in individualist terms, however. It can also mean "non-state" ownership, and of this many examples can already be found – including family businesses and trusts, partnerships, co-operative enterprise, and some forms of mutual society – all of which in some way provide incentives for the individual to seek the benefit of a wider group.[3] Thus the leading development economist Michael Lipton comments that "In a family business, the family allocates costs, benefits and risks so as to maximise expected utility to the household, not profits to the enterprise."[4]

Fourth, and in summary, we might say that the goal of a Relational Market Economy will be to achieve growth in the incomes and material welfare of nations, regions, localities, families and individuals, within structures that facilitate rather than undermine Relational proximity. For it is Relational proximity that provides the essential precondition for good relationships, and thus preserves both the individual person and the social institutions of which the individual is a member.

If we use Relational proximity as a criterion, policy concerns will move naturally in a number of new directions. (1) For there to be directness and parity, people must have the opportunity to work together in small groups and families, and if they are employed in larger organisations they must be given greater involvement in the decisions which affect their lives. Directness also demands a high level of accountability for those involved in economic enterprise and its regulation. (2) If continuity and multiplexity are valuable qualities of relationship, it follows that we will seek to protect and develop rootedness for local communities and families. Given the connection between rootedness and place, and the problems associated with establishing rootedness on the basis of employment, this suggests strongly the crucial importance of every individual having a stake in property. (3) To avoid the injustices resulting from power asymmetries in the marketplace, a Relational Market Economy will seek to move toward establishing parity in dealings between people who act as representatives of institutions, whether those institutions are companies or public bodies. (4) Commonality will urge us to promote as far as possible a congruence of interest between the groups involved in the operation of a business – for instance shareholders, managers and workforce – so as to maximise co-operation and minimise conflict.

How, then, does such Relational thinking apply to the major areas of economic concern: finance, company structure, industrial strategy, and business practice?

Lack of Interest
Relational Finance

The Relational Dimensions of Interest. We have noted at various points in this book a link between Relational dysfunction and debt finance. It is time to draw some of these loose ends together.[5]

The charging of interest in the West began with the Protestant reformer John Calvin. Breaking with medieval tradition (which had generally observed the Old Testament ban on usury), Calvin permitted interest-charging on the grounds that for a wealthy individual to pay for the loan of money was, subject to certain stringent conditions, only just and fair.[6]

It is now widely accepted that debt-finance has a number of advantages. The two often quoted by economists are that debt-finance allows money to be allocated to those who will use it most efficiently and thus increase society's wealth the fastest, and that it allows the person with energy and no money to participate in the economy more or less on a par with the person who has capital of his own. But there are at least two others.

First, since a large lender cannot know all borrowers personally, lending at interest has the bonus that it requires relatively little information – less, anyway, than the lender would wish to obtain before buying shares in a company. Partly for this reason financial institutions can mediate between lender and borrower, enabling the lender to spread the risk of lending across a larger number of borrowers. This is fundamentally the rationale for capital markets.

Second, borrowing money can be seen as bringing forward consumption from tomorrow to today – in other words, as an inter-temporal transfer of funds. This assists the life-cycle of the household, which at the stage of raising children has far greater financial needs than it does during the parents' old age. The level of interest rates should be just sufficient to ensure that there are enough borrowers to take all the funds which lenders wish to lend. At least that is the theory. In practice, the interest system produces unpalatable side-effects.

We might note to begin with that interest charging is fundamentally antiRelational to the extent that it places the more acute risks of borrowing (changes in interest rates, business failure) entirely on the borrower. Ask anyone who took out a mortgage in the late 1980s. It has also had the two further effects of more or less universalising consumer credit and indirectly increasing rates of mobility. Both carry high social costs. Credit can lead to acute distress if a borrower – suddenly unemployed, sick, or with a new baby – has to default.[7] Population mobility follows spatial investment patterns. The more efficiently the capital market works (and this efficiency is a prime goal of neo-classical economics), the more powerfully interest drives inter-regional and international transfers of capital. But the result is a displaced society, with a dispersal of family support networks and a loss of locational solidarity. Needless to say, the huge additional infrastructure costs of mobility (schools, roads, hospitals, care for the elderly and disabled who cannot be cared for by their families) are borne neither by the financial institutions that move the capital, nor by the businesses that borrow it.

Interest also exaggerates speculative booms and busts. When prices of assets in relatively fixed supply, such as housing or shares, start to rise, buyers borrow money so as to maximise their capital gain. The process spirals, with more lending leading to even higher prices, until eventually the bubble bursts. Lenders then become unwilling to lend for even relatively secure assets, exacerbating the subsequent recession. "Efficient" capital markets are a major cause of these exaggerated economic swings, and of the huge sums of unearned income associated with speculation on property, commodities and currencies.

Most emphatically, on the macro-economic level, the interest system moves economies inexorably toward aggregation. The fundamental law of nature that the rich get richer can be traced to the fact that a wealthy borrower's larger asset base, which lowers the risk to the lender, allows him to borrow more cheaply than a poor one. Consequently large companies can obtain funds at lower costs than small companies, and the resulting pressure toward giantism puts the handling and deployment of money even further outside the ambit of family and locality. In terms of economic efficiency, it also readily leads to a misallocation of funds, as money goes to the safest borrower rather than the most productive.

A policy framework encouraging Relational finance therefore moves in three main directions: regionalism, equity finance, and changes in the role of government.

Finance and Regionalism. Since one of the main problems in finance is the lack of Relational proximity between borrower and lender, it makes sense to base financial institutions – banks, building societies, pension funds, insurance companies, even stock markets – at the regional, and, where possible, at the locality/city level. The aim of this approach is to increase regional and local inter-connectedness: both city and region provide natural foci for loyalty and commonality. Just as important, the greater incidence of multiplexity, directness and continuity between business people and financiers operating at the regional and local level makes it far easier for investors to identify and evaluate entrepreneurial talent, thus overcoming the information barrier which is one of the major obstacles for businesses seeking to attract venture capital.

Significantly, despite the recent reinstatement of the region and small nation as meaningful political and cultural units, little work has been done on the operation of financial institutions at the regional level. Regional banks, however, have been studied in some detail, and their example is instructive.[8]

Regional banking is common outside the UK. Germany has 148 regional banks, and 3,600 locally owned co-operative banks, or *Volksbanken*, serving the needs of rural households and agriculture in particular. Despite the dominance of Japanese finance by the 13 "city" institutions, Japan also has 64 regional banks which in 1987 accounted for 15% of all private financial institution assets. France has 63 provincial banks. At the head of the field, though, comes the USA, most of whose 12,096 banking institutions in 1991 were organised at the regional level. Despite the problems of specialist lenders like the Savings and Loans associations, smaller American banks in general (those with under $1 billion in assets) have consistently achieved higher returns on assets than larger banks in recent years.

Two features of regional banking are especially important for a Relational Market Economy. One, regional banks lend more effectively in areas peripheral to the centres where national banks and financial services are concentrated. This is mainly because a bank finds it easier to collect information about projects and individuals located nearby: prospective borrowers are more readily assessed at close range and information spillovers within a locality often relieve the need for official inquiry. Two, regional banks lend more readily to small business. Small firms are more dependent on bank credit than large firms are, because they find it harder to raise equity finance. A recent study in Germany showed that most finance for small and medium-sized business originates from small banks.[9] Large banks, with larger overheads, prefer to lend to large borrowers.

The classic objections to regional banking in fact have little substance. It is claimed that there are economies of scale in banking, but recent studies consistently report no economies of scale in bank operations beyond a relatively small asset base ($25 million in deposits).[10] The risk of failure arising from inadequate diversification in small banks can effectively be neutralised by defining the region widely enough and by ensuring cross-sectoral diversification within it. And the liquidity risk – of a solvent small bank being ruined by a run on limited assets – will be much reduced if, as in Germany, regional banks co-operate at the national level to pool their liquid resources.

Certainly sheer weight of numbers will mean that the regulation of small banks is more time-consuming than the regulation of large ones. But this has to be offset against the advantages to the regulator of having better access to full information. BCCI, a huge bank, was almost impossible to regulate effectively because it was based in 60 countries. The laundering of drugs-money and the terrorist bank accounts were really only a sideshow to the main fraud at BCCI – an intricate scam that involved tens of billions of dollars, consumed more than 90% of the bank's assets, and escaped the notice of the world's regulators for more than a decade.

On top of economies of scale, it could be argued – though perhaps with less conviction after the BCCI débâcle – that big banks have a more solid reputation. In the UK, especially, savers commit funds to big banks because they believe the government would never allow a big bank to go under. But this is a matter of perception. After all, big banks do fail. What is required is a carefully designed explicit deposit insurance system which covers banks of all sizes and thus levels the playing field.

In banking, as in every other part of the financial sector, regionalism runs against the grain of the mega-community. The trend, visible at the moment particularly among the building societies, is toward consolidation and presence at the national level. This is partly to increase the asset base, and thus boost investor confidence, and partly to make the institution more efficient – although most industrial mergers do more for market power than for efficiency. In the short-term, from a Relational point of view, this move toward giantism in finance calls for some form of market intervention. In the longer term it will be replaced by regional finance only if consumers see regional financial institutions as both secure and Relationally advantageous.

To avoid reproducing a savings and loans scandal in the UK, regional finance would, of course, require strict rules governing the operation of its local and regional institutions. It would need to be integrated with an alternative system of financing house purchase, and tougher general supervision by the Bank of England. It would also rely, to a large extent, on the establishment of a federal political system where major political and economic decisions could be made at the regional level. In Relational terms, successful regional banking depends on a high degree of multiplexity and continuity in regional and local relationships, so that people know and trust one another in a financial context, and profit through a collective effort to expand political and economic functions at a regional level.

Debt vs. Equity. The second direction in which Relational finance moves us is toward a "debt-free" society. This does not mean a wholesale abandonment of short-term interest-based finance, for which there is certainly a place. Rather it means, in the first instance, bringing Britain into line with many parts of continental Europe in limiting the unduly prominent role played by short-term debt finance at almost every level of the economy.

For business, this would involve reorganising the fiscal system so that the current tax advantages of debt finance were removed, and perhaps transferring the advantage to equity finance. The use of equity as a basis for investment does not prevent giantism, but it does tend to increase the Relational proximity between investor and manager, sharpening the investor's concern for productivity (as opposed to mere market value) and stimulating his involvement in the day-to-day life of the firm. In addition, some restraint on a firm's borrowing capacity relative to its asset base might limit the temptation for directors to take excessive risks and also reduce the potential for highly leverage buyouts and takeovers.

The advantages of debt-free finance to the individual hardly need emphasis. One inconsistency inviting immediate rectification is that between the social costs of consumer credit and the highly pressured advertising of credit on national television. It is worth asking whether the promotion of consumer credit should not be subject at least to the same restrictions now applied to cigarette advertising: denial of access to television, and the requirement that printed material carry unequivocal warnings about the consequences of default.

How far consumer credit for CD players and clothing should be regarded as a legitimate need is a point for debate. However, in one area at least – that of housing – some form of finance facility is clearly required, and here a number of alternatives have already been suggested with a view to avoiding the pitfalls of a conventional mortgage. The government has recently put £80 million into a scheme enabling first-time buyers to purchase a house jointly with a housing association, effectively replacing part of the mortgage with rent.[11] Also, Anthony Asher, Professor of Actuarial Science in Johannesburg, has suggested that in countries like Britain, where interest rates are likely to remain high, house purchase could be brought within reach of many more people by using a salary-linked mortgage – a new investment instrument which makes it possible for pension funds to match their assets and their liabilities by lending for housing against the security of the borrower's salary as well as the value of the property.[12]

Finance and Government. One advantage of shifting political and economic decision-making to the regions is the creation of a stronger incentive to eliminate public borrowing. The greater Relational proximity operative within a region would make public borrowing – now generally regarded as a lever anonymously pulled in the Treasury – into a high-profile issue with measurable consequences for the community.

Also, it should be borne in mind that borrowing, which often takes place between countries, exercises a powerful influence on international relations. The obvious examples here are the low income countries (LICs) that were lent vast sums in the 1970s and are now unable to service their debts. But international borrowing has become a problem also in high income countries. The United States federal deficit is currently climbing at a rate of $300 billion per year. The problem is that these huge fiscal imbalances disturb the sense of justice essential to a cordial relationship between nations. A borrowing country may be tempted to avoid the full cost of loan repayment through inflation and devaluation – policies that seem to have been implemented deliberately in the US. Correspondingly, a lending country may be tempted to use the leverage of the debt to obtain other political advantages, for instance support in a conflict with another nation. What happens in LICs via the deflationary requirements imposed by the IMF is only an extreme case of this principle.

From the Relational standpoint it is particularly disturbing to hear an international banker admit that Western financial institutions do not have "even the slightest chance of influencing how or to what use the proceeds of the loans we make are put".[13] For relationships surely hold the key to this. If massive financial aid is being given to an LIC, it needs to pass between individuals or local communities who know and trust one another, and not simply be dumped into a national exchequer where internal political pressures may divert it to uses other than that for which it was originally intended.

Similarly, aid will be far more productive if it is given in the form of equity finance, since equity finance, by forcing the lender to share the risk of project failure, gives him a compelling motive to participate in project supervision: that is, it produces commonality. Some Western banks have already swapped bad debt for equities in LIC state industries. The disadvantage lies in the fact that equity finance cannot be used for projects that do not yield a pecuniary return (health or educational programmes, for example), and that, where it is applied, steps must to be taken to preserve parity between borrower and lender and so avoid the charge of neo-colonialism.

Finally, Relational finance in Britain would encourage the establishment of a Central Bank, comparable to the Dutch Central Bank, which operates independently of political control. The lack of continuity in a democracy based on five-year terms of office creates problems for the economy. Governments in Britain are notorious for manipulating the money supply for short-term electoral advantage. They expand it in the period leading up to an election to increase employment and boost consumer confidence, and then crack down again afterwards. An independent Central Bank, with continuity both in personnel and fiscal objectives, could pursue a stable price policy without fear of political intervention.

In Good Company
Relational Company Structure

Problems with the plc. To understand what we might mean by Relational company structure we will need to look again, and in more detail, at the Relational problems created by giantism in Britain's dominant company form: the plc. From a Relational standpoint, giantism is counterproductive in three distinct areas.

First, as we saw in the fourth chapter, the existence of giants in the marketplace destroys parity between firms and encourages bullying. The difficulty was expressed in precisely these terms recently by suppliers to the DIY chain B&Q, who claimed they had been threatened with the complete loss of B&Q business if they did not agree to the deduction of an extra 10% rebate to subsidise B&Q's price war with the other DIY giants Texas and Do It All.[14] That the Office of Fair Trading could not find a basis to warrant intervention shows how powerless regulators are to censure bullying tactics. Indeed few instances of it are even reported because it is so hard to prove and because the weaker party is often afraid to publicise it.

A comparable loss of parity can be detected in the plc's internal structure. As Peter Drucker has pointed out, a large corporation may have as many as seven levels of management. This kind of top-down hierarchy not only reduces directness; it also contributes to mobility within the firm, with the result that the firm's relations with any single outside agency will be conducted through a shifting succession of personnel. Jonathan Boswell is quite right when he argues that "Since inter-organisational colloquy depends a good deal on personal factors, the continuity of those involved in the interactions matters. Even the most long-lived organisations would find it hard to collaborate if their key people, including those at the 'interface', were constantly changing."[15]

In most large plcs employees are numerous and move fast. The larger the company is, the harder it becomes to achieve a sense of common purpose, and the faster people move, the less likely they are to form relationships that are continuous and multiplex. Worse – at least in terms of the company's responsibility to society – marked disparities develop in the distribution of information, effectively obscuring the true details of company policy from external regulators, shareholders, and even from lower levels of management within the organisation. As we have already seen with reference to BCCI, enforcing accountability in the giant quickly turns into a nightmare.

A second difficulty is that, notwithstanding the potential for Maxwell-style managerial abuse engendered by information asymmetry, a disproportionate amount of power in the plc lies with the shareholders. Their relationship to those who work in a company is contingent and therefore remote. Most employees never meet the pension fund managers who control large blocks of company shares, still less the individuals, like you and me, who may own pension fund policies. All too often, shareholder power is exercised not through "voice" – that is, by getting involved in the day-to-day operations of the firm – but by "exit": selling up when the going gets tough.

This, of course, affects far more than the workforce. In a fluid financial market where shareholders look for short-term profit, it is rare to find financial institutions giving a firm their enduring commitment. Thus banks foreclose on loans. It is rare also, especially in a competitive environment, for directors to put major resources into infrastructural investments like the training of staff – an irony if, as Christopher Huhne noted recently in the *Independent*, the way to bring economic success is "to make British managers and their workforces better educated, trained, adaptable and responsive to what customers want . . . "[16] Long-term growth of productivity is sacrificed to short-term gain.

Not only can staff be left inadequately trained; they can be put under severe work pressure. According to Professor Richard Whitfield, "Several studies in the 1980s reported that between one-third and one-half of workers experience regular conflict between work and family roles. Finding time for family business and family togetherness, obtaining child care and co-ordinating with school and community were the major difficulties."[17] Such tensions peak during a recession.

On a Friday evening not long ago I visited the head office of a large City bank and found all the staff still there. It was 6.30 p.m. When I asked why they hadn't gone home I was told there had been some redundancies recently and they were scared of losing their jobs.

If the employee has reason to fear his own directors, driven as they are by the needs of the shareholders, he has even more reason to fear the directors of a predator company. Businesses, as we noted earlier, are not simply economic entities. They are people, groups of livelihoods, institutions creating cross-cutting linkage and concentric circles of relationship in the local community. But from the distance of the predator's boardroom they appear only as potential sums of money. Most takeovers, therefore, have little to do with employee welfare, either directly or indirectly through capital injection and the attempt to increase productivity. More often the motive is to increase the market power of the predator and to boost the income of its managers and owners. In general, takeovers occur without reference to the ethos of the target company. The takeover of the old Quaker firm Rowntrees by Nestlé has removed control of company policy from York to Switzerland and seems likely to bring to an end an exceptional record of social concern. Sometimes – as in United Biscuits' decision to close down the consistently profitable Crawford Biscuits plant in Liverpool – takeovers occur with reference only to a narrow definition of efficiency and with little apparent concern for long-term Relational goals.

The third difficulty for the plc is the tendency of indirect relationships within the firm to reduce motivation, or X-efficiency.[18] In large measure this reflects the absence of encounter between owners and employees. X-efficiency is believed to be low in large plcs, especially among blue-collar workers who have no stake in the company and therefore little feeling of commonality with management. The search for excellence that inspires the directors may not, therefore, permeate down to the shop floor. Of course the shortfall in X-efficiency is offset in some cases by profit-related pay schemes and productivity bonuses, and in others by the indirect effect of ethnic or regional commonality, as, for instance, with the successful Mondragon enterprises in the Basque region of Spain.

There are two main elements in a Relational policy framework for company structure. First, to reduce the size of the plc, and second, in any form of company, to find ways of establishing greater parity and commonality between the various groups (including the workforce, local community and consumers) affected by a firm's operations.

Restraints on Giantism. The benefits of size-reduction in the plc are felt internally and externally: inside companies, greater directness and commonality; between companies, greater parity. But how can size-reduction be effected?

There are a number of possible measures. Perhaps the most obvious is to toughen the MMC/anti-trust legislation. Under the present system, a merger or takeover has to be permitted unless it can be shown to impair competition or be contrary to the public interest. In view of the massive power available to the big plc, and the extreme difficulties of regulating it, it surely makes sense to shift the burden of proof, so that the predator company (in a takeover attempt) or both companies (in a proposed merger) must be able to demonstrate a clear benefit in terms of efficiency, productivity, or the national interest. The amalgamation of companies, in other words, should have to be justified in ways meaningful to those outside the closed circle of the AGM.

In addition, it has to be realised how far the current business environment is prejudiced against smaller companies. This is difficult to rectify, but a number of policy options are available. Changes in the rules governing advertising (for instance, a tax on advertising in the national mass media) would substantially increase parity in the marketplace by allowing local and regional firms to compete on a more equal footing with firms that have national and international market coverage. Adjustments to tax legislation have been put forward by the Chartered Association of Certified Accountants (ACCA) as part of a package to assist small businesses in the recession.[19] Such measures can bear strongly on management decisions to divest. It would not be hard, for instance, to follow the Japanese example by charging higher rates of corporation tax to companies with higher turnovers or larger numbers of employees.

The most popular objection to divestment, of course, is that by breaking up large conglomerates and favouring small industry you actually make business as a whole less efficient through the loss of scale economies in marketing, transport, bulk-handling, finance, and overheads such as top management. It has been argued by both Galbraith and Schumpeter that large firms are an important precondition for effective investment in research and development. Large firms certainly have access to cheaper debt finance (although debt finance is clearly not an immovable fixture in the economic system). And it can further be argued not just that conglomerates lower costs by allowing resources to be pooled across industries in different cyclical patterns, but also that to compete with large firms overseas you have to have large firms at home – an argument used by top American industrialists to persuade Ronald Reagan to weaken US anti-trust legislation in the face of competition from the mega-companies of Japan.

Seductive as it may be, however, the argument for scale economies is a dubious one. Even a 1978 Government Green Paper which came down in favour of large enterprise concluded that "mergers are often found to be unprofitable by those carrying them out, and little in the way of efficiency gains seem to be realised."[20] We should not, therefore, over-estimate the value of scale economies, either in marketing, innovation or production.

In marketing, particularly, a number of the advantages attributed to large firm size could be realised by joint action and co-operation among smaller firms. Italian small firms have used joint action successfully to raise finance and acquire support services such as accounting. And the joint marketing of agricultural products by independent farm producers in Scandinavia shows that the usual firm-level scale economies of purchasing, marketing and transport can be obtained from joint marketing arrangements. The problem in Britain is the restraint placed on joint action by the Restrictive Trade Practices Act. The highly efficient administration of the Act – with 3,078 agreements terminated out of the 3,678 registered by December 1978 – has, in effect, forced ambitious company managers to seek scale economies through takeover and merger. Of course the Act is needed to prevent negative collusion between producers. Nevertheless it is an amazing anomaly in British industrial policy that mergers can proceed if they do not leave the merged firms with a market share of over 25%, while marketing arrangements are disallowed even if the agreements in total cover no more than 0.5% of the market.

The question as to how far innovation depends on size is particularly complex. Small firms are handicapped by a lack of highly qualified engineers and technicians, are inefficient in their communication with markets, find it hard to obtain funds, and suffer from limited bargaining power in the market and in dealings with government. On the other hand they also have a number of advantages. They have a greater incentive to improve established products. They are less subject to internal bureaucratic delays. And they generally invite stronger motivation and deeper creativity. Look at the empirical evidence and you will find that innovation flourishes in all sizes of firm, leaning toward the small firm in some sectors and the large firm in others. Only in sectors where small firms have a market share of less than 20% is their share of innovation sometimes negligible.[21] Since it is impossible to know how small firms would innovate if their market share increased, any proposal to split up large firms in such sectors would need to be analysed for its repercussions on research and development.

When most people think about scale economies, however,

they do not think about marketing or innovation, but of production. Huge plants, the argument runs, are needed to produce at the lowest possible cost. Yet outside the major process industries – chemicals, aluminium, steel, ammonium nitrate, sulphuric acid – there is little hard evidence to link efficiency with scale. What the author of *Markets and Hierarchies*, Oliver Williamson, calls "technical nonseparabilities" are much less widespread than is commonly believed. Even for some of the process industries, the cost penalty incurred by going to 50% minimum efficient scale is very small – an estimated 1% in the case of sulphuric acid production, and 8% in the case of a steel side-strip rolling works. Such cost increases are unimpressive compared to the gains in productivity now possible in the absence of obstructive labour relations. In most forms of production, therefore, there appears to be considerable scope to reduce both firm and plant size in the UK without incurring major cost increases.[22]

Alternative Company Structures. Not all companies, of course, are plcs. Partnerships, family businesses, private companies and mutual organisations like building societies[23] – collectively part of the so-called "third sector" – are all by nature more proRelational than the plc. They have broader aims than the maximisation of short-term profit, and in most cases they do not connect owners and managers impersonally via the market. There is no reason why these non-plc company structures could not play a far more prominent role in British business, if policies were introduced to encourage them.[24]

There are also several ways in which the plc itself could be made more Relationally constructive. Given that stand-offs between workers and managers have their source, Relationally speaking, in a lack of commonality and direct-ness, there is a strong prima-facie case for pursuing worker representation in management, perhaps after the German model of supervisory boards. George Goyder has suggested that regulators be empowered to demand a statement of company purpose. This would keep company directors more attuned to their external links with consumers, suppliers and the environment, while internal relationships could be protected by conducting a three-year social audit – although it is uncertain whether, in the case of very large plcs, an external agency could gather sufficient information to make the audit effective.

Goyder also makes the more radical proposal that plcs transform themselves into self-owning public trusts. The fundamental issue in the plc, he argues, is one of parity, for the structure of the plc bestows on shareholders "the right to exercise permanent control of the company and its policies."[25] The risk that earns this right – in effect the risk of temporarily losing one's dividend (a risk insurable anyway through the holding of a mixed portfolio) – is insignificant compared to the risk borne by the employee, who when the order book runs out is likely to lose his job. "It is iniquitous," Goyder judges, "to give control over an organisation dependent upon the daily co-operation of free men and women to absentee landlords from now until doomsday."[26]

To rectify this, Goyder proposes the setting-up of a trust on the employees' behalf, through which shares are redeemed until the company becomes self-controlling and self-disciplining. Shareholders do not lose out. They are merely required periodically to take the responsibility of reinvesting their money in fresh risk-taking ventures. Clearly this is helpful in overcoming the plc's characteristic lack of commonality. But it is no panacea for the Relational dysfunction resulting from low degrees of directness and parity. To tackle that, you must return to the issue of size.

Treating the British Disease
Relational Industrial Strategy

The Economics of Co-operation. We saw in the sixth chapter how successive governments in Britain have regarded the economy as a kind of push-button machine. Economic policy – driven mainly by the Treasury – has tended to focus on macro-economic indicators: levels of interest, levels of inflation, levels of PSBR and currency parities. Pushing the right buttons at the right time keeps the economy stable. Freeing markets to operate effectively ensures growth.

Such a model, however, has almost no comprehension of the market as a Relational system, nor does it provide any reason to ensure that "market relationships" receive adequate nurture and protection. There is little emphasis anywhere in the economy on "people", or on the need to endow the individual with such skills as will maximise her contribution to the economic enterprise. It is for this reason that education in Britain is allotted a low priority, that the teaching profession carries little prestige, and that the numbers engaged in higher education remain comparatively small.

The centrality of relationships to the economy has been argued persuasively by Jonathan Boswell. Boswell, a political economist writing within the European Christian Democratic tradition, develops the thesis that industrial growth is closely linked to co-operative relationships not only within firms, but between firms, and between industry and government. A major indicator of co-operativeness in the economy, according to Boswell, is the "extent to which sectional economic interests participate in public policy processes within a broadly democratic system, through representative institutions endowed with public rights and duties."[27] Thus he asks, "Do most workers, farmers, companies and other economic agents belong to representative national organisations? . . . While remaining fairly autonomous and separate from government, do these bodies have wide public responsibilities to carry out specific economic tasks, to work with each other, and to help implement public policies?" Such co-operative relationships, argues Boswell, are essential to secure industrial peace, voluntary pay restraint and industrial growth.

The Case for Industrial Clustering. Boswell's case for

co-operation has run in parallel with a developing literature whose central contention is that industrial patterns
themselves are changing. Pioré and Sabel argue that the
older Fordist system of mass production, with its vertical,
corporate hierarchy, is being displaced by the new technological paradigm of "flexible specialisation",[28] which
is "an epochal redefinition of markets, technologies and
industrial hierarchies".[29] Vertical organisational structures
are disintegrating, to be replaced by regional agglomerations
of adaptive, innovative, smaller firms representing a single
industrial sector and operating in a shared social environment. The functional logic of the corporation is giving way
to the territorial logic[30] of the industrial district:[31] Silicon
Glen, the Cambridge Phenomenon, the Reading–Bristol axis,
the Southern Paris "Scientific City".

Critics of the industrial district school have dismissed it as
"a new, radical mythology for the 1990s",[32] holding that
the phenomenon is far more varied and complex than the
paradigm permits, and that what we are seeing is a greater
product differentiation rather than the break-up of mass
markets. Most damning, perhaps, is the implication that the
theorists of the industrial district are utopians, unwilling to
admit that the real movers and shakers in the economy are
those who work at the level of the mega-community: the
multinationals. Thus Castells and Henderson: "The flexible
specialisation thesis and industrial district literature draw
strongly on notions of local allegiance, co-operation, and
trust relations, and have as a subtext the resurrection of
'community.'"[33]

However, the crucial issue is not whether industrial districts resurrect community, or even whether the various
industrial patterns these areas contain can rightly be lumped
under one title, but whether spatial proximity of firms –
which is the basic characteristic of the zones identified as
industrial districts – confers a measurable economic advantage. The most recent contributor to the debate, Michael
Porter, a leading authority on competitive industrial strategy

at Harvard Business School, puts forward a compelling and well-documented case to show that it does: "Competitors in many internationally successful industries, and often entire clusters of industries, are often located in a single town or region within a nation."[34] The financial services industry is highly concentrated in the City of London. Basel is the home of all three pharmaceutical giants. German optics are based in Wetzlar, Italian food-processing plants in Bologna, American large-scale computer manufacturing in or near Minneapolis. Such clustering works, argues Porter, because spatial proximity acts as a shorthand for what we have called Relational proximity:

> Proximity increases the concentration of information and thus the likelihood of its being noticed and acted upon. Proximity increases the speed of information flow within the national industry and the rate at which innovations diffuse. At the same time, it tends to limit the spread of information outside because communication takes forms (such as face to face contact) which leak out only slowly. Proximity raises the visibility of competitor behaviour, the perceived stakes of matching improvements, a local pride will mix with purely economic motivations in energising firm behaviour.
>
> The process of clustering, and the interchange among industries in the cluster, also works best when the industries involved are geographically concentrated. Proximity leads to early exposure of imbalances, needs, or constraints within the cluster to be addressed or exploited.[35]

If Porter is right, Relational theory provides a broader framework for understanding the success of this new industrial strategy. Porter goes on to point out some of the long-term risks associated with geographical concentration, and we would of course have to add to this our previously discussed reservations as to the ability of geographical proximity to guarantee proximity of relationship. The Rummidge of David Lodge's novel *Nice Work* illuminates sharply, and without unduly stretching the truth, the kind of cultural division – in effect the lack of directness and commonality – that can separate two professional spheres even when they coexist in the same town. At the same time the burden of Michael Porter's work is that industrial clustering is, in fact, the global norm for successful industrial growth, and that it is the norm for essentially Relational reasons.

Industrial Strategy in the UK. In 1989 Elizabeth Cornwell undertook a study to see whether the concept of sectoral concentration of industrial production – that is, industrial clustering – was widely understood and accepted in Britain's peripheral regions, in particular Scotland, Wales, and the north of England.[36] The findings were uniformly negative. Cornwell concluded that the aim of industrial strategy in both Scotland and Wales was to establish a broad-based economy within the region. The dangers of industrial clustering, specifically the danger of an industrial sector going into decline and dragging an entire region down with it, were felt to be so overwhelming that the clustering option was deliberately rejected. Indeed the Scottish Development Association's own review warned against becoming too sectoral in approach.[37] In consequence, however, not only Scotland but Britain in general has lacked any coherent conceptual framework for understanding the key role of relationships, either within companies, or between university and government (central and local), or for industrial development and long-term strategies for the creation of jobs.

There is an urgent need both in Britain and in the United States for the kind of Relational framework Porter has been suggesting. This points to policies which seek to identify regions with development potential, selective investment incentives into industries and university departments able to service the growth of potential new clusters, and a massive overall increase in investment in education – especially higher education. In addition, as Michael Porter stresses, there is a need for tough restrictions on mergers and takeovers to sustain a competitive industrial environment, and for changes in the fiscal system, including the way Capital Gains Tax is levied, to help ensure greater continuity in the relationship between investors and management and to achieve long-term, research-based development of manufacturing industry.

The Happy Marriage
Relational Business Practice

Relationship as Resource. Business practice is an area where Relational thinking has already made a deep impact. In one way this is predictable. Save perhaps in the financial sector, no businessperson can fully isolate the acts of buying and selling from the relationship in which these transactions are couched. You buy from people. You sell to people. Thus, long before business management became an academic discipline, shopkeepers instinctively affirmed the importance of relationships by coining that famous aphorism, "The customer is always right."

Only recently, however, has quality of relationship become a topic for systematic study in the business schools. Lord Marks stood out from the commercial crowd when shortly after World War Two he discontinued a highly profitable line in ice-cream on the grounds that discarded ice-cream wrappers on the floor contravened the M&S policy of store cleanliness – a tool he valued highly in building relationships with customers.

One of the first people to conceptualise what now goes under the name of *relationships marketing* was Theodore Levitt. Levitt was Professor of Business Administration at Harvard when he declared in 1983 that "a company's most precious asset is its relationships with its customers. What matters is not whom you know but how you are known to them."[38] Consequently, "Relationship management is a special field . . . and is as important to preserving and enhancing the intangible asset commonly known as 'goodwill' as is the management of hard assets." This view has received a more sympathetic hearing in the service industries than it has in manufacturing. Nevertheless, even among the producers of visible, touchable goods, the sale "merely consummates the courtship, at which point the marriage begins". Levitt is talking about continuity.

Relationship management could be seen as a belated reaction to conditions of business imposed by the mega-community. The initial and highly seductive benefit of an efficient national media is mass advertising – the opportunity to influence millions of individuals without having to look each one in the eye. Business relationships that did demand eye contact, increasingly conducted on a short-term basis and between strangers, drifted toward the instrumental and the manipulative. It has taken some time for the business community to find its bearings and discover that the preconditions of good business are, after all, Relational, and that the quality of relationships matters even in a sector like retailing where the buyer does not necessarily deal with the same salesperson every time he or she visits the store. As Levitt puts it, expanding his analogy of marriage:

> Buyers want vendors who keep promises, who'll keep supplying and standing behind what they promised. The era of the one-night stand is gone. Marriage is both necessary and more convenient. Products are too complicated, repeat negotiations too much of a hassle and too costly. Under these conditions, success in marketing is transformed in the inescapability of a relationship. Interface becomes interdependence.

This expectation of continuity in a sales relationship – illustrated, for example, in the sale of computer systems as "augmented products", packaged with customer hotlines, user support, efficient installation, and bulletins on regularly upgraded components and software – is now a major pre-occupation of the business literature.

"Traditional marketing gets the client in the door the first time," claims D. W. Cottle in *Client-centred Service: How to*

Keep Them Coming Back for More, "interactive marketing – relationship management – keeps them coming back again and again."[39] He estimates that high quality service firms are twice as profitable as others. On the reverse side of the same coin, a recent survey on "why customers quit", conducted for the British Institute of Management, discovered that 68% of customers are lost "because of an attitude of indifference toward the customer by the owner, manager or some other employee". Ironically, it concluded, "The average business spends six times more to attract new customers than it does to keep old ones. Yet customer loyalty is in most cases worth ten times the price of a single purchase."[40]

Landing squarely in the middle of the Relational thesis, J. A. Czepiel *et al.* argue that the key to successful relationships, both within and around a firm, is encounter. "Service encounters are a form of human interaction important not only to their direct participants (clients and providers), and the service organisations that sponsor them, but also to society as a whole . . ."[41] Similar thinking presumably underlies the decision of Glasgow Business School to run "Relationships awareness" seminars and to publish a *Customer–Supplier Relationship Audit*.

The Scope of Relational Business Practice. Relationship management clearly has its limits. It is sometimes difficult to be sure how far its practitioners genuinely believe in the value of relationships, and how far the concept of relationship management is treated as a marketing ploy and tolerated only in so far as it tends to maximise sales. One hopes that the current wave of interest in relationships, which at its best is about the inculcation of an ethos, will eventually contribute to a reassessment of company policy in other areas within the big conglomerates, and thus act as a restraint upon cynical advantage-taking and impersonalism in the market.

As to how Relational thinking can further be implemented in business practice, several options are open. Levitt notes that Gillette North America has appointed a vice-president of business relations, whose major duties include the cultivation of relationships with leading retailers and distributors. More important than creating new titles, perhaps, is to get employees from top to bottom of an organisation thinking in Relational terms. The relationships that employees – even delivery personnel – form with those outside the company are vital assets, and need to be submitted to conscious and regular review. "How can I relate well?", "Is the relationship improving or deteriorating?" and "What have I done for the other person lately?" are the kinds of question employees at all levels will benefit from asking, and a company that invests work time in allowing its personnel to come to grips with such questions, through discussion groups, seminars or sensitivity sessions, is likely to see substantial gains both in reputation and performance. So too is the company that allocates its end-of-year bonuses for relationships developed and improved rather than for the simple earning of commission. Similar, though perhaps more discreet, attention should be paid to internal relationships.

It is worth remembering, however, that Relational proximity inside and outside the firm is to a certain extent a function of the way the firm itself chooses to organise its personnel. The length of time colleagues work together, what sort of common aims departments and sub-departmental groups are given, how the structure of company operations and the layout of work space impinge on the quantity and quality of interaction, are all variables affecting Relational proximity. So too, and rather more problematically, is the need to allow upward mobility in the firm, since this affects ongoing relationships between the firm and other institutions. Since a relationship between two companies, in a legal or contractual sense, is founded on the relationship between the companies' respective representatives, it would seem important to slow down the turnover of staff in link positions, and to ensure that a person new to the job has sufficient time to pick up the relationships his or her predecessor has left behind. As Glasgow Business School's *Customer–Supplier Relationship*

Audit cannily observes, "Relationships take months, if not years to build, and minutes to fatally damage."[42]

The Outsiders
Conclusion

I have said at a general level that a Relational Market Economy accommodates competition, requires sustainable economic growth, affirms the necessity of non-state ownership, and seeks to boost income and material welfare within structures that facilitate Relational proximity.

If we follow this thinking toward its natural conclusions, we are likely to come up with a number of specific proposals.

In finance, the region emerges as the dominant level of organisation. There are also strong arguments for reducing the West's current dependence on debt finance by giving a proportionally greater role to finance through shared equity, and for establishing an independent Central Bank so that greater continuity in policy is established and the money supply cannot be manipulated for electoral purposes.

In company structure, there is a pressing need to find ways of preventing giantism in the plc, to encourage commonality in the enterprise through changes in company structure, to promote parity in the marketplace through the correction of structural bias against small firms, and to make business in general more truly representative of society's interests, both by broadening the viewpoints active in company decision-making, and by developing "third sector" forms of company structure and encouraging the transformation of plcs into self-owning public trusts.

In industrial strategy, far more encouragement must be given to co-operative company relations, an advantage implicit in Michael Porter's persuasive argument for industrial clustering. There is no reason why either option should have been dismissed in British policy.

In business practice, where Relational thinking is already

well established in the literature, the conviction that long-term business success depends on the cultivation of relationships both inside and outside a company needs to permeate boardrooms and company ethos.

Finally, in a chapter dealing with the economy, it is perhaps appropriate to add at this point a word about unemployment. What does Relational Market Economics have to say to those who are excluded from the productive economic life of the nation?

The first thing to note, of course, is that unemployment has a global dimension. In a global economy, where the buyers of products from a country or region may be located anywhere in the world, it is vital that nations and regions co-operate in every way possible to promote and facilitate world trade and to develop relationships with disadvantaged areas such as Eastern Europe, seeing them in the long view as part of a Relational economic network, and therefore as centres of future demand.

Having said that, solutions to unemployment are likely to be uncovered and financed most readily at a locality and regional level. This applies to short-term initiatives, which provide employment opportunities to see through a period of crisis (a large house-building project, for example), as well as long-term initiatives, of the kind discussed earlier in this chapter, which aim to create industrial districts or centres of excellence on a local/regional basis and for a specific industrial sector or segment.

An obvious first step to tackle unemployment within a Relational framework would be to set up regional bodies along the lines of the now defunct National Economic Development Council, whose role would be to co-ordinate ideas and initiatives from key employers, unions, financial institutions and government departments. A strong regional/locality focus might also make possible forms of voluntary taxation as a way of mobilising resources and overcoming the reluctance to spend which exacerbates recession and makes it self-perpetuating.

Such approaches, of course, underline the close interlinking of the economic and the political. An economic programme cannot be presented, even in outline, without addressing also the implications of Relational thinking for the political system. The final chapter of the book, therefore, will begin by exploring the idea of Relational democracy, and move on to suggest what Relationism might mean when applied to some other aspects of national life and culture.

Notes

1 Quoted in Brian Griffiths, *Morality and the Market Place* (Hodder & Stoughton, London, 1982), pp. 105–6.
2 John G. Greenwood (Chairman and Chief Economist, G.T. Management (Asia) Limited), *The Preconditions for Economic Recovery in Eastern Europe*, January 1990, p. 2.
3 It is possible, for instance, to encourage the holding of land property and a certain level of wealth in the form of family trusts, by making some level of property owned and managed by a family group exempt from inheritance taxes, and by allowing members of family trusts to opt out of state welfare and health schemes, enjoying commensurate income tax reliefs on the understanding that provision for these needs would be met out of the trust fund. Of course there are dangers in this. It might leave individuals without family support more vulnerable if opting out reduced the level of service for those left in. Also, ways would have to be found of protecting the interests of an individual who is not treated fairly by other members of the trust. However, if such problems could be guarded against, it is probable that the restoration of familial ownership of land and property on a voluntary basis would prove more efficient and proRelational than leaving property in purely individualistic title, since financial planning within the family group would be exercised with regard to a longer time horizon than the life-span of a single individual.
4 Michael Lipton, *Family, Fungibility and Formality*, International Economics Association, Mexico Conference, 1980, p. 2.

5 We are grateful to Paul Mills for access to his research in writing this section.

6 For a survey of the moral issues raised by interest, and its place in church history, see Paul Mills, *Interest in Interest: The Old Testament Ban on Interest and its Implications for Today*, Jubilee Centre, Cambridge, October 1989.

7 Debt is closely associated with both marital breakdown and child abuse. See A. Hartropp (ed.), *Families in Debt* (Jubilee Centre, Cambridge, 1988), ch. 4.

8 The following comments are based on work in progress by Yale University doctoral student David Porteous. We are indebted to him for allowing us to make use of his ideas.

9 See Christian Harm, *The Financing of Small Firms in Germany*, Financial and Policy System Working Papers WPS 899, Washington, D.C.: World Bank, 1992.

10 See, for example, G. Benson *et al.*, "Scale Economies in Banking: A Restructuring and Reassessment", *Journal of Money, Credit and Banking*, no. 14, 1982, p. 4. Also T. Gilligan *et al.*, "Scale and Scope Economies in the Multi-Product Banking Firm", *Journal of Monetary Economics*, no. 13, 1984, pp. 393–405.

11 John Grigsby, "£80m boost for shared home purchase plan", *Daily Telegraph*, October 20, 1992.

12 See Anthony Asher, *Salary Linked Mortgages: An Outline*, unpublished paper, 1990.

13 "Bad business for almost all concerned", *International Herald Tribune*, October 16, 1985. The person interviewed chose to remain anonymous.

14 See Roland Gribben, "Suppliers slam B&Q's tactics", *Daily Telegraph*, June 15, 1992.

15 Jonathan Boswell, *Community and the Economy: The Theory of Public Co-operation* (Routledge, London and New York, 1990), p. 98.

16 Christopher Huhne, "How to escape from our history of failure", *Independent*, September 18, 1992.

17 Richard Whitfield, *The Home Life and Working Life Interface: Implications for Training*, Training & Enterprise Council, Dorset Tec, April 1992.

18 An economist would define X-efficiency more comprehensively

as that part of worker effectiveness or productivity which cannot be attributed to resource allocations.

19 The package included allowing unincorporated businesses to claim income tax relief for losses against profits of earlier years, as limited companies can claim now against corporation tax; abolishing Class 4 national insurance contributions; allowing the self-employed to claim childcare costs against tax, as companies can now claim for facilities provided for employees; and increasing the VAT threshold to at least £50,000. See Graham Searjeant, "Small firms need help of radical tax package", *The Times*, October 31, 1992.

20 *A Review of Monopolies and Mergers Policy*, a consultative document, Cmnd 7198, HMSO, London, 1978. The document relies on and quotes two other works in this area: G. Meeks, *Disappointing Marriage: A Study of the Gains from Merger* (CUP, Cambridge, 1977); and E. Newbould, *Management and Merger Activity* (Guthstead, Liverpool, 1970).

21 OECD, *Innovation in Small and Medium Firms* (Paris, 1982).

22 See Oliver Williamson, *Markets and Hierarchies: Analysis and Antitrust Implications* (The Free Press, New York, 1975). A more sophisticated form of the scale economy argument suggests that large firms are required to manage complex and capital-intensive projects like aircraft design. However, probably much of the co-ordination needed to support them could be attained by building long-term business relationships across regional and national frontiers.

23 Clearly it would be naïve to suggest that third sector companies always live up to their Relational potential. Looking at building societies, for example, M. Rigge and M. Young (*Building Societies and the Consumer*, the Mutual Aid Centre, for the National Consumer Council, London, 1981) argue that although "the mutual status of the societies still has some value, producing more concern for individuals and collective housing needs than there would be if they were purely profit-making concerns ... changes are needed to make them more genuinely mutual ... " They suggest that local branch managers call meetings for local investors and borrowers, that investors and borrowers should receive more information about society policies, and that members should

have the elementary right to put themselves up for election to boards.

24 Possible alternatives include lower rates of corporate tax, less rigorous supervision requirements, and selective investment incentives.

25 George Goyder, *The Just Enterprise* (André Deutsch Limited, London, 1987), p. 60.

26 *ibid.*, p. 61.

27 This and following quotation from Jonathan Boswell, *op. cit.*, p. 58.

28 M. J. Pioré and C. P. Sabel, *The Second Industrial Divide* (Basic Books, New York, 1984).

29 C. P. Sabel, *Work and Politics* (CUP, Cambridge, 1982), p. 231.

30 A. Scott and M. Storpor, "High technology industry and regional development", *International Social Science Journal*, vol. 112, 1987, pp. 215–32.

31 S. Brusco, "Small Firms and Industrial Districts: the Experience of Italy" in D. Keeble and E. Weaver (eds.), *New Firms and Regional Development* (Crown Helm, London, 1986).

32 A. Amin and K. Robins, "The re-emergence of regional economics? The mythical geography of flexible accumulation", *Environment & Planning D: Society & Space*, vol. 8, 1990, pp. 7–34.

33 M. Castells and Y. Henderson, "Techno-economic Restructuring, socio-political processes and spatial transformation: A global perspective", in Y. Henderson and M. Castells, *Global Restructuring and Territorial Development* (Sage, London, 1987), p. 28.

34 Michael Porter, *The Competitive Advantage of Nations* (Macmillan, London, 1990), p. 154.

35 *ibid.*, p. 157.

36 Elizabeth Cornwell, *Potential for Sectoral Concentration of Industrial Production in Depressed Regions*, Jubilee Centre Research Paper No. 10, Cambridge, 1990.

37 *ibid.*, p. 24.

38 This and following quotations from Theodore Levitt, "After the sale is over . . . ", *Harvard Business Review*, September–October 1983, pp. 87–93.

39 D. W. Cottle, *Client-centred Service: How to Keep Them Coming Back for More* (John Wiley & Sons, New York, 1990).

40 See C. Coulson-Thomas and R. Brown, *Beyond Quality: Managing the Relationship with the Customer*, British Institute of Management, 1990.

41 J. A. C Czepiel, M. R. Solomon, L. F. Supprenant, *The Service Encounter* (Lexington Books, US, 1985), p. 14.

42 D. K. Macbeth *et al.*, *Customer–Supplier Relationship Audit* (Glasgow Business School, IFS Publications, Bedford, 1990).

9

Relational Democracy

We the People?
Relational Government

The Need for Reform. Britain's is in many ways the Château-Lafite of democracies. It has matured slowly. It is naturally stable, tolerant in its accommodation of opposing views, and – whatever you may think of the televised Commons debates – a good deal less prone to mud-slinging showdowns than its rival in the USA.

And yet, looking at it in Relational terms, one would have to conclude that British democracy has considerable shortcomings. Seldom, for instance, does much more than half the electorate turn out to vote in local elections. In the mega-community interest is increasingly directed toward the national arena, since it is here, and not at local level, that the "real" issues are perceived to reside. Yet at the same time the remoteness and inaccessibility of Westminster politics tends to spread apathy – a trend reinforced by the fact that political obligations (broadly, to ensure that society is properly organised and fairly governed) are easily forgotten in a society which, as the years pass, dedicates itself more completely to the pursuit of pleasure.

And then there is the whole style of the British political tradition. Politics at every level tends to ossify ancient class antagonisms, with the result that far less can be achieved than might be possible under a consensual model. In some parts of the country, the city council is of one political complexion, while the district and county councils covering the city's suburban hinterland are of another. To add to the confusion, the aims of these local government bodies may conflict with those of the business community. The result of this lack of common purpose is, in general, to frustrate every attempt to stimulate industrial growth.

The confrontational style, of course, finds dramatic expression in the Commons, and is institutionalized in a two-Party, first-past-the-post electoral system which, besides being a source of amazement to many of our European partners, leads to sometimes paralysing discontinuities of policy and not infrequently turns important policy issues like education and health into political footballs. The politicising does little to benefit the ordinary citizen. Indeed, as a Swahili proverb has it: when the elephants fight, it's the grass that suffers.

I am no iconoclast. But we stand at the threshold of a century that will demand far greater degrees of international co-operation, and far stronger links between political institutions and the citizens they represent. On those grounds alone I think we would do well to consider what kind of adaptations would make our democracy more Relational.

Power, Parity, and Federation. In essence Relational democracy is democracy that shortens Relational distance. It maximises directness through face-to-face encounter in decision-making, through the reduction of the vertical distance separating decision-making from the citizens it affects, and through the extension to citizens of the power not only to vote but to participate as far as possible in decision-making processes. It fosters continuity and multiplexity in the relationships linking MPs one to another and to the voters they represent, and stability of government through long-term policy-making and occupation of posts. It discourages confrontation by cultivating political cohesion and the identification of common goals both nationally and sub-nationally. And it demands that the principle of parity be built into the structure by keeping decision-making as decentralised as is reasonably possible.

Parity is the key, because a political system is at root a description of the way society distributes power. We have noted already that power in British government is largely reserved to the centre: regional and local government from the Scilly Isles to the Shetlands simply administers on London's behalf. This has long been a source of rancour to the Scots and the Welsh, who have a keen sense of nationhood and resent having their political and economic affairs run from England. And from a Relational standpoint it is intolerable because, for reasons examined in the fourth chapter, a centralised state is nearly always wedded to sectional interest and therefore open to abuse.

A decade of Thatcherism has left many commentators sympathetic to the idea of redistributing power away from Westminster. Anthony Sampson, that seasoned dissector of the British state, argued recently that "centralisation is the most visible deformation in Britain's anatomy, crippling the opportunities for reform and revival." He goes on:

> The most urgent remedy is a deliberate delegation of powers to regional and local governments, which can release immense new energies, as has been shown in France, Spain and Germany, where the *départements* or *Länder* enjoy far greater autonomy and pride than in Britain . . . Britain cannot always be governed by a small group of banker-minded people from Oxford and Cambridge whose first rule is never to resign.[1]

The sixty-four-thousand-dollar question, of course, is what you mean by "delegation". In much of the current debate delegation reads "devolution". Yet the fact that central government is willing, however remotely, to entertain the idea of devolution suggests that devolving power is not necessarily an expensive concession. Implicit in the creation of devolved parliaments is the right of central government to restore direct rule if the occasion requires. Indeed this is exactly what happened in Northern Ireland. For good reason, you might say. But that is another argument – whatever the wisdom of creating or uncreating devolved government, the one thing devolution does not achieve is parity between levels of administration. If you want to achieve parity you will have to go beyond devolution to federation.

In the context of the European debate (of which more later) a federation is generally thought of as an association formed by the joint agreement of regions or sovereign states, and governed on the basis of direct election to both federal and national/regional institutions. But federations can be born just as easily through the action of a single unitary state that wishes to give greater autonomy to its regional/national components. Such has been the case in Spain, where Basque nationalism prompted the first move toward federation in 1975, and in Germany, where federalism was more or less imposed by the Allies after World War Two. It is true to say, perhaps, that given the choice most national governments would not choose to relinquish power to the regions, which is why British government ministers who bear aloft the torch for European federalism wouldn't dream of applying federal ideas to the United Kingdom.

And yet federalism is profoundly Relational. The word itself comes from the Latin *foedus*, meaning tie, knot, or relationship – a term with the same root as *fides*, or good faith.

A federation, therefore, must have a fundamental accord between the central and the autonomous state governments. Furthermore, in the federal relationship, as a result of the distribution of powers between the central (federal) and state governments, there is not a vertical and hierarchical, but rather a horizontal relationship between the governments composing the federal whole. In this equal relationship, the central, federal government assumes the position of a *primus inter pares*. It is endowed with certain federal functions and powers, but cannot diminish or encroach upon those state powers and functions which are entrenched in the constitution.[2]

What might a federal Britain look like? We might imagine a thee-tier federalism.[3] At the top, a central government; in the middle, perhaps eight or ten regional governments (including Scotland, Wales, and Greater London); at the bottom, within each region, a collection of local governments.

Region here is used as a generic term and is not meant to imply uniformity: London remains a city, Scotland a nation. Representation would be by direct election at all three levels, the House of Lords becoming an upper House for delegates from regional legislatures. Formal constitutional provisions would be required to establish the functions of the regional governments relative to those of the central government, and to decide how disputes between the various levels of the federation should be resolved. A suitable division of functions and of fiscal and budgetary roles between federal and regional governments could be achieved in various ways, once the federal principle were granted. There are some dangers in introducing a regional tier of government. Regions would need to ensure roughly equal levels of social provision, and statutory protection would need to be given to ethnic and other minority groups, probably in the form of a Bill of Rights. Not least, although the growth of bureaucracy at the local and regional levels would be substantially offset by its decline at the centre, care would have to be taken to avoid unnecessary duplication.

In Relational terms, the bottom tier – local government – is in many ways the most important. Not only is local democracy more proRelational than national democracy, in the sense that decisions are made close to their point of implementation, and that the decision-makers are more likely to know, and be known by, those their decisions affect; the very existence of a local assembly with real powers will tend to encourage participation in the political process, giving grounds for commonality on the basis of place, and building corresponding obligations.

"Real power" at local government level, of course, demands financial independence. It is no easy task to devise a fair, low-cost method of raising local taxes. Almost any system will tend to magnify disparity. One reason why the Conservative government decided to abolish the rates was that some local councils, dominated by those who didn't own property, were expanding services and raising budgets at the expense of those who did. The poll tax removed discrimination on the basis of ownership, but even with concessions could not prevent the burden of taxation falling on the poor. A sales tax penalises those with the highest expenses, not necessarily those with most money; and an income tax, which is too complex to administer locally, undermines local government autonomy if it has to be levied at national level. To avoid disparity in local taxation one is forced either to develop a hybrid system or to establish underlying economic parities on the basis of which a single form of taxation would be fair – for instance, by extending home ownership not only to meet welfare needs (see later in the chapter) but as a foundation for a tax levied on property.

'Real power" also means real responsibility. The sociologist Gerald Suttles argues persuasively that the strength of the relationships formed by residents in a given area will be decided mainly by their sense of commonality – of being held jointly responsible by other communities and external organisations: " . . . it is in their 'foreign relations' that communities come into existence."[4] Even stable local communities – ones relatively unaffected by mobility and displacement – will not cohere unless their governments have distinct functions. In the British context the immediate need is to identify the particular areas of administration over which local government can be given greater responsibility, and in the light of this to ask what, for any one local government jurisdiction, constitutes an optimal size.

Related Nations
A Relational Perspective on the EC

The Economic Issues. It is implicit in the phrase European Community that policy-makers understand the forging of closer ties with Europe in terms of relationships. Clearly, though, the Relational consequences of greater union between Britain and her European partners are not simple.

At a general level there is a strong case for strengthening cultural and economic ties. A continent which has been the crucible of two world wars needs to build trust and confidence. Indeed the EC itself originated in the efforts of those like Robert Schuman, Alcide de Gasperi and Konrad Adenauer – all three early Christian democrats with Relational ideals – to prevent a third European war. But qualities like trust and confidence depend heavily on Relational proximity, and it is doubtful whether more widespread and frequent travel between European countries will in itself be sufficient to produce this. It seems we will only build enduring commonality in Europe by building cultural and economic links which involve greater continuity of relationship and more face-to-face encounter.

The growth benefits of economic alliance are substantial. Economic progress provides jobs, raises the living standards of those on low incomes, improves health services and education. It could be argued, in fact, that economic alliance in Europe is inevitable just because the technical resources needed to support a complex modern manufacturing project seldom exist within a single set of borders. So although Britain could, on paper, produce its own large commercial aircraft or jet fighter, the cost would be astronomical because British companies do not possess the necessary expertise. British Aerospace specialises in wings only. Given that a significant slice of the GNP is now committed to such massive projects, some form of economic alliance is almost unavoidable. If Britain did not ally itself with the EC, therefore, to compete effectively in world markets for industrial products it would probably be forced to seek an alliance with the USA, a country to which arguably Britain has greater cultural proximity due to historical ties and a similarity of language and values, but whose relative remoteness geographically would make close co-operation over the long term more difficult.

Furthermore, there is some truth in the argument that to tackle worldwide problems effectively, nations must co-operate more closely than they have in the past. As MEP Sir Fred Catherwood notes of the EC:

> We are close neighbours in an increasingly interdependent society. Ninety per cent of this community is within a two-hour flight of the rest. There is, therefore, a whole series of problems which it is better for us to tackle together – security, drug traffic, terrorism, and, increasingly, environmental pollution. None of us can solve these problems alone, but together we have a chance.[5]

He might have added the need to exercise effective control of multinationals as a further reason for closer EC co-operation. As BCCI showed, the larger companies become, the larger and more global the enforcement arm of government needs to be, and that in turn points to more centralised government administration. Without large – that is, highly centralised – government, there is an absence of parity between government and multinational. Of course, if Relational policies were implemented within Europe, the restraint on industrial giantism and wider diffusion of economic power would lessen the need for a strong political centre. However, this remains a long-term solution.

A final argument for developing closer ties with Europe arises from technical monetary considerations. The view is widely held that, with the growth of world trade, over the long haul the dollar and the DM will not be able to cope with the demands international currency status makes on their domestic economies. (Remember the strains on Britain in the 1960s when the pound was used as an international exchange currency.) One possible strategy to achieve realignment would effectively divide the world into three currency and trading blocs – the Americas, the Pacific, and Europe. If that happened, Britain would be isolated from its other markets and thrown into heavy reliance on its European partners – another argument against seeking an alliance with the USA.

None of these arguments, of course, forces us to define what exactly we mean by "closer ties". Until 1992, the EC was little more than a free-trade area, more correctly referred to by the title EEC than EC. Since the much-vaunted transition to a single market in 1992, however, not only goods but also factors of production – ownership of property, labour and capital – have been allowed to cross borders on an unrestricted basis. Land or buildings anywhere in the EC can now be owned by any EC national. Capital flows freely within the entire Community area.

Such changes topple the first in a line of dominoes. The free flow of capital between countries makes monetary union essential, or else differential rates of inflation and currency devaluation will drive capital toward the countries offering the most attractive conditions (lowest inflation, strongest currency). Similarly, there will have to be some form of fiscal harmonisation (similar levels and types of taxation in all EC countries), or else, over the years, labour and capital will flow to the countries where the tax regimes are perceived to be most advantageous. Since in most EC countries monetary and fiscal policy are *political* issues (Germany being a notable exception), and since, left to themselves, member states cannot be relied on to stay in monetary and fiscal alignment, a natural pressure develops to transfer these key political functions to Brussels – in other words, to move toward some form of European political union.

We will return to the political question in a moment. Note first of all, however, that the single market, which is in effect a further step in the institutionalising of the mega-community, imposes direct Relational costs. The de-restriction of labour movement can only mean greater mobility occurring over greater distances (indeed that is the intention), with the result that the impact of displacement on member populations will deepen. There will be more, not less, social isolation in neighbourhoods. It will become more, not less, difficult to provide personal care for elderly relatives. Married or cohabiting partners, under the stress of isolation or relocation, will be more, not less, likely to split up. This is not to imply that short periods working in European countries are disadvantageous, or that they don't help broaden vision and expand expertise. The problem is that, so often, the move is not a short "away-break" after which a family returns to its roots, but just another stop along the road to nowhere.

Also, as the potentials of the single market are realised in Europe's financial centres, we will see far greater mobility of capital. Financial institutions which previously would have looked to their own country to invest a given percentage of funds (savings, pension funds, insurance funds) will look to Europe as a whole. Economic analysis and historical experience suggest that investment will flow to the areas which are most prosperous and closest to the centres of political decision-making. It is significant that a company as small on the international scale as Pilkington Glass, with such strong roots in the North-west and such a strong social conscience, has already felt it necessary to move its head office to Brussels. Regional policies are likely to be relatively ineffective in offsetting these trends. If, as seems likely, the single market proves disadvantageous for Britain in terms of the availability of capital for investment, the areas worst hit will be the already depressed regions lying on the periphery of the EC (Wales, Scotland, the North-east and North-west) whose locational disadvantage will be only partly compensated for through the EC's Social Fund. Opening up to Europe will only exacerbate the internal problem of injustice in the distribution of resources.

European Federalism and Subsidiarity. The greatest Relational costs, however, are likely to be seen in the centralisation of political power. Here we stumble on that troublesome term "federal Europe" which is so prominent in the pro-European argument because, without admitting to any precise definition, it suggests that those who are nervous of yielding up national sovereignty can have their cake and eat it. In fact it is not clear whether the plans of the extreme pro-European lobby could accurately be described as *federal*. The European Charter sets no limits on political integration. If a projected European state is modelled, as some have suggested it should be, on the United States of America, then European nations would be adopting a political structure that in all but name has ceased to be a federal union of states and become instead a unitary state with a federal government structure. Like American states, member nations of such a federal Europe would retain the right to run separate legal systems and have separate social regulations, but ultimately would be subject to the control of a central parliament. National sovereignty would count for little, since the only areas of jurisdiction left to national governments would be those of the "social club" variety. As with devolution, the bulk of the real power would reside elsewhere.

Also it is hard to imagine a relatively centralised, US-style federation on a European scale, involving direct election to a European Parliament with sole legislative authority, that would not further erode parity between government and people. Not only are there questions of diversity in language and culture. The larger a state becomes, the less encounter there will be in political decision-making, and the further the ordinary citizen will be – in everything from food-safety rules to questions of military security – from those who make the decisions. On average, a Member of the European Parliament has a constituency of around 500,000, compared with 80,000 for a British MP. Can one person and a small office staff be sure to represent adequately the full range of views found among half a million people? This is exactly the dilemma in the USA, where the average senator's constituency will run into millions, encouraging disillusionment and frustration among ordinary citizens and fuelling the transition into media-based, impersonal, entertainment politics.

An even more alarming scenario is the future direct election of a European President, comparable to an American

President, with direct executive power over the whole 340-million-strong EC. The Relational distance between voter and President would be so great as to make accountability at local level impossible to exercise in almost all circumstances. Again, this is exactly the American dilemma. Except that in Europe the conflicts of national loyalty aroused by the necessity to choose a President from one nation would make the regional tension across America's Mason–Dixon Line look like a squabble in the playground.

In addition, what interest groups can lobby effectively in a parliament that represents 340 million and spans twelve countries? Some international trade unions are gradually being forged for this purpose. And among religious organisations, the Roman Catholic Church is rather better placed than the highly fragmented Protestant Churches. But in the foreseeable future the most powerful lobbyists are going to be the multinationals. In the Britain of 1986 it was still possible for an extensive and disparate grass-roots lobby to overturn a large Parliamentary majority at Westminster.[6] But I do not believe a successful campaign could have been mounted against the deregulation of Sunday trading if the legislation had been put forward by the European Parliament or the European Council of Ministers. Co-ordinating grass-roots resistance in ten countries would have been an impossible feat, both organisationally and financially.

Concern about a supranational Europe-state and its burden of supranational bureaucracy is usually countered with the word *subsidiarity*. Like federalism, however, subsidiarity has been dragged into the debate undressed with a definition. It is fine to claim that political decisions will be taken at the lowest possible level of government. But that leaves open the rather critical question of what powers the respective levels of government will possess, and therefore of what kinds of decision they are regarded as competent to handle. No one in Britain today would view fiscal policy as the proper concern of the region, and yet, as we have seen, it is perfectly possible to construct regional government in such a way that fiscal policy becomes its proper concern. Subsidiarity, therefore, can represent a true division of powers, or a verbal smokescreen behind which central authorities keep a firm grasp on the reins of state. In historical terms, the second is far more common than the first. Central governments have a nasty habit of attracting new roles and prerogatives, and, except sometimes in the aftermath of war, the direction of power in a state is more often centrifugal than centripetal.

Parity, Justice, and the Confederal Option. The complexity of EC union and the implications of this for the ordinary citizen should not be underestimated. "A students' introduction to the law of the EC runs to 925 pages. The official journal of the European Communities for 1990, confined to the core legislation and directives, runs to 27 fat volumes of the Law Society Library."[7] Inevitably, this leaves the individual bemused, as decisions affecting his or her everyday life are still further removed from any realistic hope even of influence, let alone effective control.

The apparently insignificant example of Sunday trading in Britain illustrates this problem and provides a good example of how Europe's centralised bureaucracy can be used to delay and obstruct justice in national courts. In April 1988, the Cwmbran Magistrates' Court in South Wales referred a case to the European Court in Luxembourg to establish whether the British Shops Act was contrary to one particular article of the Treaty of Rome. This was done at the insistence of a major retailer accused of breaking the law on Sunday trading. One and a half years later (November 1989) a judgement was handed down. When the local magistrates' court sought to apply the finding, an appeal was lodged which reached the House of Lords via the Court of Appeal and was then referred back to the European Court for further clarification. It was now May 1991. At the time of writing (November 1992), the European Court's verdict is still awaited. When it arrives, the decision will go back to the House of Lords and thence perhaps back to the Cwmbran Magistrates' Court in South Wales. During this entire period (already nearly four years) the retailer has continued trading in spite of the fact that, in theory, as made clear by the Attorney General, British law "has not been suspended".[8]

Almost certainly this will not be the end of the matter. Within weeks of the European Court's decision being applied in the British courts, the retailer is likely to seek another reference to the European Court. He can choose any one of at least four or five of the other 247 articles of the Treaty of Rome to try and get a reference, and the petition can be made from any one of over 450 magistrates' courts in England and Wales. He can trade with impunity for another year and a half, awaiting an initial European Court decision, and then if necessary appeal again. During which time he may have succeeded in stealing a considerable market share from his law-abiding competitors.

In this context it is fairly clear that, with the connivance, for one reason or another, of a national government, European bureaucracy can be used to assist the strong against the weak. In fairness, of course, the reverse can also happen. Plaintiffs who have failed to get redress in the British courts have on occasion been able to rectify an injustice by reference to Europe. But a system in which power is concentrated at the top level, leaving local officials constantly needing to refer upward to sources of higher authority, is on a European scale unavoidably ponderous and too often arbitrary or unjust in its effects. Yet how does one avoid the risks of centralised power without in the same stroke losing the benefits of pan-European co-operation?

One way forward is for Britain to seek to make Europe a confederal union rather than a federal state. The idea of confederation is well established in political history. The term was used in the Articles of Confederation of 1777, in the Union of Utrecht (1579), and in the early constitutions of Switzerland (1815–48) and Germany (1815–66). It has the virtue of placing firm bounds on centralised power, and of building subsidiarity into the structure of political relationships. What distinguishes confederalism from federalism is precisely that, as Oxford's former Professor of Government Kenneth Wheare points out, in a confederal structure "the general government is dependent upon the regional governments".[9] Subsidiarity as applied to a federal Europe would mean leaving any specific power at the EC level unless it could be shown to be better handled by national or local governments. By contrast, in a confederal Europe power is assumed to belong at national/regional level unless specifically passed up to a central body. Subsidiarity becomes institutionalised. National governments are asked to lease sovereignty, not to sell it.

Europe as a confederal union of states would have several advantages. The confederation would encourage, and indeed act to enforce, the EC as a free trade area, but would not require the unrestricted movement of capital and labour. It would have an awareness of itself as a political and cultural entity, and be able when necessary to act jointly on foreign policy, environment and aid issues, but would not force member states to adopt common citizenship, direct elections, or a unified immigration policy. Of course from a British point of view much depends on what the other member states want, and in the end Britain may be compelled to reconcile itself to living on the lower level of a two-tier Europe. Nevertheless, the confederal model provides a positive vision for the future of Europe, and offers protection for Relational concerns and priorities which the federal option does not.

Distant Voices, Still Lives?
Relational Media

Power and Ownership in the Media. The media performs essential Relational functions in the mega-community. As a means of news transmission it provides valuable information about the wider world. It broadens access to and understanding of the arts. Not least, in a society where elderly people tend to have progressively fewer encounters, it provides, by the mimicry of encounter, a sense of inclusion in the life of the national community. The link is contingent; but a contingent link is better than none at all.

At the same time the media requires careful handling. Because television exerts a powerful influence over lifestyle and socialisation, we are forced to ask hard questions both about the behavioural effects of the media generally, and about the particular impact of the TV on household relationships and the content and meaning of public discourse. As Neil Postman, Professor of Communication Arts and Sciences at New York University, pointedly observes, "The media of communication available to a culture is the dominant influence on the formation of the culture's intellectual and social preoccupation"[10] – a sobering thought in a culture increasingly dominated by the sit-com and the game show.

We will return to these themes later. The task of building a Relational media, however, begins, as Relational government does, with the problem of power distribution. Given the huge potential of the media for shaping public opinion, it should concern us, in a choice-based society where individual preference ultimately determines everything from hairstyles to the Party of government, that advertising can buy editorial sympathy and that control of the media generally lies in so few hands.

In their recent analysis of the press and broadcasting in Britain, Curran and Seaton report that: "The top five companies in each media sector controlled in the mid-1980s an estimated 40 per cent of book sales, 45 per cent of ITV transmissions, between half and two-thirds of video rentals, record, cassette, and compact-disc sales, and over three-quarters of daily and Sunday paper sales." This concentration is compounded by vertical integration into international media groups, often leaving British media interests as "the northern outposts of global media empires".

Curran and Seaton conclude: "Increasingly, the magnates dominating the British media are, in Bagdikian's phrase, 'lords of the global village'."[11]

The first priority for the media in a Relational society is therefore to reduce the potential for commercial and political exploitation, which means not only making the profit motive less prominent in media control, but insisting on a wider spread of ownership.

A list of provisional recommendations would therefore include the following:

(1) Limit the power of big advertising account holders throughout the media by giving a minimum level of subsidy to all radio/TV stations and newspapers, and restricting the amount of time/space devoted to advertising.

(2) In selling TV/radio franchises, give preference to trusts, mutual organisations and partnerships, rather than plcs – in other words to organisations which are not solely profit-maximising and whose leaders can more easily be held to account. Also, at the regional and local levels give preference to companies whose major shareholders can be shown to have regional/local links and thus to be more accessible to the public and more likely to be concerned with question of output quality.

(3) Transfer a greater degree of control over BBC programming and schedules to the corporation's regional offices.

(4) Encourage the development of Relational linkages at the local and regional level by giving greater competitive advantage to regional/local media, for example using differential levels of tax on profits, and taxing all *national* advertising.

(5) Introduce tougher rules against concentration of ownership within media sectors and cross-ownership between sectors.

Who Controls Broadcasting Policy. The 1990 Broadcasting Act has gone some way toward diffusing ownership in the media, but has done so only to encourage competition and without any explicit recognition of the pressure that concentrated or profit-driven ownership exerts on programme content. Content control is therefore largely an exercise in containment: codes of practice and regulatory bodies are set up to prevent certain things being put on air. There is little opportunity for the population in general either to influence the regulators, or to develop a sense of positive involvement with the output of its broadcasting networks. Our choice boils down to buying a paper and "seeing what's on".

The second Relational priority in the media, therefore, is to encourage a greater Relational emphasis in methods of broadcasting control. Under the 1990 Broadcasting Act, control of TV/radio programme content is entrusted to the Independent Television Commission (ITC), the Radio Authority, and the Broadcasting Standards Council (BSC). Ironically, these mediating institutions, whose purpose is to ensure that television and radio companies are publicly accountable, are not publicly accountable themselves. True, the BSC once made an effort to canvas public opinion by "discussing the main elements of the draft code with small groups of men and women selected by a market research organisation",[12] but there is no formal mechanism to ensure that regional – or, for that matter, religious, ethnic or gender – interests are properly represented. The members of all three bodies are, in bluntly undemocratic fashion, appointed by the Secretary of State. It is probably fair to say that the average complainant does not know who to complain to or where to send the complaint, and that, anyway, the thought of writing to a national body somewhat takes the edge off his conviction that complaining is worthwhile. There is little Relational proximity between watchdog and public.

An effective solution to this was put forward as early as 1968 by Manchester University's Eberhard Wedell.[13] Wedell proposed that the BBC be given a stronger regional structure and that there be regional broadcasting authorities as well as both national and regional broadcasting advisory councils. It was vital, he believed, to elect rather than simply appoint the members of such bodies, as this would ensure not only that the members were drawn from and represented a wide range of interest groups, such as the unions and churches, but also that they retained strong links with the general public. As a result, individuals would engage more positively and responsibly with broadcasting, and there would occur a "reinforcement of regional intellectual and cultural resources".[14]

Clearly such a suggestion – which could hardly contrast more strongly with the present situation – combines well with the proposals outlined earlier in this chapter for reconstituting Britain as a federation. By becoming more thoroughly regionalised, and therefore more accountable, the broadcasting media would increase its already considerable power to create a sense of regional as well as national commonality. As with the move to federalism, of course, this also has the downside of duplicating facilities and creating, overall, larger bureaucracy and stiffer regional competition for resources. Yet it would be easy to overestimate the significance of these. In an age of advanced information technology, regional television news can easily draw on national and international reports from a single news-gathering service. And there is no reason why the smaller scale and greater accountability of regionalised broadcasting should put a straitjacket on artistic freedom through chronic underfunding or overzealous supervision. Bearing in mind that we live in a society used only to consuming broadcast output, and bearing in mind also the impact particularly of television on that collective embodiment of relationships we call culture, the price of greater people involvement in the media is surely worth paying.

In addition, there is also a strong case for having national and regional media ombudspersons, perhaps assisted by a jury, whose function would be to guarantee right of reply to significant minorities, or even individuals, who feel that they have been misrepresented by radio, television or press. The remit would cover both factual inaccuracy and unfair representation, and would create greater parity between the viewer/reader and those media organisations that tend to rate the needs of the front page more highly than individual privacy.

This leads to the third Relational priority in the media.

Media Content and Codes of Practice. In the drawing-up of any code there will inevitably be debate over the proper balance between choice and obligation – that is, between the presumption of free expression and the duty to take account of public concerns. As you would expect in a liberal culture, the current Broadcasting Standards Council Code of Practice (1989) gives priority to choice: "In a free society, there must be a presumption that, like the rest of the media, broadcasting enjoys a freedom of expression restricted only for a cause generally accepted as sufficient to justify restriction."[15] What is "generally accepted" is clearly open to interpretation, but is to some degree formalised in the Broadcasting Act, which allows, in its general provisions about licensed services, for "nothing which offends against good taste or decency or is likely to encourage or incite to crime or to lead to disorder or to be offensive to public feeling . . ."[16]

A problem arises, however, in so far as the Code of Practice argues that the need for limits is less urgent than it was when, as was true in the early days of broadcasting, the viewer/listener was stuck with whatever happened to come at him on a single channel. "Those who dislike what they see or hear may now more readily change channels before adopting the last resort of switching off."[17] That is all well and good; but the fact that I exercise my freedom of choice not to watch a depiction of rape doesn't prevent a teenager watching the same programme and then raping my daughter. You will say that this draws an unrealistically straight line between media influence and behaviour, and you are right. But in making that charge you move the debate into what is surely the more relevant area: that is, how exactly the setting of limits relates to the occurrence of Relational dysfunction.

As we noted in the sixth chapter, the academic battle has been raging in this particular field for some time. But although the issues are complex, and the media, though influential, is by no means the only factor in socialisation, the evidence suggests that the Broadcasting Act's acceptance of the power of the media image not only to "offend against good taste" but to "encourage or incite to crime or lead to disorder" should be taken seriously in the Code of Practice.

In fact the Code tends to fight shy of taking any positive view of what we might call Relational health. On the use of tobacco, it is quite decided that "programmes should not encourage smoking, especially by children or young people. Encouragement may be given by identifying smoking with maturity or as an expression of sophisticated manhood or womanhood."[18] Yet on the (surely more significant) business of making love it requires only that "on television, the representation of sexual intercourse before the watershed should always be a matter for senior editorial judgement."[19]

This seems a rather weak underpinning for the Council's own professed values of the responsible depiction of women and the protection of children, discussed elsewhere in the Code with reference to issues like the depiction of rape and indecent assault. Talking only about appropriate times for the "representation of sexual intercourse" effectively both sidelines the issue of commercial pressure to represent sex, and implicitly isolates the act of sex from its possible physical, Relational, or emotional consequences – not least, the birth of children. All that seems to matter is what parts of the body can be filmed, in what ways, doing what things. And yet, even from the dramatic point of view, as Alan Plater says, " . . . the great tragi-comic drama of sex lies not in the act itself, but in the psychological paraphernalia with which we surround it."[20] There is far more to the Relational issue of sex on television, we might say, than the amount of skin on the screen. Style of representation is one matter – and there is at least a strong argument, given child-viewing patterns, for pushing the watershed back another hour. But another and equally important concern is psychological realism. If sex is depicted on screen, it should do more than appeal to male prurience. The Code of Practice doesn't go far enough to give producers clear encouragement in this direction.[21]

Finally, with respect to television, we might ask the

unaskable question about its value as a medium. It is in the nature of a commercial culture to fill every visible gap with products, and this means in broadcasting terms that viewing hours will extend and channels proliferate to the point where market forces will support no more. Whether that point, which can be fully justified on the grounds of maximising choice, is also fully in the public interest is, however, quite another matter. While it would therefore be contentious to suggest that broadcasting hours should be limited, there is, I think, a strong case for discussing, in view of Relational priorities, how much television is really necessary. It is a not entirely serious illustration of a serious point to note that prolonged power cuts are often associated, nine months later, with a boom in births. In at least one respect, then, relationships receive more attention when the telly goes off. But if relationships can benefit in a general sense from switching off, is there not a place in public debate for discussing whether, once in a while, the British people could have a national holiday from TV?

More than Money
Relational Welfare

An Alternative Model. In capitalist and social market economies welfare provision for the poor and disadvantaged is regarded as a moral responsibility. But the connection between the operation of the economy and the *need* for welfare is largely ignored. In effect the logic of the system is to pursue growth by whatever means are required, and to mop up the social mess afterwards.

One has to assume, of course, that a large enough economic surplus can be produced to finance the mopping up. But, as we noted in the sixth chapter, the "social mess" is itself a diseconomy, and the increasing drag it places on the system means that, sooner or later, the fiscal chickens will come home to roost. Part of the problem in Britain arises from the fact that social spending is already at a high level. The foundation of the Welfare State in 1948, and the ever-increasing number of pensioners who draw upon it, [22] go a long way to explaining why, since 1910, public expenditure has risen from 10% to almost 50% of GNP. With such a massive amount already committed to social purposes, the extra costs imposed by economic and social dysfunction are all the more damaging. Unemployment has risen sharply since 1980. The number of lone-parent families dependent on the state for support is estimated to be growing by 40,000 per year.

The fact that these trends – which to a greater or lesser extent are duplicated throughout Western Europe – seem likely to make the present welfare system unsustainable within a few decades constitutes, in itself, a strong argument for treating welfare as a Relational as well as a material concern. Scant attention, for instance, has been paid to the alternative model of welfare: that is, to put in place safeguards for the wellbeing and security of every locality, family and individual, and then to pursue economic growth within the framework such safeguards impose. Under this model, attention shifts from cleaning up the "social mess" to preventing its creation. The aim is a user-friendly economy.

Just as important, however, is to recognise that welfare is not, as we sometimes think, a purely material issue. There is a complex two-way link between Relational and material deprivation. We need adequate food and shelter; but we also need stability, dignity, belonging and respect. Where these Relational benefits are withdrawn (and they are often withdrawn through the influence of poverty), damage is inflicted not only on the individual's sense of wellbeing, but on his ability to function in society, his Relational skills, his ability even to hold down a job.[23] The underlying problem, therefore, is not just a lack of material resources, but a breakdown of relationships in a society which has no answer to Relational need beyond the allocation of cash.

Welfare as Self-Reliance. The person who draws a pension retains a real sense of having earned her weekly remittance, and indeed by paying her the state is only honouring a long-standing contract. In the case of unemployment benefit, however, there are ways in which, even for the vast majority of claimants who wish only to get back into work, payments become de-linked from contributions. Unemployment can last for years. Many young people are forced on to the dole as soon as they leave school, and have known nothing else. In such situations, it becomes increasingly difficult to regard benefit as the fruit of your own labour and prudence. Your contributions – if you have had the opportunity to make contributions – will not usually appear to you as a personal provision from which you are now able to finance your unemployment. More likely, you will simply feel dependent on state charity, and in a sense the facts reinforce this interpretation, for you may end up getting out of the system far more than you put in. Psychologically, however, this is intolerable: it strips the claimant of dignity. Which is why, perhaps, to compensate, we often think of benefit as an automatic right, and look on the institutions of the welfare state as so much unnecessary bureaucracy gratuitously set up to deprive us of it.

But however you respond, the fundamental problem is disparity. Claimants need encouragement to think of themselves as fundamentally self-reliant – in need of state support only on a temporary basis. Correspondingly, the economic system needs to be altered in such a way as will give this attitude substantive foundation, by giving absolute priority to the task of providing everyone with the opportunity of gainful employment. Such a project challenges our whole notion of welfare.

One way of increasing self-reliance is to strengthen the present commitment to encouraging home ownership. Most of those on low incomes spend one-third to one-half of their income on rent. Obviously not everyone wants to own a home, and the aim of increasing ownership should not involve the use of financial schemes which can lead a person heavily into debt if the house market declines or if he loses his job.[24] However, the present figure of £2 billion allocated to new housing is pitifully small, and much more could be done by the housing associations and through other forms of local initiative to provide low-cost housing for those who would otherwise never have the financial independence and security of owning a home.

A second and equally important way of achieving self-reliance is to reform methods of welfare administration. Since the introduction of National Insurance in 1911, welfare administration has increasingly forced the individual to deal directly with government, often at the national level. But there are at least two alternative models that put welfare in the context of greater Relational proximity.

The simplest proposal is to give greater autonomy and flexibility to regional and local government in the business of distributing benefits. But if local government had greater discretion in providing housing benefit, for example, a considerable amount of money could be saved by more creative thinking about the needs of the individual. I can give an example of this which is at one and the same time trivial and illustrative of the wider problem. Someone I knew wished to live in a van instead of a council flat. As this did not fit under the rules for housing benefit, he received no help. Worse, because he could not afford to pay the van insurance from his unemployment benefit, and because the police kept forcing him to move the van from one parking place to another, he drove without insurance, and after repeated confrontations and court hearings ended up, not in his van, but in prison. A small allowance toward the cost of accommodation in the van would have saved the van-owner much discomfort and the public purse a good deal of money. Nonsense of this kind is not uncommon. But the good sense needed to avoid it can only be applied where the people dealing with the case have access to those who make the rules – that is, in a local context.

You will point out, of course, that locally administered benefit also has its downside. Where each locality adapts the rules to its own particular situation there is a danger that individuals with the same problem will receive differing treatment depending on which locality they happen to live in. But then standardised procedures have their downside too. Small degrees of inconsistency between localities would surely be preferable to having millions of unemployed stuck in the poverty trap because inflexible welfare rules will seldom allow them to take part-time jobs without losing benefit.

There are other advantages, too. The higher degrees of accountability and greater familiarity with a claimant's circumstances attainable in a local welfare system will tend to discourage abuse. It would therefore be more difficult for two mothers in adjacent houses to agree to take each other's sons as lodgers, and thus to claim £64.15 a week instead of £21 – an arrangement that once even survived referral to an official tribunal.[25] Also, flexibility in negotiating with groups of relatives, perhaps by allowing them to build an extra room on to a house, might well enable families to delay or prevent the admission of an elderly person into a home – an option that, at a current average cost of £300 per week, amounts to a considerable drain on public resources.

A third way of encouraging self-reliance in welfare is for central government to give substantial tax incentives for the establishment of self-help organisations. As we noted in the fourth chapter, friendly societies flourished in Britain up to and beyond the introduction of National Insurance in 1911 – in the late nineteenth century an estimated 75% of men over the age of twenty-four were enrolled in one.[26] The strength of the friendly societies was that, being based in a local nexus of relationships, they both relied on and sustained Relational proximity. A modern self-help organisation could quite feasibly finance not only services for the elderly, sick and unemployed, but also the needs of education, training, and even leisure. Many credit unions are already established in Britain as self-help organisations to provide credit for low-income households.[27] On the international scene, Lebanon's

Family Associations provide a fascinating example of what is possible through local co-operation.[28]

There are other forms of self-help. Much more encouragement could be given to the already substantial voluntary sector, perhaps through extending matching grants schemes to encourage charitable giving. Such a form of voluntary taxation, though it would need careful monitoring, could be of crucial importance to improving quality of life in a prolonged recession. Also, a significant boost to self-reliance could be achieved if families and individuals were helped to relocate nearer to their elderly or dependent relatives. Indeed, many carers have relatives who are willing to relocate, but who are prevented from doing so because they cannot organise job-swaps or sell their houses. Expanding the voluntary sector's capacity in this way would, of course, release funds for other purposes.

The Welfare Functions of Regional and Central Government. Because, as we noted earlier, issues of parity apply also to relationships linking different levels of government, it is important for regions and local authorities to become more self-reliant in their provision of welfare support. The most immediate need is to ensure that, as far as possible, local authorities raise their own funds. This gives central government a rather different role. Because welfare needs vary so widely by area, the adoption of such a scheme would require substantial inter-regional resource transfers in the early years, and this could only be co-ordinated at the national level. Central government would also direct resources on a long-term basis to regions and localities with chronic deficits, review financial and industrial strategy as discussed in the last chapter, and ensure adequate infrastructure investment to support communication.

A further aspect of this co-ordinating role would be the provision of advice, training and other support services to help regions and local authorities administer and monitor welfare services effectively. Again, this is already happening to some extent. But in a decentralised state it would become a more vital function because experimentation with welfare approaches by different localities would require the transfer of knowledge and expertise from one area to another. In addition, since individuals can fall foul of administration even at the regional and local levels, central government would be responsible for providing ombudspersons, to give the individual claimant a means of redress against unfair treatment, and to guard against regional/local discrimination on the grounds of race, age or gender.

There is also a certain amount of direct action central government can take to optimise welfare functions. With respect to its own public service employees, it can be more flexible in adjusting working hours and providing support for those with dependent relatives. It can also put pressure on private sector companies to act more Relationally to staff in terms of mobility and hours demanded. Under a Relational welfare system, failure to comply could result in a "Relational audit" being required of the company on a biannual or triennial basis, compelling it to declare its policies on personnel involvement in family and locality affairs, and making these policies the subject of external scrutiny. Central government would, additionally, play a key role in furthering education and training opportunities, including in-service training, and in resolving wider problems that bear on welfare provision, like unemployment and relocation.

The last point bears some expansion. Clearly, an important way in which central government can encourage self-reliance and parity long-term is to prevent unwanted job mobility, and thus to enable extended family groups to relocate in greater geographical proximity. Extensive evidence exists of the astonishing level of contact and mutual support which still exists between members of extended families.[29] In many cases it is only spatial scattering that prevents them from being more effective carers. Obviously, assisting individuals or households to move from one region or locality to another will only be feasible in a minority of cases at any one time. Nevertheless, a long-term programme of assistance in relocation could be a vital stepping-stone to strengthening the ability of informal networks to provide meaningful care, and to reducing the pressure on local government resources.

Directly to Jail?
Relational Justice

Theories of Justice. Justice should be the basis of any penal system. But what do we mean by justice? The conventional image of it is that of Justicia, blindfolded atop the Old Bailey, with scales in one hand and a sword in the other. She symbolises impartiality, the thoroughness of a fair trial and punishment. The image catches much, but also misses much. Justice, after all, is not a value-free term. Its definition reflects society's underlying values, and in the British context these values are expressed in two schools of thought – the utilitarian and the retributivist – which mark more or less opposite poles in the debate concerning the nature of justice and its administration.

In the utilitarian view the just state is one which achieves, in Jeremy Bentham's famous phrase, "the greatest happiness of the greatest number". To act justly is to maximise, or at least promote that goal. For the utilitarian, then, the pain of punishment can only be justified if it is outweighed by "good consequences" – a phrase which in this case is usually taken to mean anything that reduces the crime rate. You deter the criminal, reform him, imprison him, or, if necessary, eliminate him. Such measures may be effective. Punishment often has a deterrent effect, and it can reform. On the value of imprisonment there is rather less unanimity, however, and critics claim that incarceration merely postpones reoffending and makes future criminal behaviour more likely: prisons can be schools of crime. In addition, utilitarianism suffers from certain philosophical flaws. The "pains" of one person (the offender) are not commensurable with the "good consequences" enjoyed by others (the community enjoying lower crime rates). There is no single scale on which all the required addition and subtraction can be done. It is debatable whether any one pain or benefit can be measured at all in meaningful terms.

Retributivism gets around this problem by making consequences (painful or pleasurable) irrelevant, and regarding punishment as intrinsically good regardless of any other aim it may happen to fulfil. For the retributivist, to act justly is to give the offender what he or she deserves, and the just state is one in which the principle of desert informs all punishment. The difficulty (to borrow from Gilbert and Sullivan) lies in making sure the punishment does indeed fit the crime. Desert, after all, is a complex notion which involves establishing the *harm* done by the offence, the *culpability* of the offender, and the *sensibility* of this particular offender to the proposed punishment: "a problem in three dimensions, none of which is measurable on any scale known to man".[30] Acting justly in the retributivist sense therefore becomes a near impossibility, for as Hegel pointed out, "Injustice is done at once if there is one lash too many, or one dollar, one cent, one week in prison, or one day, too many or too few."[31]

Obviously much more could be said by way of critique, but it can be observed in summary that neither school offers a complete foundation for a penal system because neither offers more than a partial view of justice. Utilitarianism evaluates justice by reference to an instant in time, not processes through time. It is therefore a construct ill-suited to taking into account the importance of relationships. Retributivism, as we have already seen, is unable to balance desert and punishment exactly. Moreover, it struggles to articulate in convincing terms the origin and validity of the obligation to punish. Any jigsaw, hybrid or eclectic combination of the theories ultimately fails to elucidate what that greater end is to which punishment is a means. In short, both utilitarianism and retributivism beg the original question: what is justice?

The Scope of Relational Justice. Here Relationism puts forward the simple thesis that justice is Relational. A just society is one whose individuals (and by extension, whose institutions) have relationships that are "good" in the moral sense we discussed in the second chapter. Crime disrupts particular relationships within society's pattern of relationships. These relationships and this pattern may not have been perfect, but they were at least of a character which society in general agreed did not require judicial intervention. It follows that the function of the criminal justice system should, in part, be to attempt to mend this damage, and to establish a pattern of relationships comparable in quality to the prior pattern — perhaps even better than the prior pattern. Punishment, which has the additional purpose of reinforcing moral awareness (fear of punishment imposes constraint in the sense in which we earlier used the term), is one of several means which can be employed to do this. In other words, punishment, among its other functions, is a means to a more positive end.

I cannot claim at this stage that Relational justice constitutes a comprehensive penal theory, though it may develop into that. Certainly it resembles utilitarianism in seeking to maximise a particular goal (quality of relationship), and retributivism in accepting that punishment, while seen as a means to a greater end, also has some intrinsic merit. At the very least, however, Relational justice opens a radically different perspective on the process of law.

If a criminal justice system embodying the priorities of Relational justice aims, as far as possible, to mend harm in the relationships damaged by crime, the first thing we might note is the number of relationships involved: victim and offender; victim and state/community; offender and state; offender and community; offender and prison personnel; offender and offender's family; and offender's family and state/community. How does one begin to pursue Relational justice in this complex of relationships?

Again there is much to say, but I must confine myself to three rather brief comments.

First, Relational justice informs our understanding of the nature of crime. While a criminal offence only exists when the criminal law has been breached, the offence itself is regarded by Relational justice primarily as a violation of the victim and her Relational Base, and only secondarily as an offence against the state. The emotional, physical or economic harm suffered by the victim of crime radiates out through her relationships. The mother of a mugged teenager is caused anger or anxiety; the children of a victim of theft may go without new shoes; the victim of rape may find it harder to trust people. Whole communities can be traumatised by a murder, the order and cohesion of society in general be disturbed by disregard of the laws – for example, against murder, theft, or more controversially, solicitation of prostitutes and Sunday trading – that represent its collective definition of punishable behaviour.

Second, Relational justice informs our understanding of the judicial process. It argues, in a similar vein to conventional civil rights, for parity between the alleged offender and the state, so that, regardless of the outcome of the case, the alleged offender is protected from state abuse – a need highlighted in the overturning of unsafe convictions, widespread concern about uncorroborated confessions, and the campaigns of reforming groups like Liberty. More pervasively, Relational justice urges that the state, which usually prosecutes on the victim's behalf, allow the victim and possibly her family and representatives of her community to participate in the criminal justice process.

Because considerable expertise is required to conduct trials at law, such participation may often be restricted to communication with the victim and her family to ensure that the victim's interest in the resolution of the case is actively respected, and consultation with community representatives over, for example, the level of sentencing. However there might in many cases be a role for mediation – face-to-face contact between victims and offenders, undertaken voluntarily, with the assistance of a trained mediator. The aims would be to repair some of the practical and emotional damage caused by the offence and to underline the seriousness of the offence in human terms. Psychologists describe how offenders put up barriers to protect themselves from feeling guilt and tend to "depersonalise" their victim. Mediation seeks to break down those barriers and, by revealing the pain caused by crime, to reinforce the meaning and purpose of punishment.

Third, Relational justice informs our understanding of sentencing, giving it three interlinked aims: retribution, reparation, and reintegration.

In Relational terms, crimes against people are more serious than crimes against property. This implies a theory of desert. Nevertheless, although punishment must be anchored in the concept of desert to reflect the responsibility of offenders for their actions, in Relational justice it is not of paramount importance for the punishment to annul the offence in a perfectly balanced equation, because punishment is not seen purely in terms of retribution. The idea of desert is complemented by a concern for offender–community, and particularly for offender–victim, relationships. Punishment isn't just retributive, it is reparative.

Reparation is the making of amends by an offender to his victim, or, in the case of indirect reparation, to the victims of other offenders. It is an important aim of Relational justice because it is a means of mending the offender–victim relationship, even if, as with indirect reparation, the mending is symbolic. It can take many forms – financial compensation, repair work, the provision of service. Even straightforward apology is sometimes prized by victims. Reparation, where made under the compulsion of a court order, serves a retributive as well as a reparative function.

The ultimate aim of the sentencing process is the reintegration of the offender into the community. Custodial sentences generally complicate this, for it is hard to train people for freedom while they are in captivity, and the effects of imprisonment linger in the form of general stigma and difficulties obtaining work. It is important, therefore, if custody is used, to gear it to life after release: education, training, activities and approaches designed to promote self-respect.

Of course the ultimate aim of reintegration is hampered in a good many cases by factors beyond the penal system's control: previous environment; unstable relationships in childhood; skill disadvantages; unemployment; alcoholism; addiction. To the extent that solutions to these barriers to reintegration exist, many of them are in the domain of social policy, not penal policy. Since reintegration is a major goal of Relational justice, human and financial resources must be made available to counteract these factors – a bare commitment to "just deserts" is not enough. Naturally, there is no guarantee of success in any approach to reintegration within the penal system. But as Chris Wood points out, "there is at least the guarantee of a system that will express better values and pursue better aims than those which it replaces."[32]

A Relational Culture
Conclusion

I have covered a lot of ground in what seems a very short space of time.

The choice of material in this chapter should not be taken to imply that government, media, welfare and justice are the only areas beyond economics where Relational ideas can be applied. There are clearly countless other issues. The administration and delivery of health services and education. The content of the core curriculum in schools. Priorities in scientific research, town planning, urban policy and environmental projects. Appreciation of literature, music and art. The role and utilisation of recreational facilities. Gender and race issues. Immigration policy. The application of information technology. The list goes on and on, and is paralleled by another list of issues relating to personal lifestyle. The structure of family relationships. Aspects of childcare. Career and housing choices. Use of discretionary time. Children's literature. Shopping habits. The use of the broadcasting media. The organisation of domestic finance. Interpersonal dialogue.

Closer attention to relationships across these public and private agendas might mark the beginnings of a Relational culture. Relational culture? How would such a thing appear? Cultures are not created by political fiat: nobody in the Dark Ages invented something called individualism and then promulgated it as an ideology – it simply emerged, a dominant colour in the seamless weaving of time. And yet, once recognised, it did acquire political force. It was reflected on, idealised, put to use. And this, ultimately, explains why I have allowed the adjective Relational to yield the rather more determined noun *Relationism*. Public policies take on the shape of their philosophical foundations. If you believe the foundations should be arranged in a different way, therefore, you will have to fight your corner in the public square. You will need to systematise your thinking and develop an ideology. You will need, in short, a word with *-ism* on the end.

Notes

1 Anthony Sampson, "No wonder Britain's in a mess", *Independent*, November 6, 1992.

2 Marinus Wiechers, "Regional Safeguards in Federal States", Proceedings of the Conference of the Newick Park Initiative on Constitutional Safeguards in Unitary and Federal States, Jubilee Centre, Cambridge, February 1990.

3 For a more detailed discussion of this, see Janet Buckingham, "Three-Tier Federalism", Proceedings of the Conference of the Newick Park Initiative on Political and Economic Implications of Unitary and Federal Systems of Government within a Democratic Framework, Jubilee Centre, Cambridge, June 1990.

4 Gerald Suttles, *The Social Construction of Communities* (University of Chicago Press, Chicago, 1972), p. 13.

5 Sir Fred Catherwood, *Pro-Europe?* (IVP, Leicester, 1991), p. 20.

6 For a detailed analysis of the conflict over the Shops Bill (1985) see Michael Schluter, *Keeping Sunday Special* (Marshall Pickering, Basingstoke, 1988).

7 Andrew Phillips, letter to the *Independent*, June 27, 1992.

8 *Hansard*, House of Commons, November 27, 1991.

9 Kenneth Wheare, *Federal Government* (Greenwood Press, Connecticut, 1980), p. 32.

10 Neil Postman, *Amusing Ourselves to Death* (Heinemann, London, 1986), p. 9.

11 J. Curran and J. Seaton, *Power Without Responsibility: The Press and Broadcasting in Britain* (Routledge, London, 1991), pp. 93–4.

12 Broadcasting Standards Council, *A Code of Practice*, November 1989, p. 5.

13 Eberhard Wedell, *Broadcasting and Public Policy* (Michael Joseph, London, 1968).

14 *ibid.*, p. 304.

15 Broadcasting Standards Council, *op. cit.*, p. 9.

16 Broadcasting Act 1990, Part 1, 6(1)(a).

17 Broadcasting Standards Council, *op. cit.*, p. 9.

18 *ibid.*, p. 48.

19 *ibid.*, p. 38.

20 Alan Plater, "The outcome is more dramatic than the act", *Independent*, November 11, 1992.

21 The question of whether or not the depiction of sex is "artistically justified" is, of course, a sensitive one. But it is worth remembering that sex can be depicted powerfully without resorting to nudity. Alan Plater, in the article cited above, notes such a scene in Alan Bleasdale's series *GBH*. "It took us into the heart of the situation, gave a poignant insight into the characters at that stage in the drama and, above all, was *funny*."

22 Between 1951 and 1991 the number of women over 60 rose by 41% and the number of men over 65 by 44%, with the result that by 1991 one fifth of the population was pensionable. See A. N. Dilnot, J. A. Kay, C. N. Morris, *The Reform of Social Security* (Institute of Fiscal Studies, Clarendon Press, Oxford, 1984).

23 Professor Halsey, for example, argues that children from one-parent families tend to do less well at school and suffer more

unemployment. See "Professor 'shudders for next generation'", *The Times*, July 3, 1991.

24 For proposals on financing house purchase, please refer to previous chapter.

25 *Guardian*, June 17, 1984.

26 For a fuller discussion of friendly societies as an alternative to the Welfare State, see David Green, *The Welfare State: For Rich or Poor?* (IEA, London, 1982).

27 Richard Berthoud and Teresa Hinton, *Credit Unions in the United Kingdom*, Policy Studies Institute Research Report 693 (London, 1989).

28 See Samir Khalaf, "Family Associations in Lebanon", *Journal of Comparative Family Studies*, vol. 2, no. 2, pp. 235–50.

29 See, for example, E. Brody, "Women in the middle and family help to older people", *The Gerontologist*, no. 5, pp. 471–80, and Peter Willmott, "Social Networks, Informal Care and Public Policy", Policy Studies Institute Research Report no. 655.

30 N. Walker, *Why Punish?* (OUP, Oxford, 1991), p. 101.

31 *ibid.*, p. 101.

32 C. Wood, *The End of Punishment* (St Andrews Press, Edinburgh, 1991), p. 119.

10

Only Connecting

Relationism
Ideology and Praxis

I use the word ideology with hesitation. To many, especially those on the political right, it has negative connotations: it is the kind of thing Marxists used to have.

In fact — and I quote the OED — the word merely refers to "ideas at the basis of some economic or political theory or system". On that definition Relationism is more than an ideology, since, to a greater degree than the ideologies of Marxism, capitalism, or even socialism, it speaks to private as well as to public life. It almost resembles a religion. And yet it does not reach that far. Beneath it lies only a set of presuppositions about the nature of human beings, which may be summarised as follows:

1. That all human life has intrinsic value and dignity.
2. That good interpersonal relationships are of primary importance to both individual and societal wellbeing.
3. That good relationships depend on the presence of both obligation and choice in the social structure.
4. That a good relationship is to be understood primarily as a morally good relationship.

All four propositions could be affirmed as intuitively self-evident, or rationalised on the purely secularist basis of utilitarian humanism. None of them demands a metaphysic.

But at the same time it is easy to see how they can be integrated with the perspective of faith.

For example, that touchstone of good relating – "Do as you would be done by" – was classically articulated by Jesus. Many Christians will see in Jesus the model Relationist, demonstrating in his life as well as his teaching how Relational commitment works out in practice. Further, the theme of relationship is integral to Christian theology, informing the idea of God as intrinsically interpersonal (the doctrine of the Trinity) and as acting to restore relationship between himself and a fallen humanity (the doctrine of the atonement). In a deep and fundamental sense, Christianity is a Relational religion.

The primacy of relationship is recognised in a similar way in Judaism. Covenant is an inherently Relational concept, and the provisions of God's covenant with Israel, spelled out in detail in the Torah, include both the Jubilee laws – and specific economic injunctions with respect to the limiting of interest and protection from debt. All of this, of course, was adopted – though not always applied – by Christianity in its canonisation of the Jewish scriptures as the Old Testament.

Not surprisingly, having drawn from both Judaism and Christianity, Islamic belief too has a strongly Relational core. There are differences of emphasis: Islam focuses more strongly on obligation and sets out distinct priorities in the ordering of relationships. But in terms of public policy much the same concern is given to promoting the Relational over the material, and this has been expressed clearly in institutional terms, for instance with the establishment of interest-free banking.

Even the non-theistic religions can endorse aspects of Relationism. In their understanding of the inadequacy of material values and of the transcendence of the soul, for example, the monistic faiths of India and East Asia all underline the failure of consumer capitalism to satisfy basic human need. African animism and Chinese Confucianism both affirm in the strongest possible terms the sanctity of kinship and the centrality of right relationship, at least within the family and the clan.

Relationism, then, with its emphasis on social and personal values in the ordering of public life, distils out an ethic upon which humanist and theist, Hindu and Muslim, Christian and Jew can all agree, and to that extent holds promise of furnishing a moral consensus upon which a modern pluralist society might be built. One could speak of humanist Relationists, Christian Relationists, Jewish Relationists, Islamic and Hindu Relationists, whose particular concerns will differ, but whose aims will in practice coincide across large swathes of public policy.

In the current political context it would be harder to speak of Labour Relationists or Conservative Relationists. Not that MPs as individuals would necessarily disagree with the root ideas of Relationism. But whereas the policy framework Relationism puts forward follows consistently from a Relational ideology, the policy frameworks of the major political Parties tend not only to draw on ideologies of a different origin but to do so in an eclectic fashion. So although particular Relationist policy proposals may find an echo in those put forward by current political Parties, in general Relationism critiques other policy frameworks and demands a reordering of priorities on the political agenda.

This does not mean that Relationist thinking is monolithic. The quality gap between suburban and inner-city high-rise housing, which will inevitably be a focus of concern for any Relationist, is nevertheless capable of generating a variety of Relational responses. It is possible to take a long-term view, arguing for the demolition of tower blocks on the grounds that they hold an excessive density of population in structurally antiRelational conditions, and accepting as a short-term cost a certain amount of residential relocation and displacement. But it is also possible to see rootedness as the central issue and to argue that, since displacement must be minimised, the way forward is to modernise high-rise accommodation through public-sector investment or private-sector job creation. Which policy is the more desirable or effective in Relational terms is, after detailed data analysis, largely a matter of judgement. Policy-makers of all persuasions work from a partial database, just because the full political, economic and social information required to evaluate a policy in advance is never available. Within a Relational perspective, therefore, there will be plenty of latitude in discussions about how much priority should be accorded to one policy relative to another.

What is striking is just how wide a range of issues invite Relational analysis and reform. If we wish to move in any significant way toward a more Relational society, we will need new financial instruments, including new savings instruments with Relationally-sensitive investment structures. We will need new ways of financing housing, greater policy-holder influence over the use of pension funds, legislative changes in company structure and long overdue adjustments to the constitutional arrangements by which we are governed. We will need to set new priorities for negotiation within the EC, and to re-evaluate the principles behind the criminal justice system, especially with respect to the operation of the prison service. Perhaps most urgently, we will need legislation to limit the dependence of the media on particular forms of political patronage or financial interest.

Ideally, we would want to see these and other issues tackled simultaneously, to make the Relational benefits mutually reinforcing. Implementing a regional industrial strategy clearly makes a lot more sense, for example, if you also establish regional banks and a regional tier of government which shares with the locality a key role in welfare administration. It is only as you embed Relational proximity and multiply cross-cutting linkages in this way that sufficient trust and confidence are built up to resource the market economy and Relational systems of welfare and justice. These are far-reaching changes. But if we are tempted to dub them "revolutionary" we should not make the mistake – particularly in the more politically volatile environments of Eastern Europe or Latin America – of thinking that they can or should be realised by extra-parliamentary means. The phrase Leninist Relationist is a contradiction in terms.

Ultimately, nevertheless, the pressure to create a Relational society must come from the people. It begins with one's innermost convictions concerning the way human life should be lived, and this means that a Relationist is not in the first instance an activist for a cause, but a person deeply concerned with the quality of his or her own personal relationships. If Relationism is an ideology, it is rooted in the most ancient of human needs and brings to the political arena the most ancient theme of literature and the arts. It is, to play with E. M. Forster's phrase, only connecting. Yet it does not ride the train of history in a rear-facing seat. It is not a plea to turn the clock back and retrieve whatever we had before the mega-community. (What did we have, anyway?) Rather, it proposes a gradual transformation of the social order; a second renaissance, if you will, but one in which the imperative to rediscover, re-evaluate and rejuvenate relationship becomes at the same time a quest to find new patterns of Relational expression within the technological and environmental realities of the dawning third millennium.

Glossary of Key Terms and Ideas

Choice

A condition under which the individual is free to determine his or her own interests without reference to the interests of other individuals or social groups of which he or she is a member.

Commitment

The individual's personal inclination to respect and/or fulfil obligations, founded on a sense of inner moral conviction.

Commonality

That condition in a relationship involving common purpose. A dimension of Relational proximity.

Constraint

Social pressure to observe and/or fulfil obligations, applied intentionally by others or unintentionally through the individual's perception of group values and expectations.

Contingent Relationships

A connection of two individuals who may have no knowledge of one another but are, none the less, linked through social, political, and economic institutions, with the result that the behaviour and expectations of one will, without any conscious initiative being taken, impact with sometimes detrimental effects on the living conditions and expectations of the other.

Continuity

That condition in a relationship involving frequency, regularity and sustaining of contact. A dimension of Relational proximity.

Directness

That condition in a relationship involving a lack of mediation in contact and, at its most intense, involving face-to-face meeting. A dimension of Relational proximity.

Displacement

The state which occurs when an individual or group makes a residential move requiring the severing or stretching of Relational links with the old neighbourhood.

Encounter Relationship

A connection between two individuals which is based on some degree of unmediated contact.

Mega-community

The complex of social groups at the largest scale, of which the individual senses himself or herself to be a member, but within which almost all relationships are conducted indirectly through the political system, the economy, and the media.

Multiplexity   That condition in a relationship involving contact in more than one context or role. A dimension of Relational proximity.

Obligation   A contract, promise, or demand of conscience or custom, by which an individual is bound in a legal or moral sense to certain patterns of behaviour which serve first the interests of a social group rather than him or her as an individual. Used without the article, "obligation" connotes the presence of obligations in general in the social structure.

Parity   That condition in a relationship involving an approximate balance of power or influence, whether or not operating from an institutional base. A dimension of Relational proximity.

Relational Base   The cluster of relationships surrounding the individual from birth to death (the most significant usually being found in the primary group or linking him or her to local institutions), which collectively govern personality development and moral education, and provide psychological stability and emotional support.

Relational Proximity

A closeness of relationship between two individuals, through which each is able to recognise the other more fully as a complete and unique human being.

Would you like to be kept informed about the work of the Relationships Foundation?

The Relationships Foundation (established as a charity in 1992) believes that wellbeing – for individuals and society as a whole – is achieved through relationships. Strengthening relationships in public and private life is a central objective which it pursues in a variety of ways:

- **Producing original research** in key policy areas.

- **Implementing 'relational' ideas** through high-level consultation and partnership with the private and public sector.

- **Pioneering fresh initiatives** to tackle national and international policy problems.

- **Promoting quality of relationships** as a priority in policy debate and working practice.

- **Running a programme of conferences and seminars**, and making available discussion papers, tapes and transcripts.

The *R Briefing* provides regular updates on the ideas and initiatives of the Relationships Foundation, and is received 5 times a year, free of charge, by all supporters. If you would like to be kept in touch in this way, simply send your name and address to:

The Relationships Foundation (charity no. 327610)
Jubilee House
3 Hooper Street
CAMBRIDGE
CB1 2NZ

tel. no. 01223 566333　　　fax. no. 01223 566359
E-mail: RF@cityscape.co.uk